Business Astrology 101:

Weaving the Web Between Business and Myth

Business Astrology 101:

Weaving the Web Between Business and Myth

Georgia Anna Stathis

Starcycles Publishing
Pleasant Hill, California

First Published in 2001 by
Starcycles Publishing
200 Gregory Lane, Bldg. C-2, #5
Pleasant Hill, CA 94523-3389

StarCycles Publishing
200 Gregory Lane
Building C-2, Suite 5
Pleasant Hill, CA 94523
(925) 689-7827
venus2@ix.netcom.com

Cover Painting, Illustrations, and layout by Amy Crook, 2001.

Book Coordination by Danielle Williams.

Edited by Stephanie Austin and Zarka Popovic. Early edits for portions of this book were in 1984 by Pamela Powers.

Chart calculations from Solar Fire created by Astrolabe/ Esoteric Technologies software. Two charts from Carol Mull's Standard and Poors 500 – Hershey's and Kellogg's.

Stathis, Georgia Anna (full birth name Stathopoulos), 1949-

Business Astrology 101: Weaving the Web Between Business and Myth/Georgia Anna Stathis

ISBN: 1-881229-26-2

Printed in the United States of America
by Baker Johnson, Dexter, Michigan.

Dedication

To my mother, Mary Diakomis-Stathis, who encouraged my creativity and to my father, Gus Stathis, who taught me to think ahead. Thank you both for supporting this process.

Hands of a Thousand Words

Nails covered with day old dirt,
Bearing no gifts,
These hands, they are.

Once a grape, now a raisin,
Like, once young, now old,
These hands, they are.

Worn and withered,
Dried and wrinkled,
These hands, they are.

Used all day,
Ready to retire.
These hands, they are.

As if in a bath too long,
Old and crumpled,
These hands, they are.

They can be described as,
The hands of a thousand words,
These hands, they can.

Contributed by:
Lauren O'Grady
Gus Nunes
Christopher Shotley

College Park High School Students, 2000

(This poem embodies the energy of Saturn and Jupiter in Gemini, 2001.)

Table of Contents

Part Three: Techniques and Strategies

Part Four: Putting It All Together

Bibliography & Appendices

Illustrations

Preface

The process of writing this book has not been easy. I began working on its contents as Saturn entered Taurus in 1998 after having had tried to start it numerous times since 1982. In previous years there was always something else that took precedence—raising my children, running a full-time Astrological practice, and keeping up with the needs of my extended family. I find the writing process exhilarating and yet it often became the last thing on my list of priorities.

After having attended another conference and perusing all of the wonderful books that my peers had written, I grew frustrated that one more conference season had passed without my book on a shelf. I left the bookstore area and boarded the escalator secretly harboring my disappointment when Mary Ursettie, a wonderful astrologer and friend sent by a higher authority in that moment, asked, "Why isn't your book in the bookstore, Georgia?" How odd that she would ask me the very question that I was turning over in my mind.

My immediate response to Mary's question was to tell her what had recently happened in my life. I had lost my brother, my only sibling and one of my oldest and dearest friends inside of the same week. The notion of time and its passage was plaguing me daily. I wanted to blurt out about all of the files of started chapters and ideas and memos and records, and the seeming lack of time that I had to sort them all. When I finally answered in a pained voice about how I had all of the material, but no one to put it together, she immediately suggested the right person to accomplish this Herculean task, Danielle Williams. Coincidentally, and there really are no coincidences, Danielle lives close to me in the

Contra Costa area of Northern California. Naturally, she happened to be available to help me.

We set an appointment for her to come to my office to gather up the boxes of disks, articles and notes that I had been accumulating since 1977, when I'd begun my practice. In strode a young woman attired in a whimsical hippie costume and when she opened her mouth a searing intelligence burned through my saturnine judgements about whether she was capable of performing the task.

After she allayed my fears about her not being able to stay on task I allowed her access to my precious life's work. Ultimately trust and faith overcame the fear and trepidation I was still holding. Danielle understood what I wanted to do almost immediately. She was excited about the prospect of doing something in Astrology that was groundbreaking (she has Aquarius rising and my Mercury and Venus in Aquarius resonated with her). I, on the other hand, simply wanted to show her the materials and outline and what I needed from her. However, she scooped it all up and walked out the door to review it. Surprisingly, I actually let her walk out of the door with twenty-five years of irreplaceable research!

I scheduled our next meeting for a month in the future. I expected that she would then tell me whether she would agree to work on the project and how we would proceed. To my utter amazement, she returned with a box in one hand, and a thick binder in the other, inside of which she had organized the data in a graphic fashion using themes of how the material could be assembled.

In one month she was able to accomplish that which I couldn't over a span of many years. I knew then that the magic was starting around this book. Over the course of the following two years we met monthly, compiling the data into a useable format. We accomplished all of the planning work as Saturn moved through Taurus, her Sun Sign and my Rising.

In addition to thanking Danielle for her marvelous efforts, I need to also thank Pamela Powers, author of a book on Chinese Astrology, who aided in the original transcriptions of the Saturn/Jupiter portion of the book in the 1980's. A big thank you is also in order to another gifted astrologer Stephanie Austin for her editing of this book. I am eternally grateful to Amy Crook, my typesetter and designer, for her clear graphics and vision on both this book and for her work on my annual calendars. The last two people to thank are Zarka Popovic for her final editing and especially Raymond Merriman who initially offered to publish this book, but strongly suggested that I publish it myself. He provided me with invaluable printing resources. So many people showed up at critical junctures to keep this project moving throughout the years that there is no way to possibly mention them all here. It is their faith in this idea and all of their patience with me that has made this possible.

Admittedly, I was nervous about writing a book on business Astrology, which focuses primarily on the vocational aspects of this discipline. It wasn't the writing of the business Astrology that unnerved me, but of how to integrate the mythologies with the vocational characteristics. Who does this? No one I knew.

My concern was that my professional peers would think that I was off of the mark in this thesis, yet I knew I would proceed with what felt viscerally and intuitively correct. Growing up, as a first generation Greek-American, in Chicago I had been exposed to Greek mythologies as a young girl. My family had insisted that both my brother and I attend Greek school twice weekly for seven years. We both hated it. Part of this grueling process however, was to read the Ancient Greek histories and myths in Ancient and Modern Greek. This remained the only part of Greek school that I ever loved or pursued outside of the confines of those classrooms.

My first book of myths was Edith Hamilton's Mythology[1] having purchased it at the tender age of seven. I had been drawn to the cover on which was the winged horse, Pegasus, who is being ridden by Bellerophon. Over the years, I have learned that Astrological concepts are best conveyed when we correlate the art of myth telling as we examine a horoscope. Clients can understand the story they are being told and the lens of Astrology slowly comes into focus during the consultation. I began utilizing this technique in my practice in the 1980's and immediately my clients responded positively to this integrated counseling approach.

Business Astrology is a very difficult area for most astrologers to grasp. The process for analyzing a company horoscope or a business transaction or the vocational indicators in a natal chart seems impersonal to many working astrologers. Why? I can only assume it is because they feel soul-less thus creating a cold, hard boundary that the astrologer must scale.

The beauty of engaging our clients with the Greek and Roman myths, and other world myths is that we can see patterns that emerge personally, politically and economically across time. When Pluto, the God of death and transformation, aligns with Uranus, the God of chaos and revolutionary thinking every 126 years, we have anarchy or political upheaval in the world (having last occurred in the mid 1960's). If we know the stories, then we understand what the words are relaying at a deeper soul level. Once we transcend time and observe the patterns, then we truly begin to understand the process. As above, so below.

This approach to business Astrology does not carry universal appeal and may be hard for advanced astrologers to embrace, as it will require some relearning and brushing up on the myths. However, for beginning astrologers it is a way to get one's arms around material that can appear complicated and convoluted. It provides a tool with which to sift through the dense rules of many Astrological traditions. It can provide you with a framework to understand the myriad infinite details by simply recalling a story.

The usage of stories and fables humanizes the material and aren't we, as astrologers, in a humanistic business? As you go through this book, allow yourself to experience the material in addition to reading it. I hope this book enables you to add business Astrology to your toolbox when consulting with clients. I enjoyed encapsulating my formulas for you to try as you take your clients to deeper levels of self-understanding.

Georgia Anna Stathis (Stathopoulos)

[1] Edith Hamilton, Mythology (Boston: Little, Brown and Company, 1942).

Chapter 1

Thriving, Not Just Surviving

Survival issues keep us from making changes in our careers and lifestyles. When we are frozen in fear of what might happen economically, politically or socially, we are kept from making overdue changes, either in our career or in our lives. We fear the sacrifices that we may have to make if we choose a new life direction. In an article written by Carole Kanchier, author of Dare to Change your Job—And Your Life, she states,

> *"Most barriers to career growth involve fear. Acknowledge your fears. Fear is the reassuring signal that you're about to stretch yourself. Fear alerts you to take action to protect yourself from loss. Underlying most fear is the lack of trust in your ability to perform."*[2]

Because Saturn is the farthest planet we see with the naked eye, its position is simultaneously significant and symbolic. Saturn represents *perceived limitation.* To illustrate the point refer to Illustration 1. Simply put, up until the time that Uranus was discovered in 1781, the perception was that Saturn was the last part of our solar system. Perhaps the ancients, because they only saw out to Saturn, made this comparison in their thinking. We really do not know, but if we work with this idea, then anything discovered after Saturn, would break open the perception, or, the perceived limitation of this ancient Saturn theory. The positive side of the perception that Saturn is the boundary of the universe is that this view shows Saturn as providing a form and structure in which we function. However, this perceived limitation doesn't allow us to see other options and possibilities that may lie in

Perceived Limitation at Saturn

Illustration 1

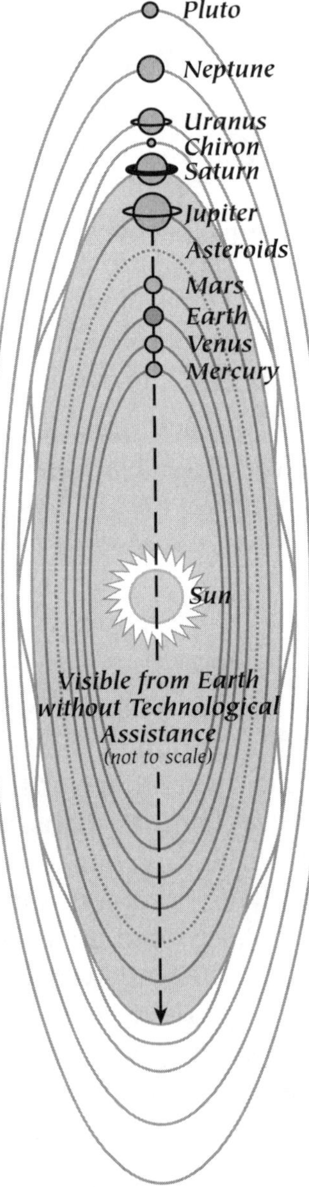

front of us, sometimes in the most obvious of places. And this view shows us the negative side of Saturn's effect.

Years ago, when I first began therapy with a wonderful counselor, I was given an example of the above concept at our first meeting. I started therapy in my late thirties when a lot of emotional issues were re-surfacing. I had the experience of a heavily laden Saturn which aspected many of my personal planets. The resulting behavior of these configurations led to my perception about how life, up until that point, was hard and that I had no support. This belief had me frozen in fear about a career decision that would change my life. I believed that people were not there to protect you (a Sun issue), nor care for you (a Moon issue) and that one had to learn to survive and care for oneself.

The first day of my meeting with the therapist, I burst into tears and frantically began searching for Kleenex as a tidal wave of emotion overwhelmed me. I searched my brief case and my purse unsuccessfully for tissue just as my therapist pointed out to me that there happened to be a box of Kleenex on the table right in front of me! The problem, I had, was very clear in that single moment. I had become so used to depending on myself that I had completely closed myself off to what was right there if I only paid attention.

This is actually, in simplistic terms, the solution for a dysfunctional Saturn that has learned to operate out of fear and isolation. Saturn's myth is discussed in the chapter on Career Cycles in this book. There is no need to revisit his stories. Saturn is tough, difficult, hard, dry, and cold. These are the first adjectives we use when describing some of the principles of Saturn. However, in Astrology as in nature, there is a positive side to everything no matter how malefic we may view the planet to be.

The up side of Saturn is that it represents focus, direction, and an ability to organize and prioritize those things that are most important in trying to get a job done. Saturn represents patience and understanding that in time everything comes around. Saturn represents the wisdom to discriminate between what is important and what is not.

The qualities that are a part of Saturn, both pro and con, seem to reflect generational themes. If one person in a family has a high concentration of Saturn energy, then it is probably true that other members of that clan have high concentrations of that planet. The psychology of the planet can run through a family for generations. For example, if someone is born with Saturn in hard aspect to their Moon or their Sun, then it may be that their formative years taught them that one must take care of oneself without assistance from anyone; to be serious and not to waste time. When Saturn is at a hard aspect to the Moon or the Sun, the parents or primary caretakers usually carry this belief system and may pass it on to their children.

Looking at the first seven years of someone's life corresponds to emotional development and is the age cycle of the Moon, which is indicative of the clan or the family. If the

Moon is negatively aspected by Saturn natally, then the environment in which the young child finds him or herself may be an environment of isolation, abandonment and frozen responses. Subsequently, this experience becomes the basis upon which we build our assumptions. If our experience was that our needs weren't met, then we come to believe that that is all that life holds for us. Our worst scenario perception may be that life is tough, unfriendly and devouring.

We are eternally caught on the first rung of survival on Abraham Maslow's Hierarchy of Needs (Illustration 2). We are unable to change that unless we consciously reframe it with a positive psychological intervention. This rung is the foundation point and its focus is existence. In order to accomplish anything you must be able to move beyond this point. It is true, of course that you can live in survival mode and still be "successful" in monetary terms. Think about how many old misers live with hardly any comfort in their environments, but

Abraham Maslow's Hierarchy of Needs

Illustration 2

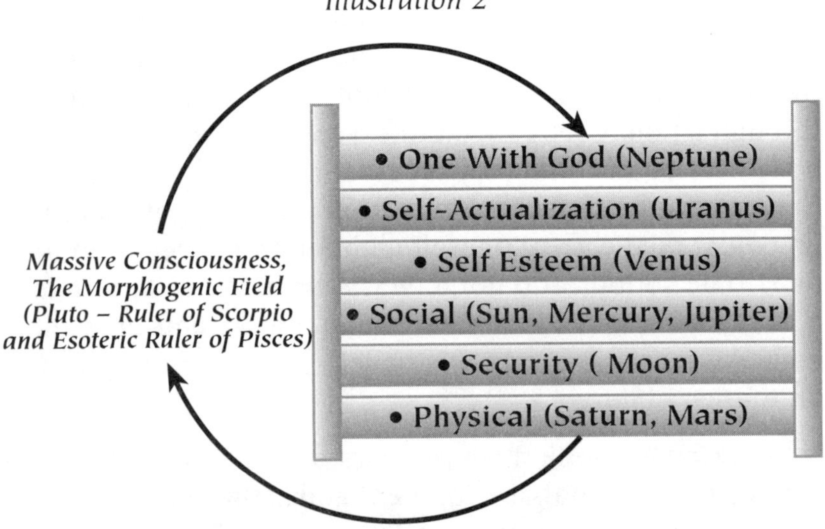

Abraham Maslow's Life Bell

are worth millions when they die. When we talk about success, we are talking about the concept of success in monetary issues as well as spiritual and emotional terms.

As you revisit the bottom rung of Maslow's ladder, which happens at different phases of life, your approach to "making it" changes as you mature. Fears that once paralyzed you have dissipated and all that remains is the healthy fear, alerting you to dangers in the world.

At this point, you have to move past perceptions and judgments and break out of the fears taught by your family and culture. When you come to this place of change there is a certain degree of courage that you must muster to move past the frozen wasteland of the survival mentality.

Robert Hand, one of the best Astrological minds of the twentieth century, states, "Saturn is the illusion that there is a reality, but Neptune is the truth that there isn't". The beauty of this quote is its great truth. There are planets and realities beyond Saturn. With the discovery of Uranus, Neptune and Pluto we expanded our base of reality and consciousness. Each discovery leads mankind further into his own psyche culminating with Pluto and the birth of psychoanalysis.

However, the basic will to survive in the world has always existed and corresponds with the visibility of Saturn in the night skies. In Maslow's model of the Hierarchy of Needs, we see an image of potentials and pitfalls. The first rung of the ladder represents the realm of the physical world. Mars corresponds with the courage to act and so Saturn and Mars co-create at this base level. I have placed these two archetypes at this juncture, since you need a successful expression of Mars to provide the courage and tools to get things done. The ability to breakout and move up requires the motivational fire of Mars. Saturn here represents what we need to do to survive.

In survival one of the first things you do is evaluate what you really need to do eliminating all other things in order to face the task at hand. For good health, you need to reassess your diet, particularly the fats, and eliminate those foods, which are detrimental to your system to lose weight. On a larger scale, to improve the quality of your fruit trees, you must prune the trees in the dead of winter, the time of Capricorn (ruled by Saturn). The more efficiently you prune your trees, the better the growth in the spring.

The same holds true for expanding your business, changing your career or creating more leisure time. The old proverb "time is money" is a Saturn maxim. When you look at changing careers and what that might require, you have to first assess your costs on a per diem basis. What are you spending? What can you reduce or eliminate to relieve you of financial pressure? What or whom depletes your energy and keeps you from getting to where you need to go? These hard questions require crystal clear (Saturn) answers.

A great pruning happened in recent years when several outer planets entered the constellation of Saturn-ruled Capricorn in the early 1990's. Major cutbacks occurred in industries; layoffs, mergers and downsizing were the standard news of the day. Just as you have to downsize your life in order to have the necessary reserve to reach the top of that new mountain of goals.

The mythical animal, the Sea Goat, which rules Capricorn, has many meanings. In more modern times we see Capricorn simply as a goat, but when we view the Sea Goat with its tail, we see a character whose challenges are doubled in terms of survival and ascension. They must first swim (the tail) from the bottom of the sea to land. At this point they need to climb onto the shore and being their climb to the top of the mountain. This is a long and challenging journey. It is a journey that requires an ambition and a drive and a willingness to withstand comfort or pleasure for the sake of achievement. The sure-footed goat climbs a craggy mountain with little to eat and a minimal amount of protection from foul weather as they ascend the mountain. Focused and willing to eat anything for survival, the goat eventually prevails and reaches the summit.

Herein lies the difference between negative manifestations of Saturn at the survival rung of Maslow's ladder versus a positive manifestation. When you allow fear or judgment to enter the equation of accomplishment and true success, then you experience two very distinct outcomes. The negative manifestation of Saturn results in depression, the inability to act (because you are so frozen you actually freeze out your Mars energy) and a general lack of motivation. You find yourself stuck in fear and unable to look beyond your societal or familial programming.

If you are overly concerned about what other people think, then you contract inward. If early programming has taught you that stepping out of the box means that you are left alone, without any forms of support, then you may think twice about pursuing your dreams, as they can be spooky. You, in turn, may start to criticize others around you as they attain successes that you are too scared to pursue. You may begin to believe that you have no alternatives to the life that you are leading, but there remains a small part of you that continually wonders, "What would have happened if I had...?".

Depression-era parents raised in difficult times have passed those perceptions on to an entire generation. How many from both of those generations opted for "practical" careers that made them "good" money in lieu of risking? How many of these survivors were really artists that never had a chance to express themselves because they believed that survival meant giving up dreams? By maintaining this philosophy, you find yourself unable to move up the ladder. In theory, it would seem that if we change our beliefs (the ninth house, which is also ruled by Jupiter who survived the devouring of

Saturn), then we change our perceptions, our fears and our careers (Saturn or the tenth house). It is not an accident that planets transit through the ninth house before they filter out publicly in the tenth!

Since Saturn is traditionally the archetype of fear, it means that at crucial moments in your evolutionary process you will be faced with the challenge of moving beyond your fears. This may come when transiting Saturn creates a hard angle of 45 or 90 degrees to Saturn's natal position, during the Saturn returns around the ages of 29, 59, and 89 or at the Saturn opposition between 44 and 46 years of age, or around 74 to 76 (see Illustration 3) [3].

The crucial element required for success is to learn how to respond to your natal Saturn and to skillfully maneuver through its often-murky psychological waters of fear and limitation. Successful resolution moves you up the Maslow ladder to Self-Actualization and Individuation.

Equally, Saturn affects the masses and their ability to move past frozen perceptions in business. During one of these recent larger cycles where transiting Saturn squared transiting Neptune, businesses changed markedly. Since Neptune is the slower planet, it had more influence than Saturn *(when deciding between the strengths of two outer planets, the slower ones have greater influence as they inhabit their part of the sky for a longer duration)*. With the Saturn and Neptune square of recent years, business structures dissolved emerging as new melded models. On a massive scale, this brought a dissolving of borders and boundaries and opened us to an entirely new generation of business models, the dot.coms. The creative elements (Neptune) in business merged with the older and more established industries (Saturn) to form a different breed of business structures.

During this cycle, a portion of the workforce changed from standard nine to five schedules in office towers to virtual work centers in their homes or at other site locations.

Internet firms, like the pioneering Amazon.com who distributes books and records throughout the world, began the model of a virtual (Neptune) business. This model set a precedent for businesses threatening to dissolve traditional merchants in bricks and mortar structures (Saturn) by relocating into the land of "virtual real estate" residing only in the minds of astute communication experts who are masters of technology.

The dissolving structures precipitate a redistribution of resources and wealth to open up the realms of possibility that only our visionary minds can create. As we dissolve traditional structures, so fall the national boundaries thus opening the way for foreign trade and offshore virtual corporations, which can drain national treasuries by withholding corporate taxes. This entire international business and trade arena begs the question as to what forms of currency will dominate in this new online market? Will we see more shared currencies as with the new European Commonwealth currency, the Euro?

As you read this book, it is important that you keep an open mind. The interplay between reality and its so-called structures and the unseen world of myth and symbolism have camps in both our left and right brains. The left brain is the camp of what we perceive is "real" and gives us much needed structures in which to operate. This part of the brain is Saturn. The right brain is the camp that hears the music, moves accordingly and is inspired and has the visions. The best combination is when both sides, the rational (Saturn) and the non-rational (Jupiter) work together, creating a kind of Whole-brain thinking, which moves us quickly from fear to feasibility. It is the purpose of this book to provide some ideas, systems and tools to encourage this type of thinking. In this way, you, the business astrologer, or you, the businessperson, may reach a better understanding on how to do this.

Saturn Cycles of Responsibility and Fear Confrontation

Illustration 3

The three faces of Saturn are: Building of Security, Achievement, and Wisdom. The illustration below shows building blocks that spiral. It is similar to the spiral of evolution that is seen in many metaphysical texts. Saturn's spiral, however, has hard edges, the squares and oppositions, which are the dynamics that provide motivation and ambition.

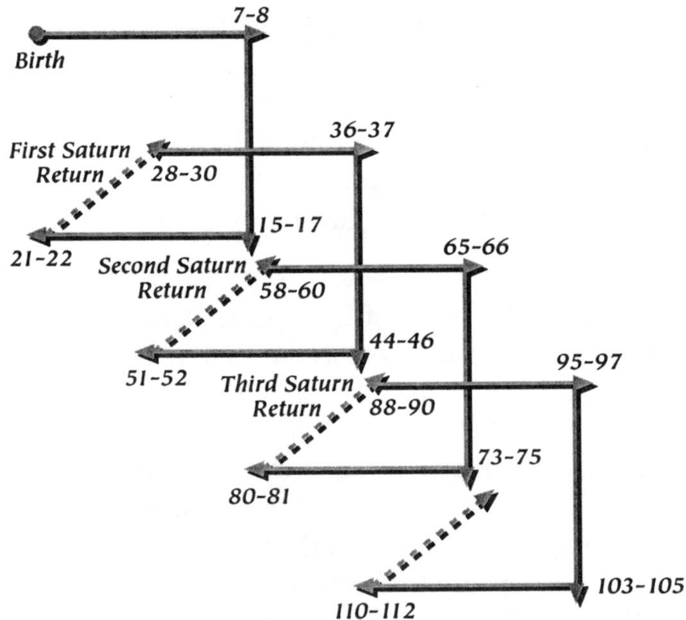

7 to 8 Years (First Quarter Square of transit Saturn to natal Saturn). First time the child exhibits separation from parent and begins path of individuation.

15 to 17 Years (First Saturn Opposition to Saturn). There is extreme tension between you and authority figures where you attempt to separate from the restraints of the status quo.

21 to 22 Years (First Last Quarter Square of transit Saturn to natal Saturn). Letting go of the past and awareness that time is passing and one must develop new skills.

28 to 30 Years (First Saturn Return). FIRST COMING OF AGE CYCLE where we work our craft, develop and refine our skills, overcome obstacles to achieve our new career or life dream. Hard work pays off as cycle ends.

*THE PREVIOUS CYCLE COMPLETES THE FIRST COMING OF AGE CYCLE—**Building Security.***

36 to 37 Years (Second First Quarter Square of transit Saturn to natal Saturn). You start to individualize your present career choices and experiment with new ideas and get organized. You establish relationships with your peers and with your community support system that will support your career.

44 to 46 Years (Second Saturn Opposition to Saturn). Cycle of extreme tension. Conflict arises around what you have been doing, the lack of time to do some of the things you wish to do and what needs to be done in order to accomplish your future. Decisions are made based on your needs versus others judgments.

51 to 52 Years (Second Last Quarter Square of transit Saturn to natal Saturn). You set things up to walk away from your old career and prepare for future retirement. Ambition shifts to vision. Taking classes, learning new skills, or engaging the help of others to expand is highlighted here.

58 to 60 Years (Second Saturn Return). SECOND COMING OF AGE CYCLE where we decide to step back and re-evaluate. It used to be people retired during this time, but many people are now starting to plan for new careers.

*THE ABOVE CYCLE COMPLETES THE SECOND COMING OF AGE CYCLE—**Achievement— and lays the foundation for the beginning of a second adult life and profession, which is free of fear and trepidation.***

65 to 66 Years (Third First Quarter Square of transit Saturn to natal Saturn). You step out of old structures, pursue new relationships with others to form groups that facilitate problem solving.

73 to 75 Years (Third Saturn Opposition to Saturn). Extreme tension is experienced because of the sudden awareness that there is conflict between what you have been doing, the lack of time to do some of the things you wish to do. Health issues may arise and you learn to let go more.

80 to 81 Years (Third Last Quarter Square of Saturn to natal Saturn). Learning and mentoring is highlighted. If health is good, you begin to allow the insights that come with the first Uranus return.

88 to 90 Years (Third Saturn Return). THIRD COMING OF AGE CYCLE. Could it be as life extension increases that this is the beginning of a new career cycle? Only time will tell.

THIS COMPLETES THE THIRD COMING OF AGE CYCLE— Mentoring and Wisdom. This is a very interesting cycle in that the first Uranus return occurs around age 84. Historically, such great figures as Grandma Moses, Georgia O'Keefe, etc., have had an awakening during this time.

[2] Carole Kanchier, "Dare to Change," San Francisco Chronicle, October 10, 1999: J-3

[3] The basic structure of this listing of Saturn was found in some old notes without a listed author. I have altered some of it to be more in line with this text. I do not have the name of the author of this and so, therefore, must state that the author here is unknown to me.

Chapter 2

Weaving the Web Between Business and Myth

When working in business delineation the traditional planetary definitions apply. The planets were named after the Roman Gods and Goddesses each representing a particular archetypal energy. As in myth, film and fable, there are heroes and heroines, caretakers, vamps, wise elders, bad witches and wicked elves. Myth not only tells a story, but also teaches a poignant life lesson.

Myths present you with a key that permits you to access the chart on a deeper level. The inability to successfully integrate the archetypes and apply them to business and financial charts is one of the reasons that people have difficulty transferring their skills from personal to business Astrology. It requires a leap from the right to the left-brain, from impressionistic thoughts to logical structures. Successful business delineation is achieved by being able to integrate the myths into the planetary interpretations of a business chart, just as you would in analyzing an individual horoscope.

As we synthesize the basic characteristics and story-myths of the planets with business possibilities, we make the information relevant to our clients. If we convey the information that we interpret in the chart through the lens of myth the client is apt to be receptive. Myth, like music, assists you in integrating the left brain function of judgment and practical experience (Saturn) with the right brain strengths of symbolism, intuition and creativity (Jupiter). Myth activates your imagination and encourages whole-brain thinking. It is from whole-brain thinking that some of the greatest ideas in the world have arisen. There are stories of Old World millionaires and inventors such as Conrad Hilton and Nikola Tesla, which support this statement. Hilton, when bidding for hotels, would rely on intuited figures that "came to him" even though they were not the numbers required to seal a transaction. Nikola Tesla, as well as Howe, the inventor of the sewing machine, had visions and dreams that completed their ideas and inventions.

The numerous points of entry into a chart are the houses. In other words, when you examine someone's fifth house you are exploring issues around their children, their lovers or their creative habits. From this perspective you gain information on how this person might handle fifth house matters. Examine whether there are planets in the house, what planet(s) (co) rule the house, where the planets are placed and what aspects they form. You may also "turn the wheel" and actually make a chart for the fifth house of this person by placing the fifth house at the Ascendant position.

For both an individual and a business, the moment of its creation is captured by the configuration of the planets that occurred at its conception. Carl Jung, who incorporated Astrology and symbolism into his therapeutic work, said, "...anything born in that moment in time has the qualities of that moment in time". The same is true for business and corporate charts. For example, you know that in the natural zodiac the fifth house is ruled by the Sun, which in turn rules Leo and represents the motivation and expression of the life force. In a corporate chart, the fifth house represents the expression and motivation of the King or Queen, known as the CEO or Sole Proprietor. It represents the success or failure of the company's advertising efforts as well as how a company encourages and rewards its employees. What activities does management utilize—corporate social functions, sports events and team building exercises, dramatic or theatrical special presentations as well as the entire smorgasbord of staff development through coaching, workshops, and seminars— to motivate their people and "play" with them?

A good example of how planetary energies may be interpreted is by viewing Mars, which is defined as the ability to harness and concentrate energy to attain goals, in an individual's as well as a company's chart. This red planet was named after the young, impulsive Greek God Ares who eventually became the Roman Mars, a strategic, brave and experienced warrior. In business delineations Mars is the assertiveness exhibited in the difference between a risk-oriented versus conservative approach to operating a company.

By integrating planets with myth in your interpretation you can successfully analyze the potential pitfalls of a company incorporated under a strong Sun/Mars combination be it by conjunction, square, or opposition. A person or company that has a challenging Sun/Mars aspect must deal with the appropriateness of the methods they summon to demonstrate their strong desires. The conjunction may express itself as anger, drive or heroism with the motivation being a penchant for taking risks or facing challenges. Whereas, the individual born with Mars squaring their Sun may be heroic and task-oriented, but their motivation is based in a wounding that may have an emotional tone, caused perhaps by the severing of a relationship with the father or other primary family members. Since the Sun usually represents the leader of the company, the opposition to Mars represents a leader who is over-reactive, argumentative, or does not listen to the information that his middle managers (corporate America's version of the ancient knights of yesteryear) provide him from field research. This inability to listen may alienate the line staff that will expend their energy on in-fighting rather than moving the company forward. When taken to the extreme the opposition may lead the company to have misappropriations in budgeting. Because of the potential for a hostile environment there may be frequent turnovers of personnel driving up labor costs and adding to the continual stress.

A highly visible Mars in a company's horoscope assists in its success, but if the company has not learned the value of a defensive strategy, then no matter how great the product and its offerings they will fail. They become like all of the other companies whose management is reactionary and does precious little but put out fires. It is imperative to learn to channel the power of Mars for maximum benefit and profit.

In mythology, the successful warriors and heroines sought good counsel (such as holding strategic planning meetings with Pallas Athena (⚴). If Pallas Athena (one of the asteroids used in interpretations) didn't agree with their cause the individuals seeking counsel would not be issued the proper strategies to accomplish their goals. If Pallas Athena is transiting the company's tenth house then it might hold true that the CEO of the company is looking for a good consultant or strategist or that it's an appropriate time to rethink the corporate strategy. If a consulting group has a well-aspected Pallas Athena in their horoscope it suggests their strengths in providing excellent counsel.

When developing a company there is a great deal of strategic planning involved to formulate an action plan with which to locate and cultivate a client base. If you are responsible for delivering and maintaining the primary accounts for your company you must temper your efforts of actively courting and gaining new clients with deepening the relationships of your loyal clients. If your primary client base, your bread and butter, perceive that your eagerness to attain new clients diminishes your capacity to service them and care for their best interests, then you will soon have them not only disgruntled but risk losing them entirely.

When there are heavy transits (meaning outer planets) or eclipses impacting a company chart the company may experience reversals in fortune. Sometimes the reversals will occur as a company expands rapidly. At other times there may be a general downturn in the economy leaving only the fittest companies to survive a recession.

A recent example of this was the recession of the early 1990's. The planets Saturn, Uranus and Neptune were all aligned in the sign of Capricorn. This period witnessed a drop in the price of goods along with a massive downsizing of corporate structures (Saturn and Capricorn issues). The recession forced businesses to evaluate the limitations of their existing structures (Saturn) and to change (Uranus) their inefficient operations (Saturn), such as the traditional time schedules (Saturn) from nine to five to "flex-time" (Uranus with Saturn). As the use of flextime and staggered work hours gained in momentum they were joined with the idea of job sharing and more team work (Neptune with Saturn) to be followed closely with the explosion in telecommuting (Uranus).

As Capricorn not only rules big business but buildings and structures it was not surprising that a parallel change in housing was underfoot. The growth of the urban village was underway (Uranus and Saturn). Co-housing (Neptune with Uranus) finally emerged in the United States after experiencing decades of success abroad. It consists of independent personal living spaces with shared assets such as common gardens, kitchens, recreation rooms and assistance with cooking or child rearing. It is the extended family (Saturn) reinvented (Uranus).

Downsizing in the late 20th century created a new workforce of independent contractors (Uranus). This model of portfolio-people created a flexible work schedule and maximized productivity while reducing labor costs (Saturn) through the utilization of technology and mobility (Uranus).

When the conjunction of Jupiter (abundance and new options) aligned with Uranus (computers and telecommunications) in 1997, laptop computers began to outsell desktop computers and at this writing are evolving into nearly weightless and wireless hand-held devices (Uranus). As the visionary influence of Neptune melds with the inspirational genius of Uranus in their pass through Aquarius, this wireless revolution is finding a foothold. We can conduct business, receive the latest in the news, check our schedules and communicate with anyone worldwide. This transformation in the work model combined with evolving technologies enables us to form a web of resource people working in real time linked through an electronic forum across continents and transnational boundaries. It lends a whole new meaning to the term multi-national corporation. This loose knit work environment allows for a greater diversity of creative input as the physical distance barrier is dissolved.

During the transiting squares between Saturn and Neptune and the squares between Saturn and Uranus from 1998 to 2000, we disintegrated (Neptune) and dismembered old structures (Saturn). With Uranus, the God of creation and invention squaring Saturn there was the birthing of "out of the box" thinking models in business. These new business formulas contributed to flexible work hours while simultaneously opening a Pandora's box of entirely new sets of problems—not the least of which is the exponentially increasing white-color crime rate, which is sure to become a pandemic when Pluto (underworld crime figures) enters the sign of Capricorn in 2008 and organized syndicates join in the melee.

Let's explore another archetype, the Moon. The Moon is associated with the first seven years of one's life and spawns the intimate relationship that an infant experiences with its primary caretaker. These lunar impressions remain imbedded in the young child's psyche throughout their life. In traditional Astrology, the Moon represents the family and the tribe. In business, it represents the employees (the company's family) and the products they produce and create.

The Moon, its house placement and aspects, indicates

the response to the product by the public. Since the Moon ebbs and flows shifting shape, there is constant movement and change in the area of employees as well as the products a company produces. Some products retain their original form, but most adapt to the ever-changing needs of the consumer. Witness the fast-paced development of computer technology in recent years; Information that once was accessible to a minority has become available to the masses with relatively little computer training or expertise.

Another thread that weaves the web of business and life is the monthly lunar cycle. This cycle has existed since the beginning of time and has been followed by hundreds of cultures to calculate growth and development. The lunar cycle lasts for 28.5 days, beginning with the New Moon and moving to the First Quarter Moon, then to the Full Moon, and the Third Quarter (also known as the Last Quarter), only to finally return to the New Moon. More on how to apply this principle to planning and trend studies is discussed in the section on Planetary Lunation Cycles.

In planning a company project, relocation or a new marketing angle it is more efficient if you pace it in accordance with the natural rhythm of the monthly lunar cycle. For example, it is always better to start projects and initiatives at the time of the New Moon, while organizing and deciding on management structures is best dealt with at the First Quarter Square, and culminating plans and releasing old forms of operations at the Full Moon. In the Last or Third Quarter Phase, you may want to regroup and reorganize to prepare to launch anew in the next cycle.

In addition, by examining the corresponding cycle of the transiting Nodal Axis, we gain information about business trends. The Lunar Nodes, like the Moon, gauge the pulse of public opinions. The Lunar Nodal Axis results from the intersection of the ecliptic (the Sun's apparent orbit around the Earth; or the orbit of the Earth as viewed from the Sun) and the Moon's orbit.

When the North Node entered the sign of Aquarius (ruled by Uranus) in late May of 1989, a Uranian dilemma suddenly developed in China. Uranus traces back to the Greek God of Chaos, Ouranos. Uranus would periodically join with Mother Earth Gaia, create numerous children, and then separate in order to be alone. He then would yearn for companionship, mate again with Gaia and have more children. The issue of Uranus and Aquarius is the issue of fusion and separation. Being one with everyone, but also separate; being detached, but joined.

Uranus represents brotherhood, equal rights, and the greater community at large. Aquarius is the sign of human rights and collective thinking. The United States had, as its beginnings, the Boston Tea Party, a revolt against England because of excessive taxation without representation coupled with an abuse of human rights.

Returning to China in the spring of 1989, we note that the student uprisings in Beijing, which ended tragically, successfully spotlighted human rights issues and abuses as the transiting North Node moved through Aquarius. Then as the transiting South Node moved through Aquarius (December of 1999), the World Trade Organization meeting in Seattle, Washington, was disrupted by rioting in the streets protesting trade agreements, again in violation of human rights issues. This occurred exactly midway through the eclipse cycle, as the North Node was in Leo and the South Node was in the sign of Aquarius, opposing where they had been nine years prior. When the North Node moved into Leo, ruled by the Sun, the challenge was in the proper concept of leadership and of doing business with heart.

As the North Node entered Capricorn (ruled by Saturn) in the early 1990's, we experienced recession cycles. Interest rates and housing values usually drop when the North Node transits through Capricorn. Saturn or Cronos was the God who brought order out of chaos. Associated with real estate and frugality, Saturn built the first justice systems and buildings.

New visions in business appeared with the entry of the North Node into Sagittarius from 1992 to 1994. Sagittarius, the Archer and the Centaur, is associated with travel, freedom and the wilderness. It rules country and western themes, truth, religion, publishing, traveling, education and Native Americans. In fashion trends backpack type purses gained in popularity while favored car models were the sports utility vehicles. There were increases in sales figures for both camping and travel equipment. In several states the legalization of Native American gambling casinos provided capital for Tribes to flex their political wills. Business travel boomed leading to streamlined designs in luggage and travel gear.

The transiting North Node moved into its own sign of Cancer from April 8, 2000 to October 14, 2001. This usually results in an increase in public desire for property and all things ruled by Cancer. The Moon rules property for both business and individual delineation and includes the already built shells of homes or proposed housing projects. We can expect that issues around property will dominate business acquisitions and consolidations. Office space price and warehouse locations will be up for review. Companies may choose to buy rather than lease space.

Since the Moon symbolizes food and nourishment and rules the stomach, there is usually an increase in food prices, a strong focus on cooking and preserving food, and trends towards new types of cuisine. In the haute cuisine industry, the strong global influence from Uranus merging with Neptune allows us to experience new culinary delights that transcend boundaries, borrowing tastes and sensations from an array of cultures, with "fusion foods". Look for a greater array of international specialty food wholesalers on-line to join the already popular on-line grocery vendors.

With Chiron and Pluto conjunct in the sign of Sagittarius, shifts in international trade agreements can be expected. The conjunction of Chiron, the teacher and mentor, combined with Pluto, the God of power and big money at the end of December 1999 also pointed to a crisis in education. The recent spate of student murders and murderers (Pluto, Lord of Death and ruler of volcanic rage) in Sagittarius (education) suggest that we need to uncover and bring into the light (another Pluto theme) why our youth are angry, feel neglected and invisible.

Perhaps the recent horrors will manifest in a renewed interest in the educational lives of our youths. Chiron was a foster caregiver so we may address a diversification of educational opportunities combined with mentoring and fostering services. The deliverance of on-demand Internet based education is beginning to transform how we educate ourselves. A number of professional development courses are available online including certifications for the real estate industry. As these online programs increase, the opportunities for vocational training versus traditional schooling may be conferred upon our youth regardless of where they are physically based.

The Year 2000 conjunction of Jupiter (ruler of Sagittarius symbolizing both the law and education) with the planet Saturn (the government and justice system) suggests the possibility of new initiatives in the educational system. Historically, this conjunction which only occurs every twenty years, has brought changes in both legal and educational systems. One way to increase the efficiency of the legal process is to further engage in the greater use of paralegals for a number of perfunctory services. Expect reforms in the legal professions and in our court systems as Pluto passes through Sagittarius.

Pluto, discovered in 1930, rules nuclear fission. Nuclear power can cause massive destruction or be harnessed for power. Industries ruled by the sign of Sagittarius are undergoing a similar transformation of power in reaching the masses. Witness the legal Merger of America Online (AOL) with Time Warner in 2001, creating new "Net-Fed" possibilities, which merge (Neptune) Networks with Communication and Publishing venues. In addition, the passage of Chiron through Sagittarius quickens the changes in education and the legal process providing wider access to the public. Already we can access an array of materials to do our own divorce, incorporation, or agreements via computers and to educate ourselves via online workshops and courses which teach everything from languages to gardening! The other realm where this will be expressed is in the need for more foreign language teachers abroad (Sagittarius rules overseas travel).

Pluto, the ruler of big business and money, is having profound changes in world currencies, including the recent emergence of e-money. The European Common market is fueling an increased concern about global trade. Whose currency will we use? Will currency become obsolete with an outgrowth of e-money? Mix Pluto with transiting Saturn (the God of rules and existing structures) moving through the sign of Taurus (associated with spending, earning power, assets and values) and the question asked is, whose monetary value will suffer deflation or will there be any hyperinflation?

The challenges and the cycles continue and by learning to frame the questions and ferret the answers through the use of myth, we can successfully navigate to identify business trends. The correlation between the planetary movements, the major conjunctions, and the nodal cycle, reveal an ongoing story that repeats throughout history with only slight variations. This integration of symbolism and timing is a weave that holds through time and your accurate use of it helps your clients.

The intention of this presentation was to show you a way to integrate the techniques of Astrology with these age-old symbols. The next chapter examines the classic angles of the zodiac, the cardinal signs and the succeeding signs of the fixed and the mutable. I also examine the less discussed solstice points of the zodiac, which hold powerful key points for each sign. Thus we begin a macrocosmic view for this book and then, slowly move to the microscopic case studies.

Chapter 3

Solstice Points, Elements, and Qualities

Solstice points are sensitive zodiacal placements that are mirror-reflections of each other totaling 30°. Using the starting point of the Winter Solstice at 0° Capricorn and the starting point of the Summer Solstice at 0° Cancer we form a vertical axis (Illustration 4).

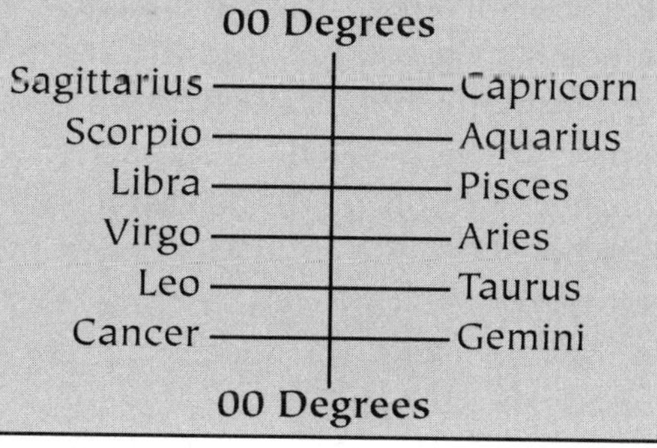

Solstice Points

Illustration 4

00 Degrees

Sagittarius	Capricorn
Scorpio	Aquarius
Libra	Pisces
Virgo	Aries
Leo	Taurus
Cancer	Gemini

00 Degrees

On either side of this axis we place the solstice point signs. Using Taurus and Leo as an example, we can set the sign of Taurus at 10°, which has as its solstice point 20° of Leo. Add these two numbers together and it sums to 30°. Subsequently, when a planet such as Saturn transits at 10° of Taurus, you know that Saturn is also activating the complementary solstice point at 20° Leo. This partially explains how easy it is to miss critical events in a horoscope. Using the above example, it would be important to scan where 20° of Leo is situated within the horoscope of the individual, the company or the transaction chart. An entire generation has their Pluto in the sign of Leo. Keep in mind that this baby boomer group was adversely affected as transiting Saturn transited through the sign of Taurus. Those that have the later degrees of Pluto in Leo were affected first by the early degree transits of Saturn in Taurus and then, as Saturn continued through its transit, the earlier degrees of Pluto were affected. Converse to what you may think!

The transit of Jupiter inTaurus also activated the sign of Leo and resurrected consciousness issues that are associated with Pluto. The word plutocracy is derived from Pluto and this planet is indeed related with money and wealth in both vocational and corporate delineations. Pluto represents the "shadow" of the personality or the company. A Pluto transit will force you to examine such business concerns as money, lending, banks and the use and abuse of corporate power.

It is important for you to note that solstice points and their corresponding elements are not always compatible with one another in the traditional sense. Let's use an example: If Neptune is transiting the solstice point of the Midheaven, then it is similar to the Midheaven being "transited" by Neptune, which translates into the company possibly considering a pending merger. If Neptune is actually conjuncting, by transit, the Midheaven the same event might occur - a merger. Another example might be that if Saturn is transiting the solstice point of your natal Mercury, vocationally this is similar to transiting Saturn conjuncting your natal Mercury, which indicates serious and focused study or a great deal of sustained mental exertion.

Elements

In Astrology there are four elements. The zodiacal sequence is Fire, Earth, Air and Water. Each chart has its particular distribution of the four elements and stamps it with a signature trait. For example, although an individual's or a company's chart may be lacking in an element, that element is on or inside a house somewhere, because the horoscope includes all twelve signs and their elements and qualities.

The first element is fire and it expresses itself through energy and inspiration. The signs of Aries, Leo, and Sagittarius are in the fire sign triplicity. A triplicity, like the Holy Trinity, represents balance. Where Aries is found in the horoscope is where the expression of heroic and courageous acts will occur. Here is where you experience the fire to blaze your own trails and fight for what you desire, as you are ardent about attaining your goals. For example, it takes a very Martian or Aries-oriented company to courageously move forward and enlist people who can teach and train their organization to innovate, particularly as we enter the 21st century. A successful independent company has to have, as its base, the Martian energy to move aggressively into new ventures and particularly to overcome stagnation. Martian energy is bold. Its main lesson in life is to learn to think before it acts. This ability to plan, to edit, to work through the details comes with Aries' solstice point in Virgo. When cutbacks are necessary, then a company needs to "prune its corporate trees" and re-strategize. It is imperative that it has the capacity to cut off (Aries or Mars) swiftly and meticulously (its Virgo solstice point) all that is no longer useful or contributing to the core product line and the income it generates. What may seem as cold and bold really is just a move toward a healthier, leaner, efficient (all Virgo concepts) organization.

Leo, the second fire sign, represents loyalty, consistency, strength and the fires of the heart. It isn't as fleeting as Aries energy; it stays with things longer, waiting for them to develop over time. Out of this emerges the creativity that Leo is known for and the playfulness, generosity and good humor that feeds on creative expression. Leo is sometimes seen as a slow element and this is primarily because it falls in the fixed or stabilizing mode of operation (Modes are discussed later in this chapter). Leo appears to be a gambler and a risk taker, but unlike an Aries, which takes action for action's sake, Leo lays tangible foundations before speculating or gambling. Thus, Leos are considered lucky, but their speculations are generally the result of a long process of weighing, measuring and researching the probable outcomes of a calculated gamble. This relates to its solstice point in Taurus, which infuses it with the principal of value and stability. The underlying question for a Leo is, "...is this worth (Taurus) it to me?" Leos must feel comfortable (Taurus) with the potential costs of a risk or speculation before they will agree to proceed.

In Sagittarius, the third fire sign, we experience the culmination of the fire energy. Sagittarius represents the leap of faith required for the and striving for a higher spiritual ground. It is the fire sign that has the capacity to envision infinite possibilities and to propagate those visions across cultures and national borders. Sagittarius is the fire of perfection and the freedom to experience an ideal. It has an adventurous quality similar to Aries, but is not as brave or courageous. It is as playful as Leo, but less creative. Its solstice point is Capricorn, ruled by the planet Saturn, which exercises caution regularly.

The freewheeling Sagittarius has, as its counterpoint, caution and fear the attributes associated with its solstice point in Capricorn. Sagittarius battles with its exuberant need to expand and experience life as it pushes against Capricorn's solitary and precautionary nature. This is the challenge of the Sagittarius, to leap forward in faith and with idealism, but a clear, structured plan in place.

With strong Capricorn or Saturn placements in the horoscope, continuous battles between freedom (Sagittarius) and responsibility (Capricorn) and the struggle to attain the correct balance are waged. Ideas and thoughts, when given permission to run free and are supported may inspire people. These joyous inspirations don't require structures or sacrifices in the literal sense yet act as bridges to higher realms of thought. Sagittarius has earned a reputation for being the ideal teacher, trainer and salesperson, as Sagittarius wants to expound its beliefs.

To sum up the differences between the various fire elements think of Aries as the first flash of fire; Leo as the comet itself; and Sagittarius as the tail of the comet.

The complementing element for fire is air. Air represents thought and communication. The three air signs are Gemini, Libra and Aquarius. Air has the capacity to mentally climb above a situation and view it from a detached, logical perspective. Air types can first move furniture in their living room around in their heads and actually visualize how it will look before straining to move it. Air's ability to perceive ideas in an unusual way and then to execute them is excellent. Air's detached manner in approaching problems can lead others to perceive them as detached, cold and unfeeling.

The air attributes are highly valued in business as their agility to move from one perspective to another with grace and ease while accurately analyzing all ramifications. This is an innate skill that can be capitalized upon. Air isn't confined by rules and its presence is found in the charts of those who work in industries that require problem solving and facilitation, marketing and sales, communications, and independent contractors.

If you have a high influence of the air element in your chart or your company's chart, then you are active, social, experiential and visionary. All of the air signs like to debate the merits of various proposals and to staunchly defend their positions, but how they do so is different for each of the three.

The Gemini approach resembles that of the bumblebee going from flower to flower, pollinating and cross-pollinating ideas and thoughts with various people and organizations. Because their scope is so vast and they talk to so many people, and because they have a capacity to adapt to whomever they find themselves with, they may struggle with loyalty or consistency. When they become bored with the activities, they may just as quickly switch or go over to the other side. However, they are not inclined to do this unless they truly feel that there is some sort of security that lies at the foundation of that decision. After all, their solstice point is Cancer, which is a sign of safety and security.

The sales industry is known for its high turnover. If a sales representative or agent, after trying his or her hand at one thing, really feels that they aren't being offered enough future security, they will change firms or projects and regroup seemingly effortlessly. Where Gemini is in your company's chart is where there is variability and constant flux.

Where Cancer is situated in the horoscope is the landing and cultivation point for Gemini. If your company has a great deal of Gemini energy, then you have a company that has, as its primary product, some sort of information service or research that can be sold or taught to others. This information provides a base for new growth (Cancer) that requires nurturing and cultivation. In the global marketplace information is the pollen that is carried from industry to industry and germinates idea after idea (Mercury). As we gain instant communication in business sectors of other countries the potential for resource sharing becomes unfathomable.

Information and the connections required for accessing information falls under the umbrella of Gemini. Gemini types have facile minds and flexibility in thinking that generates new ideas and problem solving with a deftness that slower minds can't conceive.

Taking these newly formed ideas and developing the right teams to implement them brings us to the realm of the next air sign, Libra. Libra is one of the action or cardinal signs. Libras have a reputation for their indecision. It is true that they see both sides of any argument and carefully weigh one point against the other rarely taking allegiance to any one position. However, if we move past that cliché, then we can appreciate that the air sign of Libra is about fair resolution or agreements that parties can live with. Libra is driven by a need to compromise and maintain cooperation; they are the original teamwork designers.

The scales of justice represent Libra. When the scales are unbalanced Libras expend a great deal of energy in re-balancing the scales. Sometimes if things are too peaceful, Libras will instigate a situation that creates disagreement or tension to intentionally throw the scales out of balance so that they may busy themselves with the task of bringing harmony. It is no accident that many military strategists and generals have a heavy dose of Libra in their charts.

A strong influence of Libra or the asteroid Pallas, which has a similar energy, in the horoscope, suggests an ability to work with or inside of the justice system. Libras excel in negotiations and contractual agreements, as well as in industries that are focused on esthetics. They are often at the vanguard of the fashion industry, interior and exterior design firms, architectural firms, and any work that requires a talent achieving some ideal state of perfection.

This ability requires inspiration and appropriately the solstice point for the sign of Libra is the sign of Pisces, ruled by Neptune, the planet of idealization and making dreams realities. There is a strong affinity between these two signs, even though they are of different elements; Libra is air and Pisces is water. In traditional Astrological literature, Venus one of the rulers of Libra reaches its highest expression (exaltation) in Pisces.

What these two signs have in common is the quality of duality (see chapter on Houses, p. 129). Both signs have a difficult time of making decisions by being able to relate to both sides. The air energy of Libra appears cool and removed, but with Pisces as its solstice point, there is a deeper capacity to merge two different worlds, or two different ways of thinking and acting.

This is why Librans typically find success in management and in working with people as well as manipulating environments. Personnel managers, human resources and employee benefits specialists, labor negotiators as well as textile and jewelry designers are all vocations that require emotional empathy (Pisces) to satisfy the client. Bringing the right people together at the right time and under the right circumstances are important skills. The following successful interior designer (Illustration 5) has the ability to listen to her clients' needs and successfully integrates their vision with her own. This partnership of expertise and ideas creates en-

Illustration 5

Female: Designer, Feb. 20, 1947, 9:40pm CST + 6:00, Altona, CAN, 49°N06' 097°W33'

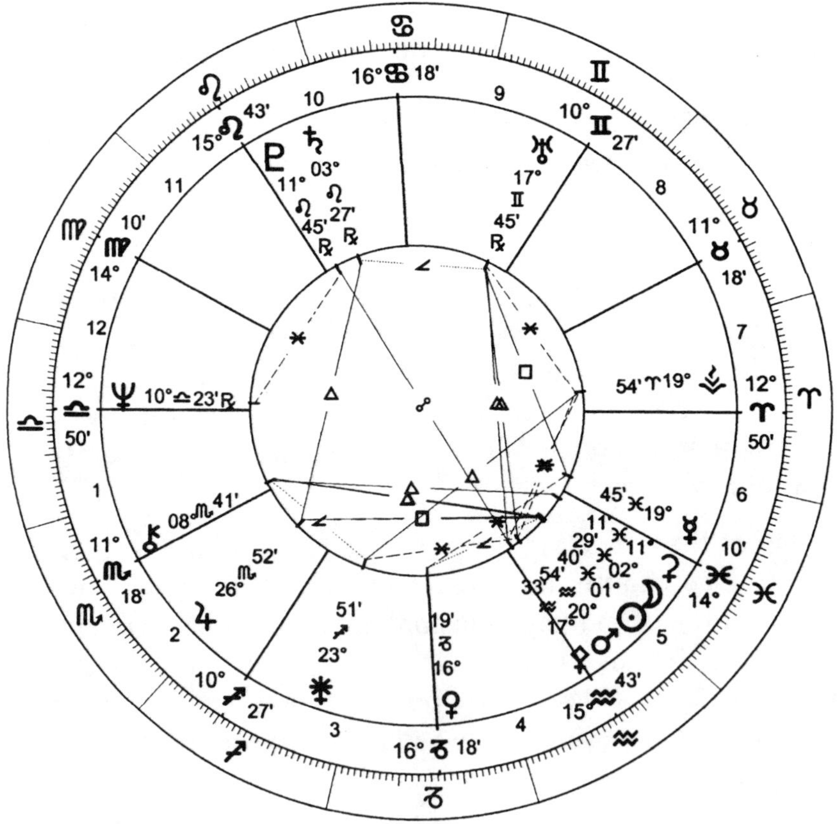

vironments, furnishings, and interiors that are highly desirable. Note the complement of Pisces and Libra (solstice points) in her chart, particularly the Mercury and Neptune, which strengthen her imagination. The Mercury placement in the sixth house encourages precise thinking as well as problem-solving capabilities. It suggests an ability to communicate ideas emanating from the twelfth house (Neptune) to the client represented by the sixth house. The "intuitive" or "psychic" ability of the Pisces solstice point is the glue that connects the creative dots and brings Librans to successful fruition in their chosen enterprises.

In the example of the designer her Mars is placed in the sign of Aquarius, the carpenter or the one who works with wood. Aquarius is the last air element. Where Libra works very hard at putting people and situations together, Aquarius is its antithesis and seems to break things up. For an Aquarius the motivation is to take things apart and place the respective pieces into new situations. This sign simply thinks differently. The solstice point of Aquarius is Scorpio, which is represented by Shiva or Pluto, the destroyer and creator of the world. Scorpio or Pluto energy represents all of those bad witches that didn't get invited to any mythic parties, but showed up anyway! The essence of Pluto-ruled Scorpio, Aquarius' solstice point, is to transform and to kill that which already exists by recycling it with a fresh perspective. Aquarius presents as an anarchist, but they are really innovators. In the Scorpio solstice point we see a deep desire to change, destroy, transmute and retool. Isn't this a type of anarchy or revolutionary activity? The difference between the Aquarius and Scorpio is that the Aquarius is emotionally detached to outcomes and processes and people. Whereas the destruction and rebirth activity that is generated by Scorpio stems from deep seated feelings about all situations.

Solstice points complement and dance with each other so that it becomes difficult to distinguish where one begins and the other ends.

In competitive business, the question is always, "...how can we build that better mousetrap/government /company?" These questions correspond to Uranus and Pluto the rulers of Aquarius and Scorpio. They perpetually ask whether there is something new and different and more effective which reflects an evolution in consciousness. How can we integrate this question to derive a unique product or service?

Aquarius explores the outer regions of undiscovered possibilities. Uranus the first planet beyond the visible solar system rules it. (Refer again to Illustration 1, p. 9). In viewing the illustration, we see that Saturn is the visible perimeter of the solar system, which for thousands of years was the reference point for sky navigators. Fittingly, Saturn rules boundaries and limitation. How shocked people must have felt when suddenly, with the advancement of telescopes there was a planet that lay beyond what the naked eye could discern. Uranus, the first outer planet to be discovered was thought to be there because when planets reached a certain point in the sky, they would abruptly be thrown out of orbit. Its physiology was even different in that this was a planet that orbited on its side as opposed to all of the inner planets that rotate on a vertical axis.

It is through the air signs which rule the mind that we birth ideas and these ideas are fed or inspired by the fire signs, but it takes the earth signs to form and execute them daily. The signs of Taurus, Virgo, and Capricorn are the earth signs. Earth is the practical element. Earth people are the builders and the planners. Their preferred mode of operation is order, logic and structure. They are the ones apt to nag at a meeting that there needs to be a new organizational chart made. The earth element is slower than fire or air, because it operates in three-dimensional space. Three-dimensional space, by virtue of its nature, is limited in speed and movement. The fire and air elements operate outside of three-dimensional space. So without the earth element we would never be able to translate the world of fourth-dimensional ideas into third-dimensional manifestation. Hence the paradox of the curse and the blessing of the earth element. How to create new forms within the confines of concrete reality is a constant challenge in today's business world.

These challenges are ever present as we try and integrate brick and mortar businesses (third-dimensional) with virtual businesses (fourth-dimensional). We can only do so much in our three-dimensional realities, in our three-dimensional retail stores, and our three-dimensional offices. The "concept" of an office and workspace has radically changed in these last few years and now, more than ever, because of the benefit of technology, we can work and communicate from any place in the world. We have our portable phones, our portable computers, our pagers, ad infinitum. We can work all of the time from the time we wake to when we sleep if what we do is contingent on concepts rather than physical assembly.

It is the realm of making work tangible that concerns all of the earth signs. They evaluate whether there is the cash flow to make the necessary changes or acquisitions and then administer them. The one who holds the moneybag often has a strong placement of Taurus in the horoscope. Taurus rules values and all that we hold dear including cold cash.

At the end of the twentieth century, we are having a spiritual crisis as Saturn passes through the sign of Taurus. The revolution in values began as Saturn passed through the sign of Taurus and squared Uranus in Aquarius thereby requiring us to use our imaginations in solving the larger questions of what has meaning and how we can mobilize our resources, including new technologies, to do that specific work. The materialistic values that were so very dear in the early eighties are being revisited as the onset of old age befalls our millions and millions of baby-boomers questioning their spending patterns with their histories of consumption (Taurus) and the relevance to their futures (Aquarius). This revolution in consciousness, which expresses itself through the body politic, is the domain of the earth signs. Thus, what Taurus makes and spends, Virgo then organizes and manages, and finally Capricorn reuses and economizes.

The basis for comfort and pleasure that is associated with Taurus has as part of its roots, the fact that Leo is Taurus' solstice point. In Leo there is a connection between ego, beauty, comfort and spending. When one feels good or looks good, one is able to give and create expansively. Taurus attracts money, is good at managing it and making it grow. It is a fertile sign signified by its annual celebration in the spring with what was called Beltane. Beltane is one of the May Festivals that is associated with our more modern May Day. These celebrations symbolized and paid tribute to the seduction of nature through a series of fertility rites as offerings to the Gods to guarantee the plentitude of all of creation.

Taurus energy requires comfort for peace and creative, challenging projects (taking this from its counterpoint of Leo) in order to sustain interest and happiness. A strong Taurus influence in the chart requires adequate compensation for their work, however they loath working just for a paycheck.

The sign of Virgo is content to take a series of seemingly unrelated items or facts and to assemble and organize them into efficient, useable systems. Virgo is associated with the small intestine of the body, which is the organ in the body that assimilates the various nutrients from our food and parses that which is useful against that which is not.

This may be why individuals with a concentration of Virgo in their charts spend hours sorting and processing information. The sign of Virgo is known for its long hours of devotion and duty. They have tremendous drive and resiliency to adapt to discomfort which may be the influence of its solstice point in Aries, the trailblazer and warrior.

This is indeed a good combination in that Virgo is quite

flexible and when new ideas come in from Aries the Virgo can act on structuring them in a useable form. Virgos are adaptable and can manipulate the data or the structure to fit an expected outcome. Manually dexterous, they can sort through a myriad of minutia (Virgo) quickly (Aries).

The sign of Capricorn is associated with the mountain goat that always has a goal. Capricorn energy can withstand tremendous pressures if they whole-heartedly embrace their goal and believe in themselves (their solstice point of Sagittarius). This earth sign is notorious for its ability to reuse and recycle as well as manage that which already exists.

The recycling movement gained momentum while the North Node was traveling through the sign of Capricorn in the early 1990's. The movement gained acceptance in our society, as Jupiter, Saturn, Uranus and Neptune were moving through the sign of Capricorn.

It was not just the recycling industry that felt the reverberations of these outer planet giants in Capricorn. Multinational corporations started to cannibalize one another and suffered shakeouts as they shape-shifted to form new paradigms in global operations. Capricorns are big-picture players. Where a Virgo will try and deal with the entire minutia, the Capricorn will present the direction of the company. Capricorn energy can appear as aloof and all business. Often found in executive management they may seem rigid, judgmental and authoritative, but scratch the exterior and you'll discover the solstice point of Sagittarius, filled with the warming fire of following a vision. Capricorns make great mentors. They have an ability to bring people together in ways that facilitate productive change. They have high expectations and are willing to sacrifice pleasures and comforts to achieve those expectations. They can live austerely in order to achieve their goals.

Concrete and tangible forms are the interests of earth, but not the interests of the water element. The innate, intuitive ability of the water element is what binds the other elements together. Water is a three-dimensional element and requires a container to hold it or else its motion ebbs and flows like the ocean and its tides. Since water has the unique capability of changing form it can move between and around the other elements. Its movement is continuous and wearing, pushing or dissolving that which lies in its path. Witness the tremendous power and impact of hurricanes, mudslides, tidal waves, and overflowing rivers.

If you have a lot of water in your chart, you might do well in an industry that values and profits from the development of your creative ideas. The water element is full of feeling and introspection that goes deep within to find the kernels to feed a creative enterprise.

Water is prominent in the charts of those who have heightened skills. They can envision the process of transformation from the third-dimensional form into fourth-dimensional space. This is why a high concentration of water is commonly found in the charts of artists, psychics, healers and people in occupations that change things from one form to another. Therefore, the individual or company that has a strong influence of Water in their charts can act as a catalyst for change.

For a water personality to maximize output they need a strong foundation from which to operate. Perhaps the firm always makes sales calls in the morning, this structure enables the water to focus its energy during those calls and then to do more creative or fluid work later in the day. Without structured routine water people can become scattered and frustrated.

The three water signs are Cancer, Scorpio, and Pisces. All are responsive and receptive; their talents include the ability to integrate diverse ideas. The sign of Cancer is often associated with security, the family, and long-term holdings, motivated by a deep need to create a family or home. Those of you in the industries of real estate, restaurants, film, and any industries having to do with family and comfort are found with a high concentration of the sign of Cancer or a strong Moon placement. The sign of Cancer is one of the most tenacious of all the signs. Subtle in your approach, you will approach a goal by moving sideways towards it, almost imperceptibly, until you've captured it. You are the folks that always have the extra bank account or penny box saved for a rainy day. You are world-class stashers, the kings and queens of garage sales!

Your solstice point Gemini is cerebral and provides Cancer's second voice when negotiating and taking on new challenges in your business. The Gemini is always telling the Cancer that it can mix this idea with that item, stirring up things. This marriage of the minds and emotions gives Cancers an ability to appeal to public sentiment. They are great at reading what Joe Q. Public wants to spend his money on.

Whereas the next water sign, Scorpio seeks to know, understand and change everything. They delve deeply into others desires and are marketing mavens because they analyze (to death) what the public wants. There is an innate need to find out, to research, to discover the real truth about anything they are interested in. This borders on obsessiveness and has created many compulsive personalities.

Scorpio energy is extreme, a result of its Aquarius solstice point, and holds high expectations. Working for someone who has a lot of Scorpio in their charts can be a life-changing and demanding experience. If you listen and observe them in action, you can learn a lot about wielding power. You will learn how to investigate, ask questions, think and strategize. Over time they prove themselves invaluable to management with their loyalty and searing intellect. It is the Scorpios who are prepared to beat competitors by having evaluated all of their weaknesses before a big meeting. Having Scorpio personnel can give you a competitive advantage.

The element of Pisces, the last water sign, acts much like a conduit for the organization to regroup, to heal and to reflect. If you have a lot of Pisces or Neptune in your chart you require a lot of space and time to dream and to incubate new ideas and inspirations. Pisces' solstice point is Libra. Pisces energy has to feel as though the spiritual part of themselves as well as the physical and mental are in balance (Libra), in order to operate successfully. You also need to have people to whom you can assign projects since focusing tends to be one of your challenges. Like a river that is overrun by heavy rains, you must have inlets where you may disperse your energy efficiently.

Pisces realm is the world of the arts, music and all forms of including operating substance abuse programs. You hold a unique position in the world of business because you act as the missing link of inspiration, which catalyzes others into new thinking patterns.

Pisces or a strong influence of Pisces represents the lone wolves in the world of business and corporations, requiring your own space in which to work and a strong manager who can support and understand your creative efforts. However, you may be misunderstood as you communicate in an indirect, diffuse manner causing unintentional confusion for coworkers or superiors as they try and pin you down for specifics. Time can be another problem for Pisces in that you operate outside of the physical realm of time. Punching a clock and having a report done by five can be far too restrictive. You will deliver a high-end product, in your own time.

Qualities or Modes & Aspects

Qualities are the mode of operation for each individual, company or event at its initiation. Qualities show the modality of the individuals or company rather than their style of operation, which is described in element expression. This is the basic difference between the elements and the qualities.

The three qualities are cardinal, fixed and mutable. They fall into different elements, but express the same kind of energy. Since they occur at the angles or the 0°, 90° and 180° distances to each other, their nature is stressful and provides motivation.

The cardinal cross is associated with the cardinal points Aries, Cancer, Libra and Capricorn and the natural rulers of first, fourth, seventh and tenth houses of the horoscope. Positions on these axes are considered angular. The nature of cardinal placements encourages initiating a myriad of projects and risk taking. The cardinal points are ambitious, independent, and pioneering. A high emphasis of cardinal energy in the horoscope suggests a vocation that requires challenges and a seat of the pants response to stay interested.

People with primarily cardinal placements are good initiators, but may not complete things well. They respond negatively to what they may perceive as menial positions unless there are mitigating factors in the horoscope. Cardinal people are great at coming up with new ideas and keeping up with the latest trends and cycles. The cardinal individual is the one who sees the future and poises your company to reap the benefits. This person needs to have a solid team underneath them to follow-through with the actions that they are bound to start.

The negative side of cardinality is that it can be self-centered and rash. They must learn to strategically plan their course of actions. Their prime directive in life is trailblazing new ideas and models. When they learn the art of delegating then they operate at their optimum capacity.

The fixed signs are comprised of Taurus, Leo, Scorpio, and Aquarius. In the natural wheel they are found in the succedent houses, which are the second, fifth, eighth, and eleventh, respectively. These are the houses that are the midpoints, or, resolution phases of the wheel and fall between the cardinal houses and the mutable houses.

The fixed qualities represent the ability to bring into form that which is an idea. They finish what the cardinal people in their fervor start. They have the practical know-how on where to go to get what needs doing, done. They serve as excellent resource people and have a fierce determination to succeed in their endeavors.

This group sculpts ideas into matter. To keep them satisfied they need to be valued, since each one of these sectors relates to the second house or phase from each one of the cardinal points or houses. The natural second house, associated with Taurus, has to do with cash flow and spending and the values that shape our personalities. The same holds true for the fifth house, which represents the creative babies of our minds and bodies or those things, which our families (fourth house) value. In the eighth house, we join with others to share resources, sexuality, and all sorts of mergers. The eighth house is the second from the seventh, which is the house of partnership and value sharing. The eighth house, associated with Scorpio the eighth sign, represents the forms of partnership holdings, such as investments, shared loans, legacies and inheritances.

The eleventh house which is associated with Aquarius, friends, colleagues, and community, is the second house from the tenth, thus indicating the best type of friends and associates as resources for your business. We often find the right jobs or right connection through an associate.

If you work as an independent contractor, it is important to have a strong mix of fixed signs in the chart. However, if there are too many fixed signs and not enough cardinality then you will get comfortable operating your business in the same way and may never update your equipment, marketing campaigns, or try new management techniques because you have always had success with the way things are. The term, "If it ain't broke, don't fix it" was probably first articulated by someone with a concentration of fixed planets.

It is equally true that if you lack the third quality, that of mutability, then you may be inflexible and unbending. The mutable element is important in that it is the element of flexible transitions between one phase or cycle and another. Using the natural zodiac, the mutable signs are associated with the cadent houses the third, sixth, ninth, and twelfth and with the signs of Gemini, Virgo, Sagittarius, and Pisces. These cadent or mutable houses are the transition vehicles that move us from one quadrant of the chart to the next. They are the transition signs that connect the fixed signs back to the cardinal signs. These "bridge" signs represent education, service, systems, methods, intuition and flexible thinking patterns, all necessary components that shape-shift our consciousness over time.

Mutables connect people and ideas with one another to facilitate and act as agents for change. In an organization, the mutable personality is usually the mediator, facilitator, and information gatherer that plug people and concepts into the proper channels. If you ever meet a good Hollywood agent, they are probably chock full of mutable planets and placements. They excel at juggling information and knowledge, but need the cardinals to initiate and the fixed people to build something of lasting value.

Using This Information

The first step to success in an organization is in recognizing the qualities and the differences between these three groupings. If there are systemic problems in the organization we can examine the imbalances of the various modes. For example, if an individual has a great deal of mutable air energy in their chart (primarily a Gemini signature), then this person may not be best suited as a manager who restructures the organization, unless of course they have a trusty fixed earth (primarily a Taurus signature mode) assistant who successfully utilizes the contacts that the mutable air manager generates.

To sum up, keep in mind that to keep a company successful you must balance new ideas and possibilities (cardinal) along with the process of getting at least a few of them implemented (fixed) and derive assistance from outside sources or consultants to sell the idea or refine it (mutable).

Signatures

Similar to a final dispositor, your signature signals an area of strength. (*NOTE: A dispositor is a type of "distillation" of the chart. For example, if the Sun is in Gemini, we look at the sign of Gemini, and then we find Mercury, the ruler of Gemini, and where it is in the chart. Say, for example, it is in Cancer in the horoscope, and then we look to the Moon, which rules Cancer, and then find it in Aquarius and then look at Uranus...etc. What this does is gives us a "trail or trails" of how the energies pour one into the other, giving us a dispositor, or, underscoring theme(s) of the chart.)* This is true for both individuals and companies. To calculate signatures, for example, if the highest number of qualities is mutable and the highest number of elements in the chart is earth, then the signature of the chart is Virgo. The element that is strongest and the quality that is strongest are placed side by side and thus we discover the signature of the horoscope. From this particular signature of Virgo, we know that the individual or the company has the ability to assimilate and digest divergent bits of information, as would a researcher, or writer, or holistic health analyst or computer programmer.

Using another example, if the highest number of qualities is cardinal and the highest number of elements is water, then the signature would be Cancer embodying the capacity to sensitively assess a situation and to take bold action based on review of the assessment. People who accumulate things, like bank accounts, collections, and various properties have a strong Cancer or Moon influence in their horoscopes. Motivated by security and safety for themselves or their clans they act more on how things may feel rather than what they may think is best.

By comparison another water sign, Scorpio is more stagnant taking its time to seep into a situation. Its quality is fixed which lengthens the decision-making process as they are prone to wanting background research and they will engage in protracted weighing of pros and cons before taking any one particular action. Consequently, this is a useful signature for strategic planning in business.

They may wait a while before making a decision, but once the decision is made, they have the fortitude and the endurance to bring it to completion. Scorpios will want to make solid investments and as they may invest more money than others in each transaction they are sure to be thorough in their research to protect their investment. They excel at due diligence. They may take the firm's assets and plunge headlong into what may appear to others to be a risky venture, then go right to the edge and hold that position for a long time. They usually win big over the long haul.

Now that you have a clearer understanding of the sensitive points prepare to learn how to utilize the power of rulerships. Rulerships synthesize the activities that occur in the various areas of the chart. Little is written in modern texts or taught in Astrological classes on classical rulerships, but without understanding their importance you will never reach a level of sophisticated analysis. Rulership theory and a fundamental understanding of Horary Astrology will increase your learning curve in horoscope analysis and will help you find critical answers when testing out complicated corporate or vocational questions.

Brain Teasers

Following are some charts with different signatures. They are in sequence: a Program and Lecture Coordinator; the Professional Artist; the Marketing Director; and the Owner/Developer of a very successful employment service. Do any of them have a specific signature? What are their elements and what are their qualities?

(See Illustrations 6, 7, 8 & 9)

Illustration 6

Female: Program Director, Sept. 14, 1930, 4:35pm PST + 8:00, Napa, CA, 38°N17'50" 122°W17'04"

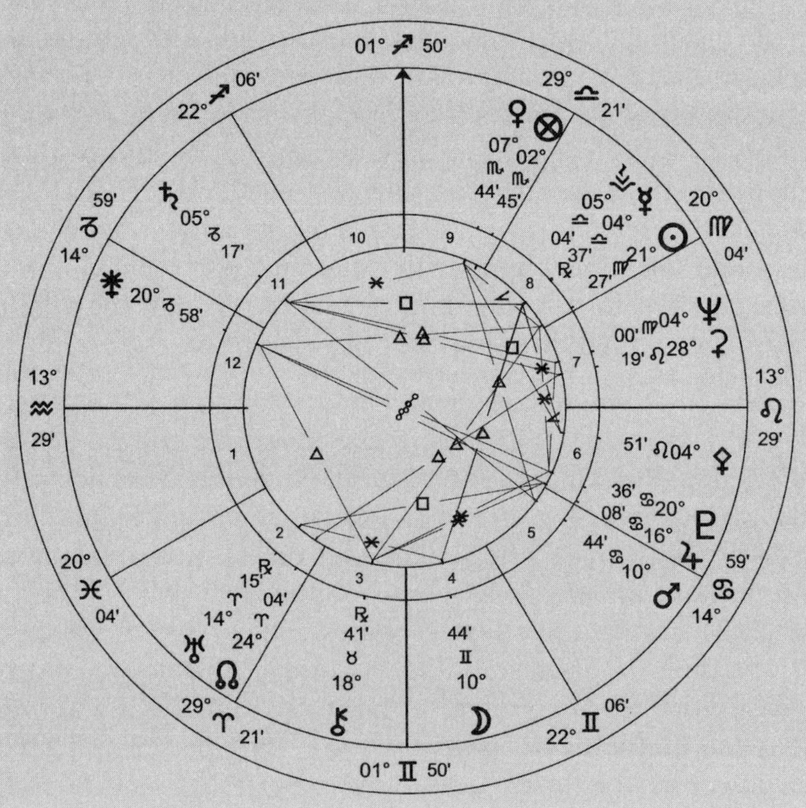

Illustration 7

Female: Professional Artist, Oct. 22, 1944, 10:35pm EWT + 4:00, Toronto, CAN, 43°N39' 079°W23'

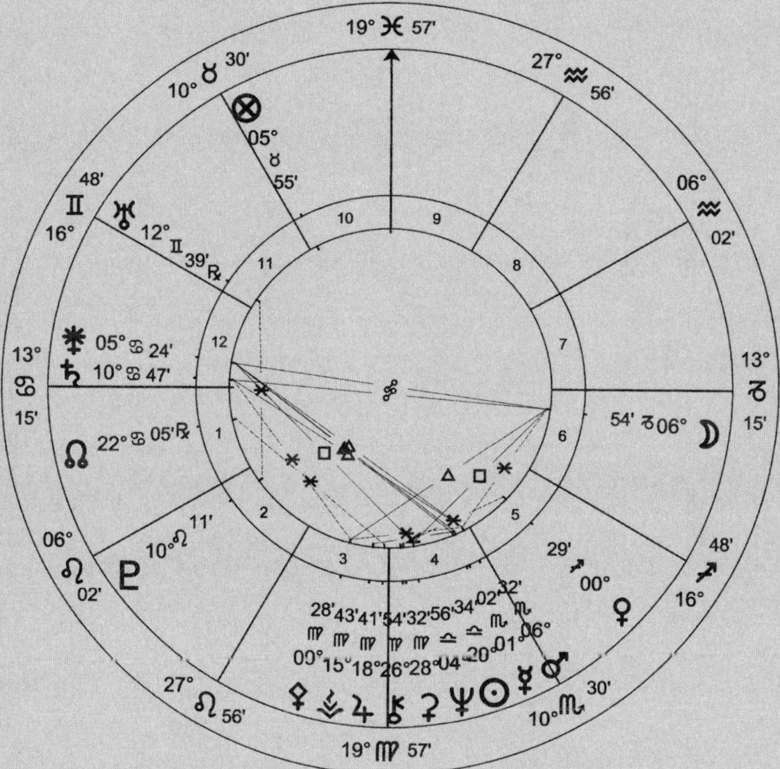

Illustration 8

Female: Marketing Dir. Bldr., Dec. 31, 1937, 12:03pm PST + 8:00, Portland, OR, 45°N20'27" 122°W37'

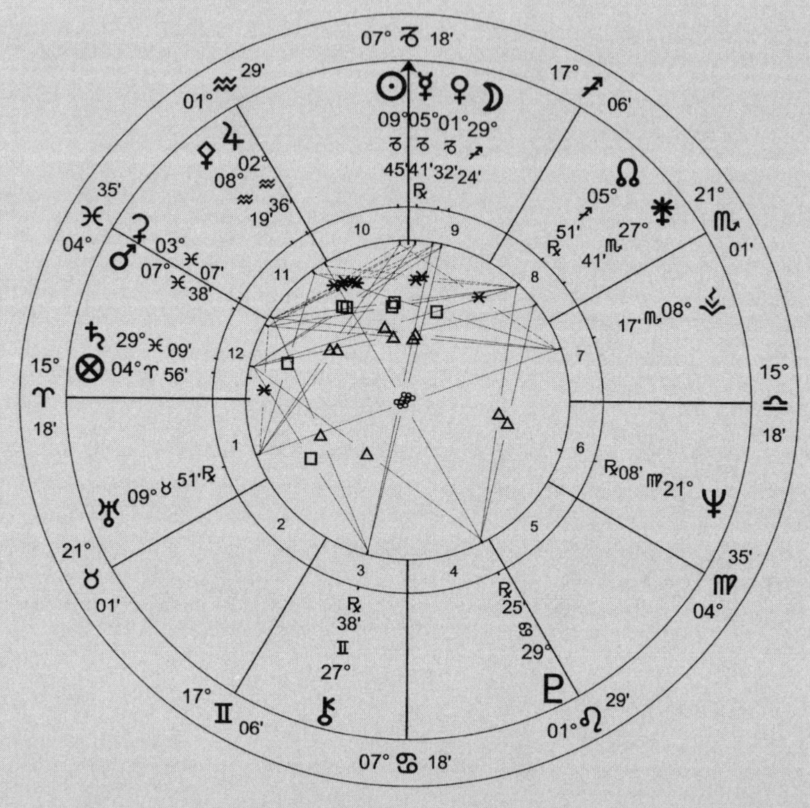

Illustration 9

Female: Owner/Director Employment, Nov. 22, 1946, 9:00pm + 5:00, Eagle Lake, ME, 47°N03' 068°W36'

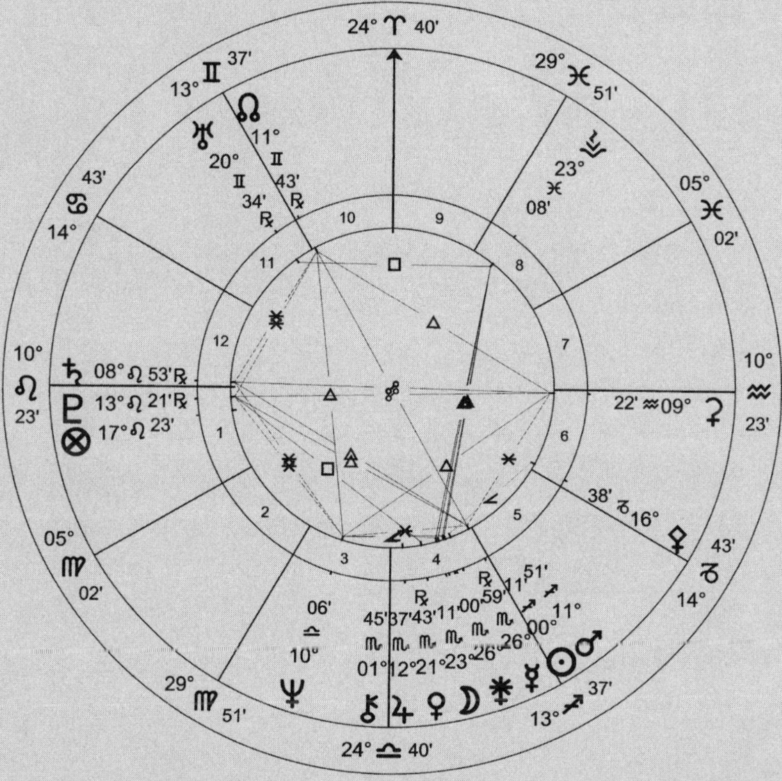

Chapter 4

Rulerships

Rulership delineation is a technique that is not frequently mentioned in the study of the various methods of interpretation. It is sometimes only after years of study that the usefulness of this technique becomes apparent.

Astrology is often taught as a two-dimensional subject. We watch transits and look at one house and its sign to see if there is a planet there or not and if so, how those two factors connect. Many people stop there. However, if you really look at the chart, it is far more complex. We can see subtler levels of meaning by using the system of rulerships. This method allows you to open to greater possibilities as we study a chart in depth. This is where rulerships come into play.

Rulerships can be defined in many ways. There are traditional and modern delineations of rulerships. A study of the many systems and methods are of great value to the practicing astrologer and this study lends itself to many different avenues of interpretation. One of the oldest studies of rulerships is the study of Horary Astrology and it is recommended that every astrologer study this method of prediction even if they don't continue on with it. It has very specific rules and regulations and requires a good amount of time to master. However, even if you never become a Horary astrologer, the experience of working with rulerships is paramount to successful interpretation of both individual and company charts.

Studying Vedic Astrology is also another way to expand your knowledge of rulerships, particularly when we focus upon the houses. My experience after studying Vedic Astrology for a couple of years is that some of the delineations used in the Vedic system work very well in Western delineation. One example of this is using the twelfth house as representing the area of enlightenment. The twelfth house in Vedic is also the house of foreign countries. I have used both these interpretations in Western delineations many times with a very positive result.

We can use an example of simple predictive or planning delineation using rulerships in the following example. For example, if you have the sign of Gemini on your tenth house of career and outer world standing, then you not only look at the sign of Gemini and its meaning, but you also take a secondary look at where the sign of Virgo falls in your chart. The planet, Mercury, rules both the signs of Gemini and Virgo.

When Mercury retrogrades three times a year, for three weeks at a time, the houses it rules are affected. It is important that you not only view the house through which Mercury is retrograding, but to always include in the interpretation the houses that are ruled by Mercury for in-depth analysis.

When you review a horoscope that has, for example, the sign of Gemini on the tenth house cusp, (the Midheaven, which indicates careers and connections to authority figures), you note where Mercury is placed natally. Some of the questions you might ask are: Where is the ruler of the tenth house, Mercury, placed in this chart? Is it in an angular, succedent, or cadent house? Is it highly aspected? Are the aspects primarily positive or negative aspects? Do they create more or less tension or motivation? In what sign is this planet? What degree? Is it about to progress from one sign to the next, thus changing the climate of the house(s) that it rules?

It is important to view other data other than what you immediately see in a chart. For example, on what day of

Days of the Week

Illustration 10

Sunday	Sun
Monday	Moon
Tuesday	Mars
Wednesday	Mercury
Thursday	Jupiter
Friday	Venus
Saturday	Saturn

the week is this person or company born? Was it a Tuesday or a Thursday? Those days of the week have rulerships. Tuesdays are named after the ancient Norse god of war, Tiw. Thursdays are named after Jupiter, or Thor in Viking mythology. The day influences the individual, the company, or the event. (Illustration 10).

I have a friend who at one time was an executive for Safeway Stores. He commented one day that he noticed that many Safeway tragedies occurred during those weeks in which Monday was a holiday and the workweek began on Tuesday (a Mars day). Incidents such as the warehouse fire in Richmond, California were cited. It didn't help, of course, that the original Safeway chart was incorporated under the sign of Aries and that its original owner was an Aries, also! Mars rules Aries as well as fires and assertiveness. The days of the week influence events. A partnership that forms on a Tuesday (Mars) may not be as successful as one that forms on a Friday (Venus).

Age Cycles

Illustration 11

0-7 Yrs	Moon
7-15 Yrs	Mercury
15-24 Yrs	Venus
24-34 Yrs	Sun
34-45 Yrs	Mars
45-57 Yrs	Jupiter
57-70 Yrs	Saturn
70-85 Yrs	Uranus
85-99 Yrs	Neptune
100 + Yrs	Pluto

How old are you? Another method we use in rulerships is the concept of age cycles. Are you 14 or 56 years of age? Different ages embrace different age cycles. At what ages are you experiencing life cycles such as Saturn returns or Saturn oppositions? Are there similarities? Identifying them and putting them into chronological order helps your interpretation. (Illustration 11).

If you look at a company's chart and you know that it is technologically astute and progressive, it probably has a prominent Uranus. You might not necessarily notice Uranus as a prominent influence in the horoscope but when you begin the task of rulership delineation you may understand more how important the planet really is. If there are heavy transits to Uranus then you know something is coming for this company because of what you see in its chart.

Illustration 12

Event: *eBay First Trade, Sept. 24, 1998, 9:30am EDT + 4:00, New York, NY, 40°N42'51" 074°W00'23"*

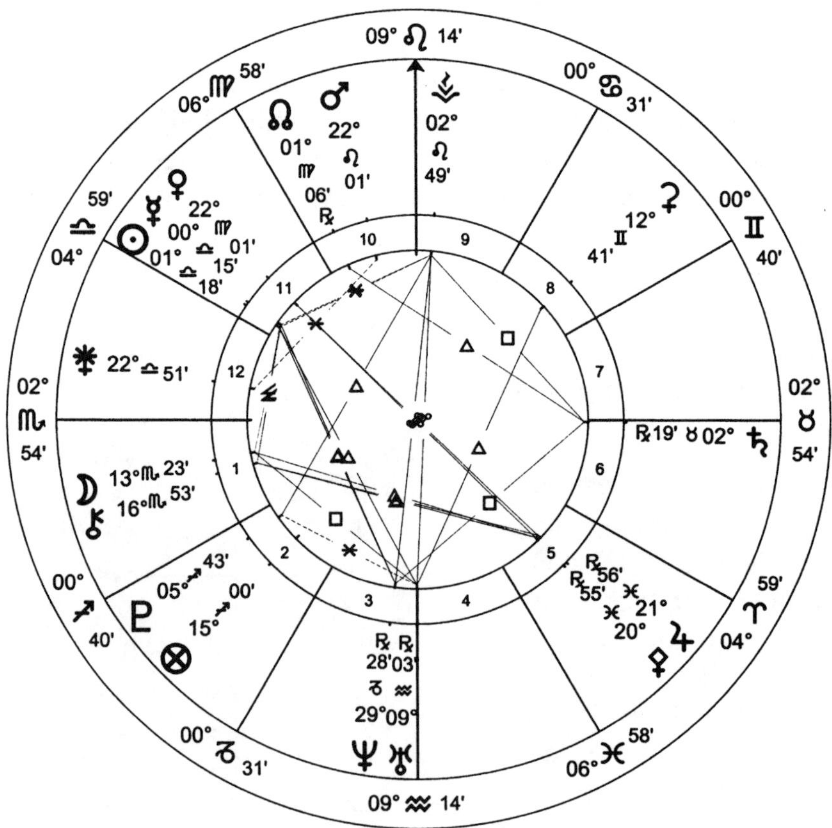

As an example, we can use the first trade chart of eBay, Inc., September 24, 1998, 09:30 AM, EDT, in New York City, New York. (Illustration 12). This information is from Bill Meridian, the author of Planetary Stock Trading.[4] eBay is one of the first on-line auction sites from which several models have derived since its first trade. In keeping with the idea of rulerships, there is an angular Uranus on the fourth house cusp at 9° of Aquarius. Uranus squares the Moon (representing the product and the public) at 13° Scorpio, which is in the first house, another angle. This chart's Uranus also squares the first trade's Saturn at 2° Taurus, which is very close to the seventh house, another angle. Three angular hits with the sign of Aquarius on one angle and ruled by Uranus, associated with the computer industry, is a perfect example of a very powerful rulership.

Other ways of using rulerships are delineated by examining current eclipse hits. Is the planet ruling the eighth house of a company chart being transited by a conjunction of a current solar eclipse? Is it being squared or opposed? This would naturally create a stress, which leads to an awareness of problems and then change regarding the company's eighth house. This will occur over the course of the subsequent third, sixth, ninth, or twelve-month period after the eclipse. If an eclipse is a New Moon (Solar eclipse), then the sequence will hit upon the following New Moon in the above-mentioned increments. If the eclipse occurred at the Full Moon (Lunar eclipse), then the sequence will hit upon the following Full Moons in the above-mentioned increments

The eighth house of a company chart includes information pertaining to the company's frozen assets, its losses or gains through the death of the corporation, financial responsibilities, private conferences, board of directors, credit, dividends, trade secrets, net earnings, insurances, handling of legacies, nonprofit status, donations to nonprofit organizations, financial conditions involved in partnerships, mergers or lawsuits, financial relations with competitors, competitor's financial condition, revenue from investments or liquidation of frozen assets, loans and income from sources not under immediate control of the organization, or the company treasurer.

When an eclipse transits a planet in a house, the domain of that house is being highlighted. However, a richer interpretation is possible by including the house that the planet rules.

Following is the chart of an excellent psychotherapist born on November 18, 1946. Ascendant: 19° Taurus 53'. (Illustration 13). This chart is ruled by Venus, which is placed in the seventh house of relationship. Note also that Jupiter, the ruler of her eighth, income, is placed in the sixth of health and health services, as is Chiron. This woman has been in the county health services for almost thirty years. She also maintains a private psychotherapy practice. Her primary motivation for becoming a psychologist stemmed from her early childhood experiences. Note the placement of Pluto, the ruler of Scorpio her Sun sign, as well as the ruler of psychotherapy, natally placed in the fourth house. Note the ruler of her fourth house, her family, placed in the seventh house of relationships with others. Service is one of her primary purposes as well as relationship counseling. She has a unique ability to come up with unusual suggestions and solutions (Aquarius Midheaven).

Her Taurus Ascendant approaches the Capricorn decanate of the sign of Taurus (Ascendant rounds off to 20° Taurus). Saturn rules Capricorn, work, and career, and conjuncts her Pluto (psychotherapy) in the fourth. Saturn is also the ruler of her ninth house, (philosophy and belief systems), as well as the more ancient ruler of the sign of Aquarius, which is her Midheaven sign. She is intelligent and uses unusual and eclectic methods in her consulting. Uranus, the ruler of her tenth, is in the second house of earning power.

Her secondary interest, which is beginning to be a new

Illustration 13

Female: Excellent Therapist, Nov. 18, 1946, 4:23pm PST + 8:00, Maywood, CA, 33°N59' 118°W11'

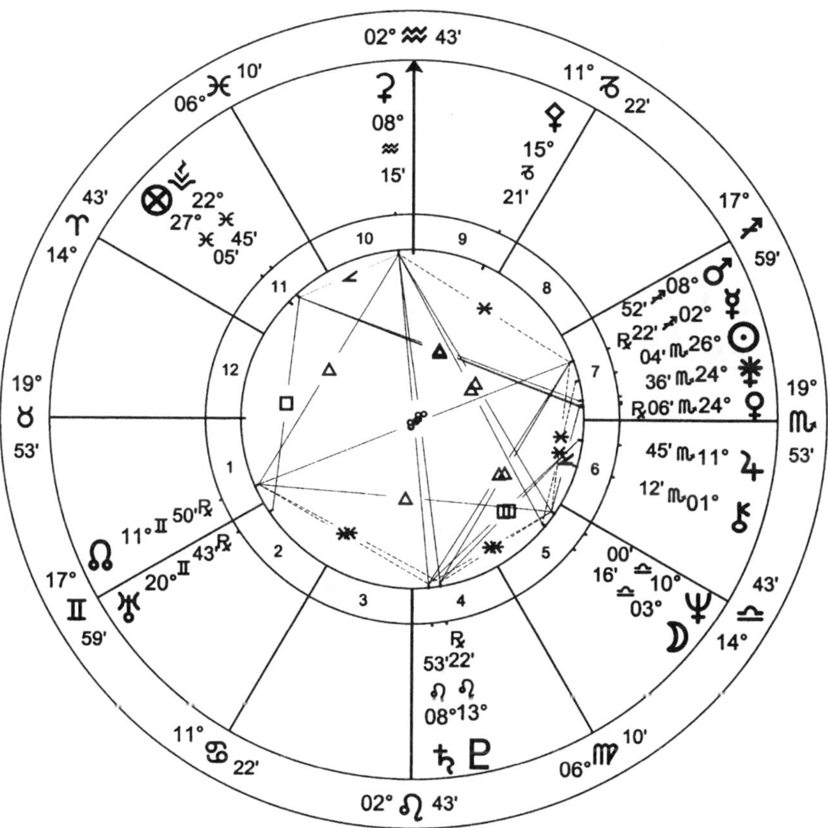

career focus, is cooking. Note the placement of Saturn, co-ruler of the chart, as well as the ruler of careers in the fourth house, a Cancer house. The fourth house and the sixth house are associated with the food services businesses, or food supply businesses. As an added note, her spouse (represented by the seventh house ruled by Pluto placed in the fourth house) was in the food service business for years. Her friends, whom she calls family, enjoy cooking with her. Cooking and designing recipes are her hobby (Moon rules food and is placed in the fifth house of hobbies). As the transit of Saturn passed through her twelfth house and entered her first house, she started her part-time catering business in a very low-key fashion.

This is an appropriate choice, considering that Saturn, which rules the ninth and the tenth, crossed the Ascendant, which is the place of new life and new birth. Traditionally, I have observed that regardless of what house Saturn rules in the chart, that when it passes over your Ascendant, you begin a new career. Sometimes you start the new career as soon as the transit is complete while at other times the process moves more slowly. In this case, Saturn had been squaring her natal Saturn as a last quarter square thus breaking down structure. This indicates that there is a high likelihood that at the second Saturn return she will retire from her profession and enter the catering business as her second career.

Throughout the last ten years of practice, I've witnessed that whereas people used to retire at the age of 58 through 60 twenty years ago, that now they choose new careers. This is due to better health extending the productive lives of people. It has been my observation that the second career that begins at the second Saturn return is more in tune with the individual's spiritual and soul quest. It may have been a desire during the first Saturn return, but due to fear, the individual was unable to make that choice until the passage of time and the development of wisdom (both being Saturn characteristics).

Her Jupiter, which is the ruler of her eighth (income), and the ruler of her eleventh, (friends who act as assets for your business), is placed in the sixth house of services. This has helped her psychiatric career and is helping to start her catering career. She has Ceres (⚳), the grain goddess, in the tenth house of public acknowledgment. Ceres is common in the charts of people who have interests related to the food business. Her Ceres is in the sign of Aquarius suggesting a global outlook, which is echoed in the eighth house Sagittarius placement. Her catering business will probably focus on foreign cuisines. She plans to develop "theme" catering to support the foreign influence.

The above is a simple delineation of someone's chart using rulerships. What do you see in this chart? What other possibilities or ideas first present themselves to you using this technique? As we proceed, you will note how this is used in company and event charts.

Now begins the deeper study of the planets, their myths and stories and the symbolism that weaves them together. Initially, the exploration of the myths may seem out of context since this book is about business Astrology and its analysis. However, the roots of the planetary meanings translate into all the branches of Astrology, which include such disciplines as medical and mundane Astrology. Once you grow familiar with the basic myths and stories, chart interpretations become easier as you will readily recall the stories associated with the planets.

[4] Bill Meridian, author of Planetary Stock Trading (New York: Cycles Research and Publications, 1998) Second Printing) Information directly from Meridian.

CHAPTER 5

THE MYTHOLOGICAL SIGNATURES OF THE PLANETS

VOCATIONAL & BUSINESS INDICATORS

☉ SUN ♌

THE KINGS AND QUEENS OF THE CORPORATION

The Sun represents the life force of the individual or the company. The Sun of an individual as well as a company represents the driving force. This is particularly true if the Sun is placed in an angular position in the chart.

My experience has been that if the Sun is in the first house, then because the first house is the Aries house, the individual may be in business for him or herself and show some type of public prominence by the time they are 35 years of age. Contrary to that, the individual who has their Sun in the tenth house, the natural Capricorn house may not go into business or even reach a peak of self-maintained success until after 45 or 50 years of age.

The Sun's placement in someone's chart is where they "shine". It is also where they go for inspiration and a shot of new vitality. The part of the chart in which the Sun falls is where we find ourselves taking risks and gambles, which relate to the Sun being the natural ruler of Leo as well as the fifth house. Gambling and risk-taking are both important elements in business. Therefore, the assignment of the nature of taking risks from the head of the company, who like the King or Queen of the realm, must make the final decisions for the people.

In a company's chart, the Sun represents the chairman of the board or the person in charge. In a sole proprietorship it is the owner. Where the Sun is placed in the chart is where there is a positive influence from former leaders of the company, from the individual's father, or paternal models in life. It can show where those individuals can help influence one's career or company.

If we look at the Sun from a mythological perspective, the Sun represents the search for self-actualization as represented in stories of the Holy Grail. There was a search for God, the "Father", and the "Holy Spirit". The search for the father is a myth mentioned many times over in the works of Liz Greene and Joseph Campbell.

The story is characterized in one of the films in the Indiana Jones series entitled, Indiana Jones and the Last Crusade, where Indiana Jones is searching for his father who is, in turn, searching for his life-long passion, which is the search for the Holy Grail. The search for Self is very important for anyone in pursuit of their right career, their true work in this life, their authentic creative expression. The essence of that search is encoded in the sign and house placement of the Sun Sign of the company or individual. The modality of the Sun Sign is also important.

Remember the three modalities: cardinal, fixed and mutable.

Cardinal signs (Aries, Cancer, Libra and Capricorn) are the starters, trailblazers that see things in a new and pioneering way. An individual who has a cardinal Sun is someone who isn't naturally patient and who has to work at finishing what he starts.

Part of their motivation is to be recognized. They are renegades who attempt to do things that most people wouldn't attempt. Cardinal types require some sort of edge, an adrenaline high, a living on the edge in the pursuit of their work.

They are usually at their best working for themselves where they may have autonomy. If they are smart, they know they need assistance in finishing the myriad projects they generate. They need someone who can finish what they start and assist them in prioritizing and focusing their ideas. In other words they are great starters, but lousy finishers!! One of their greatest challenges is to think before they act and measure the various outcomes of their decisions. This can also apply to those individuals who have a lot of angularity in their charts.

This is where a healthy and mature Mars comes into play. Mars is the knight waiting to be the king or queen who symbolize the individuated Sun. Mars and the Sun have to learn to work together. This is difficult when we see hard aspects between the individual's or the company's Mars and their Sun, like squares, semi-squares, oppositions, and any of the aspects whose degrees total to the number 9 (See Illustration 14, p.211—Another View of the Lunation Cycle Using Hard Aspects—in the chapter on the Lunation Cycle).

Hard aspects between Mars and the Sun dissipate energy, at the same time that it drives energy. Impulsive action is sometimes a problem with this configuration. This is one of the most dangerous things in any business venture, in any career decision, or any major invention. This configuration encourages taking risks, which is important in successful business transactions, but acting without thinking, without examining the possible outcomes of choices can be dangerous. The placement of the Sun in an individual horoscope and the house in which it is placed are indicators of what gives a kind of light to the individual's life or the company's life. It is where you or they shine.

> ### Brain Teaser
>
> Where is the Sun placed in your horoscope? Where is it placed in your company's chart or where was it placed at the time that you opened the doors to your company? This indicates the place from which you may draw energy, particularly when things are slow or when you feel lost. For example, the Sun in the eleventh house may suggest that by reaching out to friends for support or inspiration and by doing the same for them, you find a new way.

Moon

Products and Employee Relations

The next step is to look at the Moon in either a company or individual chart. First let's look at the symbolism and the archetypal energy of the Moon. The Moon is unique. Always changing its shape, the Moon shifts from one constellation to the next every couple of days creating coastal and emotional tides. The Moon is the only "planet" that has no light of its own and, therefore, reflects the light of the Sun, which in business or vocational charts represents the leaders of the company. The Moon represents the "Cosmic Mother" in myth, the mother that nurtures as well as devours. All ancient Goddess statues represent primal women as full and round in shape like the Moon. Like the female cycle and form, the energy of the Moon ebbs and flows. Life begins, waxes and wanes.

The Moon in a personal chart represents the containers of the body, the breasts, the stomach, and the womb – the containers. That is exactly what it represents in Business Astrology, too! Containers have many forms. There are the containers that enclose the family, the house, therefore, the housing industry. There are containers that enclose food, which represent the food business or restaurant business.

In traditional Astrology, the Moon represents the tribe, the family. In business, it represents the public and its response (don't we all respond to the Moon)? Therefore, the Moon in business represents the public's image of the products of a company. It appears prominently in any individual or company dealing with family products and services. Many people who have prominent placements of the Moon or, the sign of Cancer, which it rules or the sign of Virgo, which is its esoteric ruler, find themselves drawn towards these areas.

The Moon can represent the females in the company. Some people think that the Moon in a company horoscope represents the employees, particularly any employee that assists in the "birthing" process of the company's products. Using this theory, the employees will "reflect" the energy of the Sun or the leaders as mentioned earlier.

Mythologically, the "Cosmic Mother" collaborates with images of certain Goddesses as Kwan Yin and Black Madonna. Kwan Yin is the ancient Chinese Goddess of nurturing. Black Madonna is an ancient Christian image, which incorporated the earthiness of pagan Goddesses with the Christian ideal of service and selflessness. The expression of these Goddesses through a business or vocational chart suggests an ability to take care of the public through its products or through its service and suggests that it takes care of its employees. A strong placement of the Moon in a company chart suggests a company that has a great deal of holdings in cash, stocks, or investments and implies a know-how on how to get things done, addressing the correct details, implementing new techniques as well as methods. Some people would look to Mercury for this ability and Mercury is examined for this purpose, too. However, because I also look at the Moon and how it rules Virgo in the esoteric school, I have found that the Moon can play a large part in details and systems.

Original company charts such as Hershey Foods, incorporated October 24, 1927, in Dover, Delaware (Illustration 15), have their Moon in the sign that rules its product. For example, in the original incorporation chart of Hershey Foods, the Moon is in Libra, which is ruled by Venus, which rules sugar and chocolate. In the original incorporation chart of Kellogg's Foods, incorporated on December 11, 1922, in Dover, Delaware (Illustration 16), the Moon is in the sign of Virgo, which is one of the signs that rules grains. Kellogg's main product, when it started, was Corn Flakes.

Illustration 15

Event: Hershey Foods, Oct. 24, 1927, 9:00am EST + 5:00, Dover, DE, 39°N09'29" 075°W31'29"

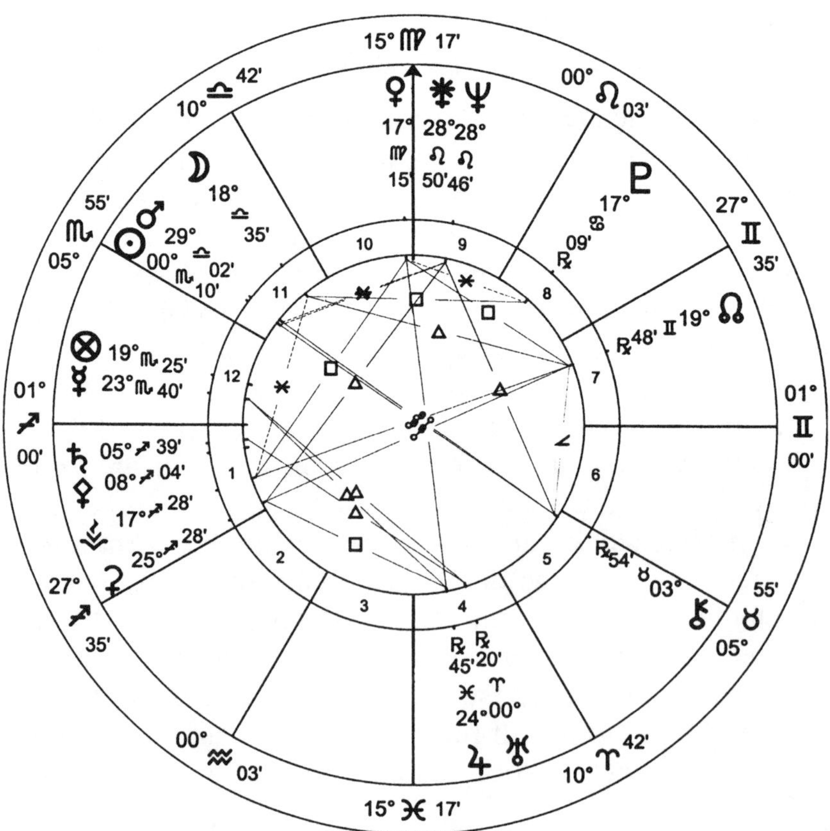

Illustration 16

Event: Kellogg's Foods, Dec. 11, 1922, 1:00pm EST + 5:00, Dover, DE, 39°N09'29" 075°W31'29"

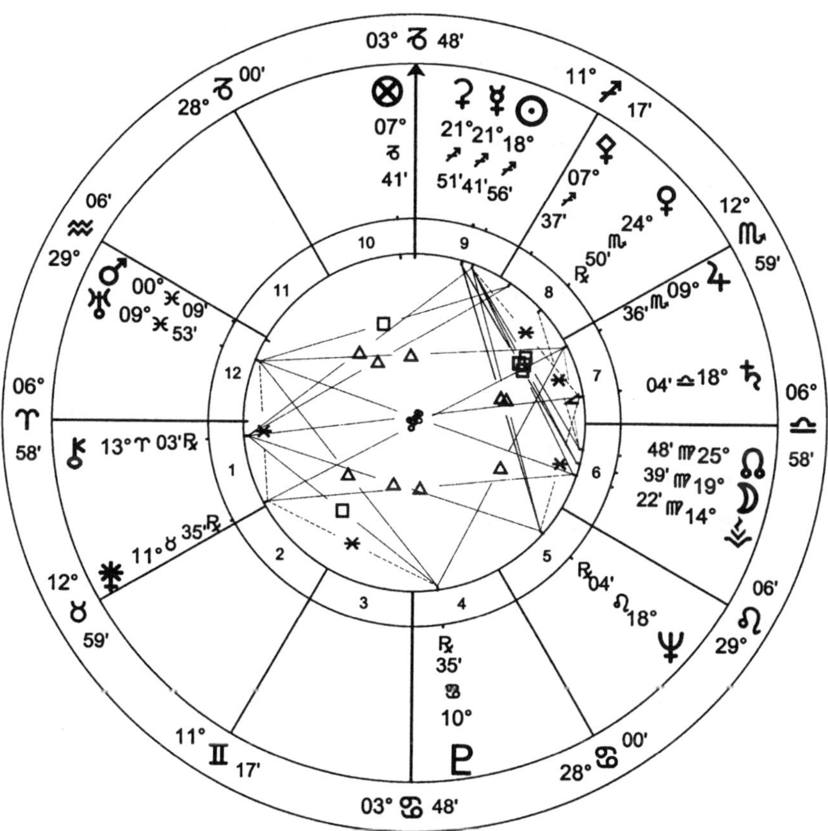

The Moon in a horoscope is very strong, yet subtle. For example, when you walk into a traditional Eastern Orthodox Church, you are struck by the huge byzantine domes, particularly of the main dome, which is often painted with Mary, the mother of Jesus Christ. On her lap is placed the Holy Child. The image is striking in that the larger of these two is always Mary, the Mother or the Moon.

A similar mythological figure is the Roman Goddess Ceres or Demeter, as she is known in Greek myth, the Goddess of fruitfulness and bounty. It is beautiful Demeter who feeds the earth and produces the food and flowers. Because of the loss of her beloved daughter, Persephone, she goes into deep mourning. Her deep loss translates into famine and starvation for the world. The people of the earth beg Zeus to return Demeter's beloved daughter to her so that they do not starve. He pleads with Pluto, his brother, who is the God of power and the underworld and Pluto agrees to allow Persephone to return only half of each year to her mother, because she has already eaten from the pomegranate, the fruit of the underworld. This action claims her as Pluto's, at least for part of the time. The other half of the year she returns to her mother. This story is also the basis for the story of the seasons. When Persephone remains with her Lord, Pluto, her mother, Demeter or Ceres, is in mourning and she stops producing fruit and flowers and we have fall and winter. However, when she returns for the other half of the year, Demeter rejoices and brings back the fruit and the flowers and we have spring and summer.

The above mythological characters have as their base, the Moon, the symbol in your horoscope that represents your early childhood experience, your family, and your tribe. Extrapolating the association into business is not that big a leap. The key is to translate these meanings into contemporary terms. Thusly, the idea of businesses that deal with food and food supplies, restaurants and restaurant supplies, food brokers, larger grocery store chains, which are contemporary expressions of ancient myths.

The movie business is associated with the Moon, as is Neptune, which is discussed later in this chapter. Since the Moon has no light of its own, it reflects the light around its environment and this, in a way, is how we experience movies. People see movies in different ways. It all depends on what "filters" you use. When you go to a movie, you are in a certain mood. The word "mood" comes from the Moon. Fittingly, as the Moon changes shape and signs, you shift to different moods. A movie can change your mood, too. The environment of the movie changes your emotional response.

Since the Moon is known for its changeability, then a highly placed Moon in an individual's chart may indicate emotional changeability, as does a highly placed Moon in a company's chart. This could indicate that the company may shift from one idea to the next. If properly channeled by doing demographic studies for marketing their products, then this can imply a great deal of success. However, if there is no plan, no structure in which the water can flow, then it can imply that the company's focus may tend to be off. Highly placed Moons in company charts may also indicate a strong feminine influence or feminine energy in the company and may, as a result of this highly measured percentage, have those industries ruled by the Moon as primary markets for income.

Brain Teaser

Look at the Moon in your chart. Is it angular? Is housing and food an important part of your life? Do you find yourself care taking people inappropriately? Does your company's Moon have strength? Does it listen to the public's input as to which direction to take?

☿ Mercury ♊ ♍

Trade, Commerce, and Communications

Mercury is different from the Moon. Having no particular gender, nor particular loyalty or place association, Mercury is the neutral party that transfers and translates communications. Its existence is for the sole purpose of generating ideas and sales and to convey information. The more highly developed the company's or individual's Mercury, the more easily it is to either process information or convey it.

When you read the ancient myths of Mercury, the trickster child of Zeus, you recognize immediately that he is the archetype of rapid change. Pictured with winged feet, he moves in and out of the different worlds unscathed. Mercury rules the spoken and written word, advertising and printing. A company with prominent Mercury in its chart or an individual, who has the same markings, has a mobile and facile tongue and wit.

My thesis for my M.B.A. program, asked as its hypothetical question, what planets or archetypes are highly accented in the charts of advertising specialists?[5] Research revealed that Mercury was prominent and often placed in the second house, which is the house of values and possessions, but also the skills and talents that we have that earn us money.

Those of you who have a lot of planets in Gemini or Virgo, which are signs both ruled by Mercury, are people who need variety in your chosen work and you can juggle several things at one time. In fact, when you don't have a lot of different challenges, you may get bored and soon move on to other things or find yourselves in a type of inertia from which you can only break free if you are juggling several balls in the air at the same time.

The Mercurial personality produces a good facilitator, a good editor, a good teacher, and an even better trainer that works with formulas and systems. Teaching techniques and methods can be a boring task. The gifted teacher must also have a very good sense of humor and a variety of approaches, both requiring a sharp Mercury!

Mercury is prominent in the charts of writers. Especially writers of shorter pieces such as lyrics, newsletters, and teaching and training manuals (third house) as well as guides, tables, escrow papers, rental agreements, and the more practical types of writing (sixth house).

A company having prominent Mercury in their chart is a company that may deal in such industries as telecommunications, advertising and sales. The sales arena is the place where we find quite a few Mercurial types. In fact, one of the biggest mistakes that many businesses make is placing some of their top salespeople in management positions. Thinking that these ace salespeople will do a great job, the company is often disappointed to find that the multi-faceted (Mercury) salesperson may not be very organized and that "follow-through" is not always one of their strengths (something required of a good manager).

Mercury facilitates connection and communication. It is the cog in the wheel that connects us with each other. It connects this idea with that idea, and possesses an almost alchemical ability to network people together. This is the one of the planet's greatest gifts. A powerful organization with a good structure is the perfect foundation for Mercury energy. The strength and workability of this structure facilitates and enhances Mercury's abilities and skills. The more structured a company and the more autonomy they give to their Mercurial types, the more they allow mental freedom to their Mercurial types to bring in new ideas and to sit in on discussions of how to make things work more smoothly. Mercurial types are known for their ability to assimilate vast amounts of information and reformulate them into useable nuggets.

Brain Teaser

Is Mercury on an angle in your chart? Do you speak or travel for a living? Is it highly aspected? Is focus sometimes a problem for you? Were you in a position that gave you more movement and freedom in the past? Have you had stressful aspects to your Mercury over these last few years? Do you struggle with details or do you analyze and edit on a regular basis?

♀ Venus and Pallas Athena ⚴

♉ Aesthetics and Negotiations ♎

The ability to collaborate, to merge, to negotiate is the essence of the planet Venus in a company's chart. The same is true for an individual chart. A strong Venus makes you attractive and enables you to draw to you what you desire. A highly aspected or angular Venus can further this ability. Classically, the planet Venus is the planet of seduction and desire.

A well-placed Venus is an indicator that a company's style is that it tries to conduct business in an esthetic or fair way. Its surroundings are often elegant, particularly if Venus is placed in the fourth house or rules the fourth or first house of the chart. Conversely, if the company has a retrograde Venus, then it may indicate difficulties in the ability to attract to it that which it needs. It may also offer rather unpleasant surroundings. The offices may have bare bones furnishings. A powerfully placed Venus can have the opposite effect. The placement of Venus suggests how to set up a situation for a company so that it is more likely that the company can attract what it wants.

Venus in difficult aspect to Saturn brings a sense that you have to work hard for everything while sacrificing along the way. It can also indicate delays in success. It is the perfect marker for the professional Madame, too! There is a sense of having to obey the rules in order to attract what you desire. Desire requires a price. The Venus/Saturn person is willing to pay the price for success and achievement.

This combination of Saturn with Venus can indicate expensive tastes, i.e. "Rolls Royce" desires versus other lesser automobiles. For that reason, cash flow (Venus) may often be affected in trying to achieve the ultimate in pleasure or life quality.

Conversely, a hard aspect between Jupiter and Venus may

suggest overindulgence by you or your company. It might suggest a company that has difficulty managing its cash flow or overspending. Jupiter square Venus may also suggest that the "product" is valued for its ability to create pleasure or its price may be over-inflated. Throw Mars in and you have impulsive actions accompanying the above behaviors as well as the ability to stir up the resources and gather them when needed.

Adverse aspects to natal Neptune may indicate negatively, credit or debt problems and makes the company susceptible to mergers or takeovers. The positive manifestation suggests that you or your company identify and act on idealism and have a capacity to manifest visions as part of your product line or your company's over-all purpose. In addition, it indicates the ability to intuitively gather the right people to do the job, the right suppliers, and the right materials.

A well-placed Venus or highly aspected Venus may suggest working in the following trades: textiles, the law or justice system as well as sugar manufacturing, copper production, jewelry or any type of fashion design and adornments such as purses, accessories, and even household furnishings.

Pallas Athena (⚴) sometimes interchanges with Venus placements and is associated with weaving, justice, and the law. In Greek mythology, Pallas Athena emerges from her father's head. This happens right after (Jupiter) Zeus, Athena's father devours her mother, Metis, the Woman of Wisdom, his pregnant consort. In full armor and brandishing a war cry, Athena springs forth out of Zeus' head. Her birth is an example of parthenogenesis, a noun meaning the development of an egg without fertilization. The Parthenon, the temple of Athena Parthenos, in Athens, Greece, is named after this phenomenon as well as Athena's virgin-Goddess status. Athena becomes the Goddess to whom the heroes and heroines go for help and assistance and for the wisdom of strategy for which she is known. If she believes in your cause, she advises you on a strategy and provides you with the tools necessary for success. A virgin-Goddess in the sense that she is an individual unto herself, Athena is also a master weaver and mentor for the weaving and textiles of ancient Greece. Her capacity to weave together stories, ideas, concepts, and plans is known. Prominently placed in your horoscope or your company's horoscope, she can be of great help in these areas, but also quite ruthless as well as determined if not balanced by other factors.

The Goddess Aphrodite (the Greek name) or Venus (the Roman name) also descends from her father. Her father's name is Uranus also known as Ouranos in literature. His son, Cronos or Saturn, slaughters Uranus, the sky God and the God of chaos. Uranus' testicles are thrown into the sea and out of the blood are birthed the Furies at the same time as Venus, symbolizing the life giving power of passion and the aggressive quality that accompanies desire.

In an individual chart, when you have a strong Libra or Venus, textiles, weavings or fabrics may be your work or hold your interest. Strong Venus placements are found in the fields of apparel, lingerie, upholstery, fashion, cosmetics, and all of the beauty and skin occupations. Interior design, painting, negotiation and mediation, and social function organizing are wonderful career choices for those of you born with a strong Libra or Venus.

Venus was neither a mean nor a weak figure in mythology. As the Goddess of attraction, she got exactly what she wanted! She was willing to step over dead bodies to get what she wanted, but she did it in such a way, that her charm overcame any objections or kept the door open for further negotiations. If your Venus has more of a Taurus bent, either in an earth sign, placed in one of the earth houses or is highly aspected by earth planets (more organic in scope), then it may focus your interests towards physical and organic industries such as the herbal business, agriculture, farming, land development, or building comfortable homes and furnishings.

Using these associations, Venus in a company or career chart indicates your desire to gather resources, to be comfortable, to pursue creative ideas and make them a reality. Because Venus assists others in making their lives more comfortable, Venusians can help others with defining their values and developing their resources. This relates to many diverse occupations whose range includes banking, savings and loan businesses, to marketing and advertising, to design and environmental work. Comfort is a strong motivating factor behind Venus in an individual or company chart. Your company is motivated to provide comfortable surroundings for your employees or wonderful benefits so that your employees are productive. Venus represents the appeal of a company, what will be attractive to its employees and what it values.

Both Venus and Pallas have similar meanings. They both descended from their fathers—Pallas from her father's head and Venus from her father's genitals. Both Goddesses have strategic abilities and strong motivations. Both Goddesses express themselves through textiles, weavings, negotiations, and strategy.

The difference, however, is that Venus is charming, seductive and alluring. She uses her sexuality to achieve her aims. Pallas Athena is direct, forthright and blunt. She has an edge to her presentation and a mind that cuts through the problems and challenges quickly. Venus feels while Pallas thinks. Venus is very amoral and Pallas is moral. Venus is less judgmental than Pallas, affording her fewer enemies. The morality of Pallas Athena is harsh, strict, without a lot of extraneous social pretenses. Pallas Athena does what she needs to do to get the job done, regardless of peoples' feelings.

Brain Teaser

If you are fortunate enough to find an accurate transaction chart, whose correct time and date of birth as well as location of birth are precise, then review it. Was the transaction successful? If it was a real estate chart, was it a pleasant negotiation or a difficult one? Was the property correctly valued for the price paid?

Where was Pallas Athena placed or Venus? What kinds of aspects did they have? Were they angular?

♂ Mars ♈ ♏

Motivation, Strategy and Action

Business delineation differs from personal delineation. You approach corporate or vocational delineation with an objective perspective, using the meanings and the symbolism of the planets in their purest forms. For example, Mars represents assertion and aggression. In business delineation, we look at Mars as the key planet signaling what motivates an individual to work or a company to prosper and thrive. Mars shows us why you get out of bed every day and go to work and it shows why a company keeps doing or not doing what it needs to do to be a success. This is an important thing to know when offering career counseling to your client. You have to ask the client, what motivates you, what makes you angry, what makes you react, what makes you fight for what you believe in? Correct delineation of Mars answers these questions.

A person who has a Mars in Gemini has a very different motivation than someone who has a Mars in Pisces. The

Mars in Gemini personality is driven by the search for information and communication. The Mars in Pisces individual is driven by the need for space and solitude. The Mars in Aries personality loves the challenges of climbing those new, unexplored mountains.

In business Astrology, the planet Mars is seen as the "buying barometer". If you are interested, you take action. If you take a risk you have to take action. The Dow Jones Industrial Average has some of its best days when there are favorable aspects of transiting Jupiter to transiting Mars. On the contrary, it has some of its worst days when transiting Mars is aspecting transiting Saturn through hard aspects. It can also drive the price down, which is also the right time to buy in certain cases.

A strong Mars placement in the chart (highly aspected, angular, parallel or contra-parallel to several planets) can denote a competitive, athletic, risk-taking personality. Drums and percussion are represented by the planet Mars and though many musicians have a strongly placed Neptune in their horoscopes, drummers and percussionists usually have a strong Mars. Any vocation that results in scarring or wounding, such as warriors, soldiers, martial artists, racecar drivers, hunters, and people who deal in guns, knives, and heavy artillery generally have strong Martian influences.

A strong Mars life is characterized by a childhood in which you were forced to leave your family and went on your own on a contemporary "walkabout". While on this search, you discovered yourself and what made you tick. This walkabout is not, however, without its challenges. You are injured, hurt, challenged, but that strong Mars doesn't give up, because in the end, you search for those undiscovered places and things that only a true Mars personality can handle and process.

Mars in your horoscope challenges you to become a

master strategist in whatever arena (house) you find it in and whichever house it also rules. It is in this area of the chart that you cultivate that environment for greatest success. Mars in your third house (ideas, communications, working with your hands, asking a lot of questions, researching, writing, thinking) indicates areas in which you may be wounded, but if you become strategic, as well as patient, can achieve as well as surmount tremendous obstacles. The location of Mars in your chart or your company's chart is where you are asked to be brave, to get up when you fall, and to not react when things associated with this area of your chart is not responding to your appeals. Mars in this area of your chart asks you to constantly reassess the value of what you are doing in this area, if you have lost interest or if you need to further improve your skills and abilities.

The paradox of Mars in this area of the chart is where you always struggle and are challenged to be brave and strategic. It is where at any turn, you can be wounded and hurt, but still must continue in order to achieve and trail blaze new areas of this part of your chart. The location you find Mars in your individual horoscope as well as your company horoscope is where you struggle, have to stop and re-group, be on the cutting edge, and exhibit bravery in the face of battle.

Brain Teaser

Go through your client files and pull the charts of the self-employed clients. What does Mars look like in their charts or their company's chart? Is it angular or highly aspected? Did they start their businesses or leave their businesses during heavy Mars transits?

♃ Jupiter ♐ ♓
Visionary Thinking, Marketing, and Public Relations

Jupiter (the Roman name) or Zeus (the Greek name) is the prevailing God of the Pantheon. As such, he symbolizes possibility and vision. It is from his head that Athena, the Goddess of Wisdom, is born. Jupiter is the son of Saturn. In fact, he is the only surviving child after his father, Saturn devours all of his children in his attempt to not lose control of his power and authority. Saturn the planet with rings and the farthest planet visible to the naked eye is associated with perceived limitation.

Jupiter is called the God of luck and possibility. This is because when his father, Saturn, devours the children, he does it in fear. Jupiter survives and eventually takes over after Saturn. Saturn, the father of Jupiter, is associated with the rational linear left brain, while Jupiter is associated with the right brain, the intuitive part of the brain, which hears music and sees colors.

In Viking lore, Jupiter is known as Thor, the God of thunderbolts. The day of the week we call Thursday is named after Thor or Jupiter, and is the day of the week most associated with expansion. Jupiter in a company chart signifies the company's ability to have a grand vision and expand. Jupiter's placement is where they have the most return for their efforts, and where they are most gifted and protected. It is an indicator of the capacity to work with people beyond the known culture. Since Jupiter is associated with the ninth house of the natural zodiac, which includes foreign cultures and foreign belief systems, a strong Jupiter in a company or career chart could indicate business involvement on a world platform.

In the new global marketplaces, any companies or individuals that have a strong Jupiter signature may be perfectly suited to work in international travel, international marketing and trade, publishing, both nationally and internationally. A company with this marking could be known for its open views and hiring practices. There may be a great deal of legal involvement or use of legal practices as part of the products or services.

In your chart, Jupiter is where you are lucky and fortunate and where you hold grand visions or where the grand visions hold you. This area of the chart is where you hold your idealism and where you may profit handsomely if you harness and work with the challenges of your Saturn.

Brain Teaser

Watch the stock market during times of big Jupiter transits. Note the sign that Jupiter is transiting for the marketplace to be flooded with the things that that sign rules. Does there seem to be a lot more interest or is there an oversupply of the products which that sign rules? For example, when Jupiter transits the sign of Pisces, there is more oil and petroleum but is it over-priced or in demand? When Jupiter transits the sign of Cancer does the price of housing go up or down? Is there a glut on the market of over-priced houses?

♄ Saturn ♑

Managing, Structuring and Building

The classic mythology of the planet Saturn (Cronos to the Greeks) is that of a father who devoured his children. On first viewing this image is horrific, but upon examining the story closer, you can get a better sense of how Saturn works in company and career charts.

Saturn is one of the children of Gaia, the Earth Mother, and Uranus, the sky God. Uranus is always mating with Gaia and conceiving children he does not remain around to help raise. When he separates from Gaia and leaves, she is left to raise the children by herself. After a while Uranus returns to mate with Gaia and conceive yet more children. Gaia becomes frustrated with this erratic commitment of Uranus and so she sends their son, Saturn (Cronos) to kill him. Thus is birthed the metaphor of bringing law and order (Saturn) out of chaos (Uranus).

In business, you need some sort of order and structure. In the myth, Saturn builds the forms and puts together the justice system. He is the original general contractor. Appropriately, Saturn represents building, construction, stone, masonry, ice, hard work, and, the concept of time. There is an old business saying, "Time is money", and this statement is a perfect embodiment of the planet Saturn.

When Saturn is placed on an angle or prominently in your chart, you may take a longer time to reach success as the classic "late bloomer". It is a battle hard won. You have had a great deal to overcome and will often stop at nothing even in the wake of barriers and blocks if your Saturn is supported by elements of the chart.

Capricorn is like the mountain goat that faithfully walks to the top of the mountain alone, in the snow and wind, with little sustenance. They reach success in life if they maintain faith and hope in their lives. This relates to the solstice point of Capricorn, which is Sagittarius, and is ruled by Jupiter. Saturn was also the ruler of Aquarius before the discovery of planets beyond it. My experience has demonstrated that using Saturn as the ruler of Aquarius works, particularly in specific predictions as it is often used in Horary Astrology.

Since Saturn is associated with the mountain goat, it warrants an examination of its original image, which is that of the

Sea Goat. The Sea Goat is a mythological creature that has the body of a goat and the tail of a fish. It begins its life at the bottom of the sea, the symbol of the unconscious, and it swims its way to the surface where it uses its goat's body to climb to the top of the mountain. This image evokes the blossoming forth of consciousness later in your life. Out of an unconscious state is birthed conscious possibility that happens while you develop concrete forms, structures and disciplines.

Since Saturn rules building as well as management, which includes time management. If your Saturn is highly aspected you may work in these professions as well as work with the elderly or any products or services that involve senior citizens. As baby boomers turn 50 years of age at a rate averaging every 7 seconds, businesses or services aimed at seniors can only improve as this large market ages. Witness the recent growth of assisted living facilities throughout the U.S. Since the planet Saturn is associated with either high-end products or services as well as quality versus quantity, Saturn supports anything that works with quality control or imparts a high-end service.

Saturn also rules real estate, whereas the Moon rules property. Because of this, when Saturn is being aspected by progressions, transits, and eclipses, this can activate real estate interests.

In a corporate chart, Saturn expresses itself as the rules of the company. Saturn also represents its fears, or where it may limit itself. If you remember the image of Mr. Scrooge, in the Charles Dickens story, A Christmas Carol, you remember a negative manifestation of "management" in a company that is associated with a negatively expressed Saturn. Yet that same Saturn can also express itself as fortitude; a company that survives when all others do not; a company that works on very little to get ahead and maintains high profit margins and low debt ratios.

The original Johnson and Johnson Company, which is delineated in the chapter on Corporations, is one of the oldest incorporations, having been incorporated in 1887. It has survived many disasters through time (Saturn) and still continues to be profitable in the marketplace. Its natal Saturn is conjunct its natal North Node, denoting the staying power that is indicative of strong Saturn placements in individual or corporate charts.

Brain Teaser

Looking at a company chart or a first trade chart, where is Saturn? If you know anything about the management in this company, then how would you judge their effectiveness? Looking at Saturn in a client's chart that is struggling with a career or life decision, where are they frozen in fear or in what area do they work very hard re-constructing themselves over time? (Refer to chapter on "Thriving, Not Just Surviving".)

⛢ Uranus

Innovation and Technology

Modern organizations have to have a bit of wizard in them to make a difference and shine. The Industrial Revolution occurred alongside the discovery of Uranus in 1781. Uranus is the planet associated with those "ah-ha" experiences or those big ideas that we all have. It operates somewhat as an electrical shock in consciousness. It is the energy associated with such inventions as Alexander Graham Bell's telephone, Elias Howe's sewing machine, and Bill Gates' Microsoft.

Uranus is associated with magic and alchemy. Think of Michelangelo's wonderful painting on the Sistine Chapel entitled "The Creation" where the hand of God touches the hand of Man and humanity begins. This is the energy of Uranus.

Uranus, in mythology, was the Sky God, an archetype that is present in every creation story. Out of Uranus came everything else. In the Greek stories, he is called Ouranos. Uranus would come together with Gaia, mother Earth, to have children and then without warning, quickly depart. This image describes the process of creation as an energy that fuses and separates. Where Uranus is in your horoscope is where you experience incongruities, sudden changes, where you grasp onto that area of your chart and, just as suddenly where it leaves you. Its placement implies an area of your chart or your company's chart where you are unique, invent or, where you think in a non-traditional futuristic ways.

Uranus rules the sign of Aquarius, the sign of group and global consciousness. Aquarius' opposite sign is Leo, which is a sign that describes more of the individual's expression. Uranus symbolizes group expression, the networks, the people who know the people who know you and the ability to receive work from referrals. However, even though Uranus rules groups, Uranian energy doesn't really want to be a part of the group. Uranians have the ability to tell the group what to do and give viable solutions to heal their problems and issues. When that task is complete, it just as swiftly departs as it arrived. This is the same type of energy of some of those groundbreaking actors such as James Dean, who had a new and unique style of presentation, presented us with that style, and just as quickly were gone, but not before pioneering an entirely new genre of acting. This is very similar to the story of how Uranus merges with Gaia, quickly creating new progeny and then just as quickly departing.

Just as in the story, the effects of Uranus in your chart are where you wake people up, where you do not conform. This is your storehouse of knowledge where you are comfortable in challenging the status quo. In other words, Uranus shakes things. Along with its charismatic appeal, it has the power to sway and convince others of that same new insight.

Everyone, companies included, has Uranus placed in a house or field of experience where it is best expressed. Uranus in your tenth house of career, or the sign of Aquarius, the sign which it rules, placed on the tenth house cusp may indicate that you are seen by the world as a revolutionary. You challenge authority figures, bosses and parents (all denoted by the tenth house) to think differently. Although you effect a change, it doesn't guarantee that you will remain in that position of change, for as quickly as you stir things up, you may just as quickly be gone. Why? Because your job as catalyst is complete or you may be bored and no longer feel mentally challenged.

Your energy challenges people. If there is a like-minded intelligence and the organization is ready for change, then your maverick thinking can be of great benefit. However, if your ideas are too far ahead of the group, then you may not be able to continue in that position. Uranus can make those unprepared and uncomfortable as it always challenges and threatens the way things are done.

The placement of Uranus on any angle or highly aspecting an angle, can act the same. The nature of Uranus is to shake things up, to question tradition and authority. One of my young clients who has natal Uranus in her first house is studying facial and skin care in Paris. She recently said, "They just never have my major!" Uranus is the planet prominent in charts of those who march to the beat of a different drummer, are visionary, future-oriented and who start the new trends and ideas.

Uranians are revolutionaries. Since the planet Uranus takes approximately seven (7) years to move through one constellation at a time, these are the people whose careers seem to be on seven-year cycles. As a result, these individuals may head down one career path that excites and inspires them, but then, because they learn quickly and get bored easily, may suddenly have a yearning to move on. With the first hints of change, they send out a psychic signal that can bring groups, acquaintances or friends in who offer them new possibilities, new roles, and new experiences. Often this new direction is very different and extremely foreign to their previous life roles. And yet the new role fits if their interest is stimulated and their individuality is allowed to shine through.

The Uranian individual is torn, like the God, Ouranos, between belonging with others who are in more traditional roles versus being autonomous and individualistic in their lives. They never really fit until they accept the fact that, in fact, they are different. The awakening to this possibility is triggered in their early twenties, but when transiting Uranus opposes their natal Uranus, then they truly awaken to their soul's purpose. Their work usually finds them; they don't find the work. By letting go of trying, or fighting, and just being okay with trying something new that inspires them, the opportunities present themselves and they figure out their direction. Many anarchists and entrepreneurs have strong placements of Uranus. Uranus is usually in the picture when a sudden departure from a company occurs or when there is a sudden change of direction.

Prometheus is associated with Uranus/Aquarius. The name, Prometheus, translated means, "he who has foresight". Prometheus was the God who stole the fire of creativity from the Gods and gave it to the people. Because he believed that it would be of great comfort and use for the "people", he was condemned. He was tied to a rock and by day an eagle, the symbol of enlightenment, ate away at his liver. The liver grew back at night.

I have found that people who struggle with their visions and creativity sometimes struggle with liver problems. The struggle for enlightenment presents itself through physical illness and, sometimes, mental illness. Those that have major conjunctions of Uranus to the personal planets and angles such as the Sun, Moon and Ascendant may also suffer from manias or hypertension. They can have a mind that is going too fast in a world that is still stuck in third dimensional movement and thinking. Geniuses have these placements and many geniuses throughout history have struggled with manic depression and cyclic behaviors.

There is a great challenge in the charts of Uranians similar to the struggles of those who have prominent Chirons (Chiron will be discussed later). They do not want to be part of a formal movement and yet want to invoke lasting change. One of the spiritual lessons for Uranians is to temper their tendency towards extremism by learning to find a viable middle ground working within groups to create change. Resolving this disparity can result in individuals who concurrently work at several different jobs or types of work at one time. Part of what they do may be more traditional while another is more in the pursuit of creative freedom. People who have strong influences of Uranus in their charts are the corporate anarchists, the ones who do everything a little differently, and if they are blessed with a strategic nature, they can often maneuver a company into progressive new products, services, or a new direction. They are given autonomy as a reward. Their foresight moves them through doors that open for no one else. This is when the possibility of corporate magic can occur, when leaders of the organization recognize the need for change and engage those who are able to facilitate the change.

The action of one Uranian individual within a company can trigger a long-needed revolution for which this individual becomes a leader unless, like Prometheus, change is so terrifying to the "corporate Gods" of the company, that this individual is forced to leave the company. With Prometheus the Gods realized their wrongdoing and released him from the rock whilst Chiron took his place. It follows that any individual or corporate revolution has a certain number of casualties. Careers and traditions may be sacrificed for the greater good. The Promethean employee is left to lose his liver by day and grow it back by night perhaps with a stronger ability to "digest" that which was previously intolerable.

The American Revolution illustrates the possibilities of Uranus as a far-reaching agent of change. The American Revolution was a war that involved a very common Uranian theme, human rights where all are created equal. Uranus is the archetype for human rights, freedom, and independence. The old-world businesses of yesteryear have been forced to move into new models, as downsizing occurred during the passage of Neptune through the business sign of Capricorn. As more individuals left their companies and began their own businesses or worked as independent contractors, the form and structure of business changed radically. When such ideas as Tom Peters' theory of Management by Chaos were birthed, it introduced a new paradigm of business called team management and team leaders, a democratic way of working. Ultimately, the success of a company in the new Millennium will be based on individual contractors joining together for specific projects...a type of temporary company whose form is time and task specific. The whole team is really very temporary. The kinds of people that these companies hire must not only manage the fire of anarchy and creativity, but, ironically, must be grounded in the world of Saturn.

Saturn's realm is the world of structures, law and order. It was Mother Earth's plea to her son, Saturn, to bring order out of the chaotic unions with her consort Uranus. It was Saturn who brought the order out of chaos. Though these two archetypes are diametrically opposed to each other, it is the successful integration of these two: of anarchy and freedom that best calls in the qualities of Uranus. It is the saturnine form that creates the chamber wherein the alchemical process of innovation (Uranus) is possible. The question is how do we make these two worlds come together? The answer is found in the mythology of Chiron.

Brain Teaser

Following is a chart of an individual options trader. Where is Uranus in this chart? What comments can you make about the Uranus placement and aspects? If this were your client, what would you tell them about their innovative ability?

(Illustration 17 - An Options Trader)

Illustration 17

Male: Options Trader, Jun. 4, 1950, 8:13am CDT + 5:00, Chicago, IL, 41°N51' 087°W39'

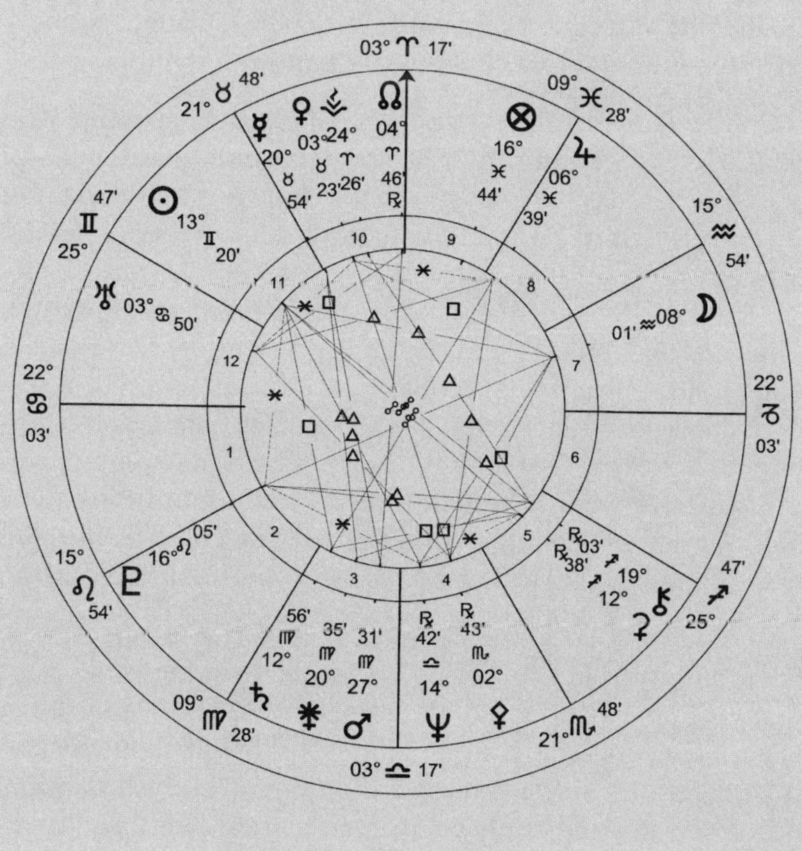

⚷ Chiron

Linking Opposites — Hybrid Thinking — Crossing Between Traditional and Non-Traditional Thinking

Chiron is often referred to as the Rainbow Bridge because he orbits between Saturn, which represents tradition and what we think is "reality" and the planet, Uranus, which represents revolution and foresight. Its orbit is approximately 50 years. At either an individual or a corporate Chiron return, individuals and businesses undergo a profound metamorphosis. Joyce Mason, a known authority on Chiron says, "Chiron is like Pluto, except it leads you more gently". It is a comet, discovered in 1977, during the beginning of the holistic health movement and coincided with Elisabeth Kubler-Ross presenting a new concept of death and dying.

Chiron is a complex archetype. He is both isolated and social. He is a centaur, half human and half horse, born of the union between Cronos and a mortal nymph, Philyra. He is a maverick and an anarchist. However, unlike his fellow centaurs, he is unusually intelligent, perceptive, and sensitive. He also is wild and in this way similar to his fellow centaurs. His lustiness and the ability to tear flesh indicate a strong split within the personality of Chiron, creating a hybrid. Wherever he is placed in your chart is where you experience maverick or unresolved views, which may plague you until your 50th year at which time it offers you the tremendous wisdom of seeing beyond the shackles of your mind to invent a methodology that works for you or your company.

According to Melanie Reinhart[6], Chiron was rejected by his mother and abandoned by his father. In some versions of the myth, he was adopted and raised by Apollo. Regardless, his early youth is spent alone in the cave in which he discovers and refines new ideas and thoughts. Chiron has many questions, which can only be answered in solitude, in a "cave" experience. His process is similar to that of Jesus in the desert. When Chiron emerges from his cave, he emerges with new views and new solutions that come after the experience of isolation. This specific knowledge is what separates him as a force with which to be reckoned.

Apollo, who befriends Chiron, is a patron of medicine. Chiron, also known as the one who taught Asklepius, the first physician of Greece, became one of the greatest of mythical healers. He taught his craft to others and became a mentor for the children of the Gods such as Hercules, encouraging their special gifts and talents. In one of the stories he is wounded in the ankle while witnessing a wedding in which the other centaurs come down from the hills marauding the wedding guests. Hercules' many arrows, all dipped in the blood of the Hydra, inadvertently pierce the ankle of Chiron and though Chiron is able to heal everyone else, he in the end is powerless to help himself. Hence, the often given name of the "wounded healer". Because he is half-God and only half-mortal he cannot die. He continues to help others while trying to find a cure for his own pain.

In horoscopes, Chiron seems to be strongly placed in the charts of foster caregivers, adoptive parents, and those working in the healing arts or in hospice situations. He is found active in times of individual and corporate transitions the times when major decisions can create life or death situations, similar to the nature of Pluto.

Taking the example of foster care providers or consultants, this concept is an alternative to the traditional family. It is alien to nature. However, through time it has always been an alternative that fits neither here nor there in terms of traditional expectations. There is a great deal of pain involved in placing youth with those that are not their parents. Sometimes the situation does not work. In general, it is an alternative way to deal with troubled families. It requires a new thinking for not only the children, but for their birth parents that may continue to participate in the life of the child, while someone else raises their child. It is an alternative that many times works because it gives space to the families to work on their problems. Granted that the system isn't perfect, but it is a hybrid concept in terms of families.

Because Chiron lived in two worlds, the world of mortality and the world of divine possibility, the struggle is always in that part of the horoscope to come up with a way of living that best suits that placement. Because there is a very high intelligence associated with Chiron, its placement in either an individual chart or a corporate chart indicates that there can be some unique insights coming out of you, the individual, in that area of your chart or in that area of your company's chart, which offers solutions not derived from traditional models.

When found in a horoscope at a prominent position, the individual might be a healer — either emotionally, physically, intellectually, or spiritually. This interpretation may be a corporate consultant who comes into a troubled company. The Chiron personality knows exactly what the company needs to do and suggests the changes, but may in fact, be unable to keep track of marketing his own practice or not be paid for his or her services accordingly. It can be a holistic practitioner who ventured into the world of holistic health because of an ongoing health problem and whose search for a cure moved him or her beyond the limits of traditional allopathic medicine. The same can be said of drug or alcohol counselors who experienced trauma in youth with an alcoholic parent and end up counseling alcoholics as an adult or, they may themselves be recovering alcoholics, drug users or overeaters who altered their habits. If natal Chiron highly aspects the major personal planets, particularly the squares, conjunctions, and oppositions and involves, the Sun or Moon which sometimes represents the parents, the individual may struggle to heal their relationships with their father or mother in adulthood.

The Chironic person exhibits a unique intelligence at a

Illustration 18

Female: Chiropractor, May 22, 1955, 9:11am PST +8:00, Olympia, WA, 47°N2'17" 122°W53'58"

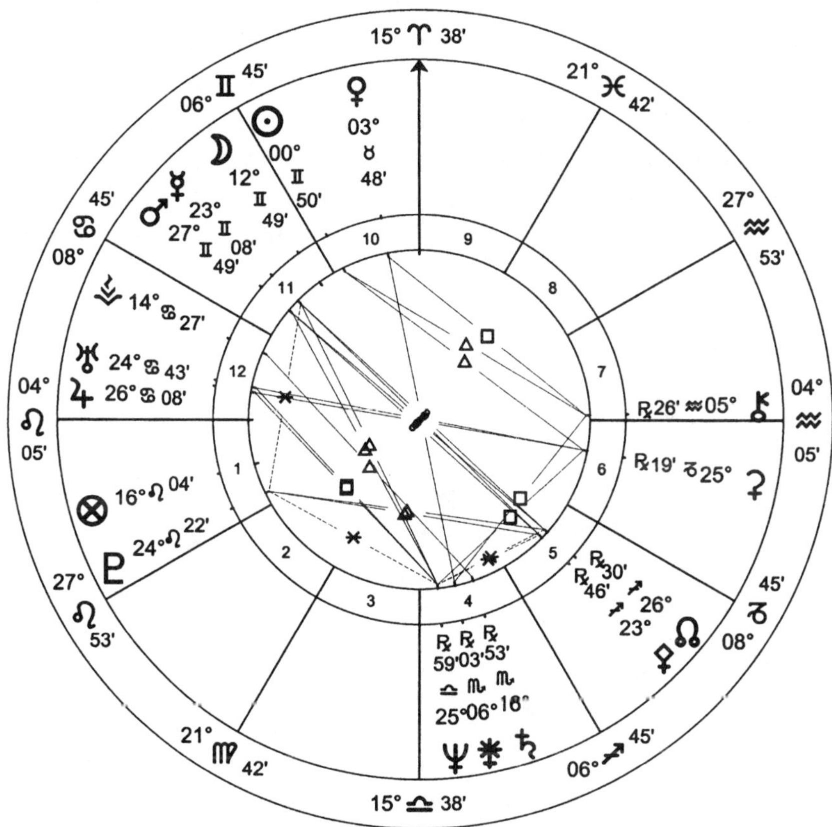

young age and this awareness and sensitivity can trigger an early wounding. This wounding is a necessary experience for their future work in the world. Following are two charts, one a chiropractor who experienced a severe eating disorder in her youth and as an adult specializes in nutritional studies. Note the seventh house Chiron squaring natal Venus in Aries in the tenth. Venus rules the fourth, home family, security issues. The second chart is that of a foster care consultant who places young people in foster care due to serious dysfunctions in their birth homes. This individual, too, had a difficult, neglected childhood running the streets at a young age. This individual witnessed friends die young because of violence on the streets in the neighborhoods in which he grew up. (See Illustrations 18 and 19).

Where Chiron transits a company chart the area experiences a crisis, which on the surface may appear to be tragic, but is what is needed to heal or revise the situation. This situation is triggered by a crisis similar to the Pluto transit. Where Chiron is placed in a company chart is the same as the experience for the individual. This is an area of weakness, the weak ankle of the company and needs continual attention and support.

Illustration 19

Male: *Foster Care Consultant, Nov. 15, 1948, 3:32am PDT + 7:00, Berkeley, CA, 37°N52'18" 122°W16'18"*

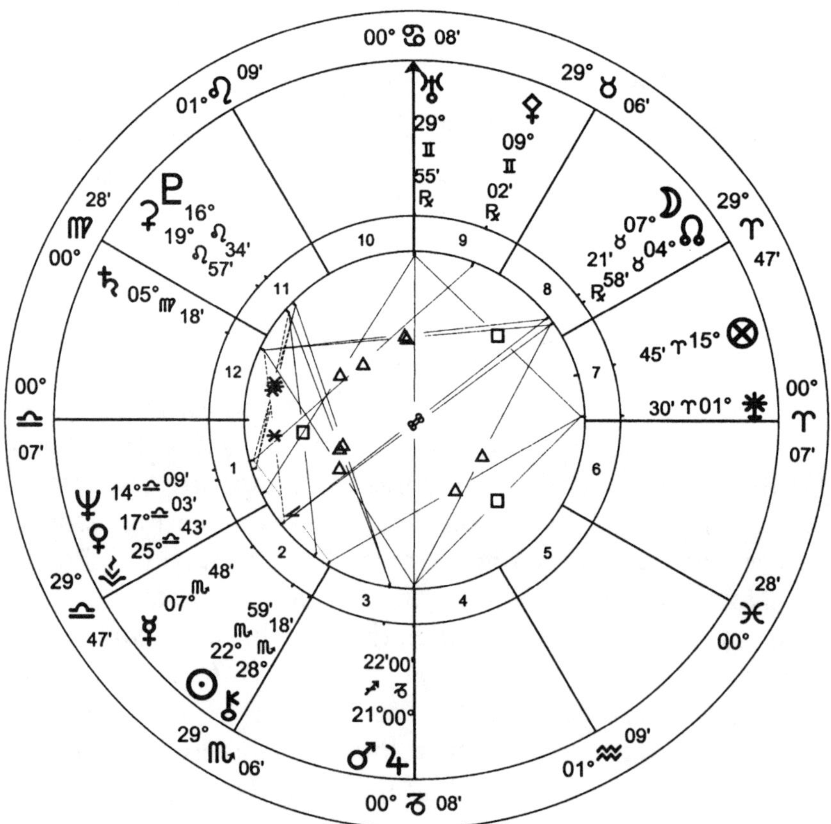

Following is an example. In the buy-out chart for Safeway Stores, August 29, 1986 (Illustration 20) the Sun is in the sign of Virgo. In 1986, Kohlberg, Kravitz, and Roberts, a New York investment firm, purchased them. The sale was approximately 6 billion dollars, one of the largest at that time. Subsequently, the company became privately owned. This continued until 1991, when they released about 40% of the company in a public offering. In 1994, while Chiron traveled through Virgo, Safeway downsized laying off nearly 2500 upper management executives. The Sun represents the lifeblood of a company and Chiron represents a critical issue and correction, a wounding and healing.

Illustration 20

Event: Safeway Buyout from KKR, Aug. 29, 1986, 12:00pm EDT + 4:00, Dover, DE, 39°N09'29" 075°W31'29"

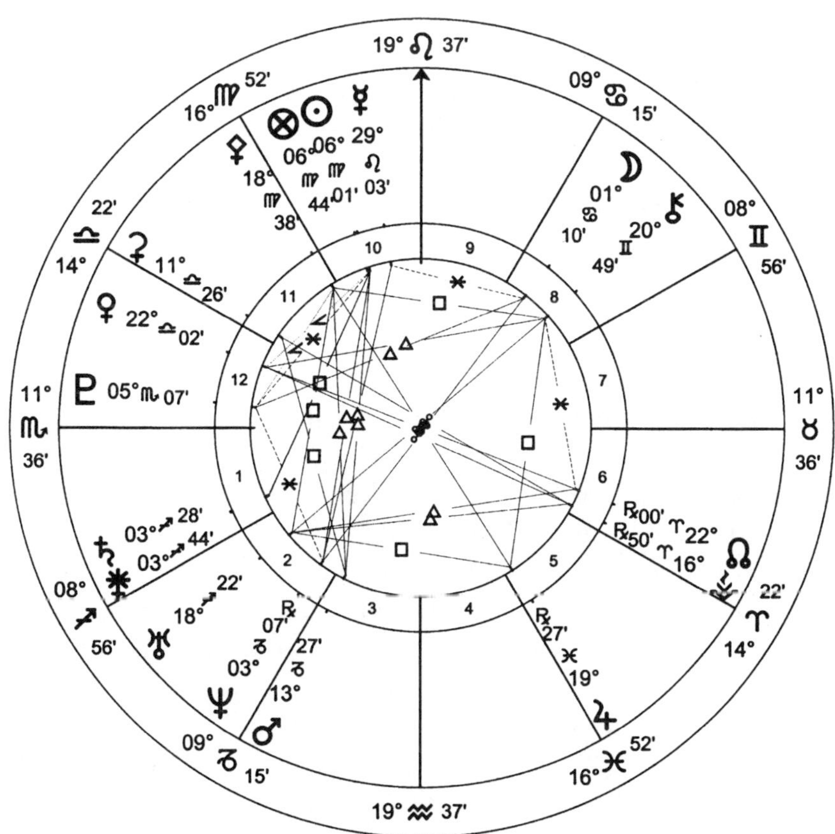

Illustration 21

Male: Former Safeway Executive, Apr. 5, 1950, 0:39am PST + 8:00, Orange, CA, 33°N47'16" 117°W51'08"

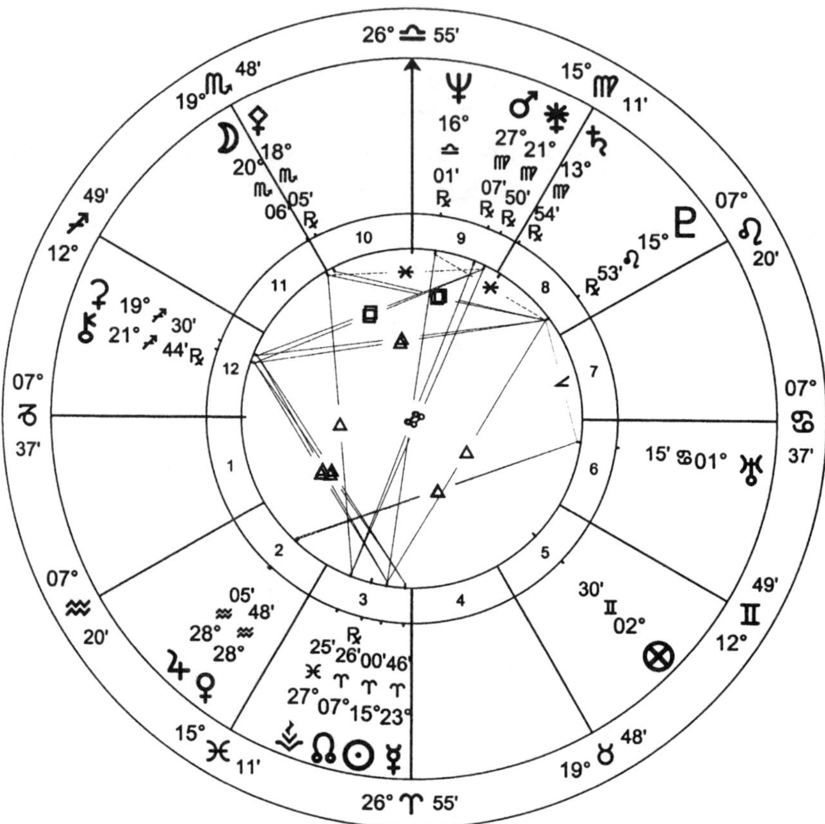

One of their executives, born April 5, 1950, was caught in the crossfire of this particular situation (Illustration 21). As Chiron transited his Saturn, (the ruler of his chart, and, also the ruler of one's business), he was forced to re-organize his life and find new employment, which ultimately was more suited to his personality. During this same time, Pluto was transiting and creating a square to his Venus, the ruler of his tenth house. He experienced both a professional and personal crisis; his life took a downward spiral after being in such an elevated public position. For a Capricorn Rising, this was devastating. It was actually a situation that took several years to resolve.

While looking for work, he began a favorite hobby, painting, tiling and transforming peoples' environments (transit Pluto square his Venus). This also gave him an opportunity to work with his hands, another attribute associated with Chiron. For a while, he was employed by a very large organization, which worked with AIDS patients, but after one year he was laid-off because of the organization's lack of funding. Ultimately, he found work in city politics as a public information officer (ninth house activity); similar to the political work he did for Safeway. Through this transition he has been able to regain a balance between his personal and professional life. During this entire cycle, he was also able to work with clearing personally painful psychological issues, which in the end, released him and moved him into a very good situation in which he hopes to teach, consult and write.

In summary, Chiron represents a merging of "the intuitive and the instinctual" [7], as stated by Joyce Mason, a Chiron specialist. When this split is healed, the individual or the company is able to be who they truly came here to be and no longer feel alienated or rejected. They take their place in the world as new thinkers when they have moved past the confinement of their own judgments.

Brain Teasers

Continue to view the charts presented in the text of Chiron. What other factors do you see that would have contributed to the changes mentioned in the text? How does this information apply to your Chiron in your chart, your true vocation, as well as a company in which you are interested?

♆ Neptune ♓
Vision and Mergers, Redistribution of Resources and Debt

Neptune is associated with several different Gods, one of which is the God of the sea, Poseidon (to the Greeks) or Neptune (the Roman version). It is long known that the universal solvent is water and this is exactly how this planet works in the vocational charts of individuals or in corporate charts. The Neptune placement in the chart is where a lot of re-processing occurs during the life of the entity. It is where we see altruism. It also indicates the area of the chart where there are no boundaries. This manifests as either negative or positive energy depending upon the perception and the ability to filter properly.

The negative manifestation is where there is a sense of being lost, a sense of over-idealism, and over-inflated influences. On a positive note, it is where there are no boundaries in terms of imagination. It is where one may re-create themselves and their identity over and over. An indicator of creativity and intuition, a strongly aspected Neptune, or a Neptune or Pisces influence in the chart encourages mergers and acquisitions. It has the capacity to create in the individual or company an appropriate vision, which manifests externally as a merger.

Neptune is the planet that represents mergers and re-organization. It is where one can take old and worn out resources and transform them into new and useful possibilities. Mergers, a type of symbiosis, occur when a company or individual chart intersects that of another's and can go no further than its present form unless they join forces. The resulting merger eliminates worn-out systems and methods, thereby eliminating some of the past.

When a heavy debt factor is present a company is open to a merger. Like the myth of Poseidon, the God of the seas, the company or the individual finds himself lost at sea and realizes that they need to become part of a larger body.

Since Neptune is the God of the seas, it represents nautical products or occupations. It also rules oil, petroleum, paint, rubber, tin, and gas. Neptune is associated with Dionysus, the God of wine, ecstasy and madness, who mesmerized the women and drew them into an ecstatic frenzy (similar to rock and roll idols and the young people that they influence). The ability to mesmerize and influence the public into purchasing—advertising and its resulting buying trances is associated with Neptune.

Neptune rules the drug and pharmaceutical field as well as holistic and traditional healing fields. Hospitals and institutions that work with those less fortunate, prisons, adoption agencies, cults, and homes for people whose mental faculties are impaired, are all Neptune ruled. Agencies or organizations that work with addictions such as tobacco, alcohol, and drug may include Neptune as part of their chart make-up. Neptune rules Pisces, which, in turn is associated with the feet. Shoe industries, stockings, leggings, podiatrists as well as fields that work with illusion or controlled imagery such as make-up, cosmetics, photography, music, dance, and acting are all Neptune ruled. Any industry that works with the unconscious such as dream analysis, hypnotherapy, and Jungian symbolism, is also Neptune ruled as well as over-inflated prices, over-inflated ideals, over-inflated ego, and heavy debt.

Brain Teaser

When studying mergers in the news, where was transiting Neptune in the company's chart? What was hitting a company's Neptune? Does the company chart indicate debt levels that are high? Does your client's chart, whose company is merging, show heavy Neptune transits to their chart, to their tenth house or the ruler of their tenth house? Is that a transit coming up?

♇ ♇ Pluto ♏
Power, Money and Mass Production

Pluto represents the power in the company or in the individual and where Pluto is placed is also the source of many transformations and resurrections during the course of your or its lifetime. Pluto is associated with your wealth as an individual and a company as well as where that wealth may be hidden. The placement of Pluto in the chart shows where the greatest transformations can occur and the doorway that leads to those transformations is directly equal to how willing and courageous you or your company can be in the face of adversity. Pluto's placement in the chart represents the pools of contacts we have as resources for future transformations.

Individuals and companies that have a highly aspected or angular Pluto or many influences in Scorpio have tremendous ups and downs in their lifetimes. There are numerous examples of people who have been bankrupted or experienced huge losses in their lifetimes yet have persevered to rise to new heights, much like the phoenix that burns to ashes and then rises again to greater power and consciousness.

If you have a highly aspected Pluto your primary gift is that of transformation. You can apply this to such fields as the environment, the economy, in social systems as well as in the field of transforming technologies where you are challenged to take systems, people, and methods that aren't working and turn them around. You can be a type of corporate shaman and you arrive at this ability through your own experience in your professional as well as personal life. Since Pluto is related to the word plutocracy, strong Pluto influences in the chart may indicate dealings with money and finance. This requires a type of surrender to its power and its darkness. When we surrender our fears, our secrets and our addictions, Pluto gives us back our power and "gold", which is the treasure or gift we receive when we sacrifice old patterns and fears to new creative possibilities. It is the return we receive when we make decisions particularly financial and psychological decisions in business. It is the gift received when, with fortitude, we exhibit courage and risk making creative changes long overdue.

Pluto was the wealthiest of the Gods thus the associations with wealth. Like the Shamans of ancient times one of the rites for becoming a shaman was to be buried in a pit of snakes. If you survived, you were able to move between the worlds and become Shaman or Medicine person. This is how Pluto operates in the world. Pluto is the dark character found in all fairy tales. The wicked witches, the evil wizard, the Darth Vader.

In the fairy tale, Rumpelstiltskin, Rumpelstiltskin helps the young maiden make gold out of straw to please and meet her obligations to the King and his son, the Prince. She is required to pay something for each favor that Rumpelstiltskin bestows upon her. When she has nothing more to give, she pledges her first, not yet conceived child for one last favor. When Rumpelstiltskin returns after her marriage to the Prince and the birth of their child, he comes to "collect" his payment, the infant. She has pledged something very dear, but she has received a "loan" and now it is time to pay. This is what happens when we contract for a home mortgage or borrow funds. At a later time we must pay for the power that was given to us to transform our lives by repaying the loan.

We might think of Rumpelstiltskin as wicked. But neither Rumpelstiltskin nor Pluto are really wicked. Both require return payment for the capital they invest in you or in companies. As my Scorpio daughter once said at a very tender young age in response to the question, "Was Rumpelstiltskin a bad guy?" Her thought-provoking answer was, "Rumpelstiltskin wasn't really a bad guy, he was just a good businessman!"

Brain Teaser

Where is Pluto in your chart? Where is it in your favorite company's chart? Has it been the area where you have experienced the greatest pain in your life? Have you or your company passed your Pluto square? Are you in that transition now? What did or are you learning? In the long run, wasn't it the most profound transformation in your life? After a long abandonment in this area, did you return transformed? Later in this book, there is a chapter on Corporation Delineation. When viewing Johnson and Johnson's chart, a Scorpio, work with their Pluto and see what you discover.

☊ North & South Nodes ☋

The Significance of the Nodes in your Horoscope
The Challenge of Career Direction
"Uncharted Territory"

The Nodes are associated with the path of the Moon. The Moon has no light of its own and reflects the light of the Sun. It is related to our home environment, what feels safe, what we remember based on our environmental experience, particularly in the first seven years of our lives when we are in the Moon Phase cycle (see chapter on Solstice points and Equinoxes).

The Moon represents our security needs. What gives us security and makes us feel safe correlates with the style that we engage in order to pursue our life's ambitions. It is important that we are aware of our childhood experiences, of what we saw as security, because those memories, whether good or bad, are the driving force behind our adult individuation. Viewing the North Node and its placement as the "Uncharted Territory" of your path, gives you insight into "What will I be when I grow up?" The North Node continuously pulls us in the direction of its house placement throughout life. It forces us to journey into new territories until we become familiar with them and comfortably settle into them.

When you view the North Node as the challenge in your life or the risk you need to take in order to get to wherever you are going, a new clarity appears. Using the South Node as the counterbalance to your North Node provides further insight. The South Node symbolizes all the qualities and experiences of ourselves that we bring into this life. This includes such things as tools, memories, and knowledge that aid our trek into the unknown territory of our North Node. There is a fine line between using the learned knowledge of previous experiences that help us grow versus the negative manifestation of the South Node, which gets stuck in the past, because it's easier, comfortable, and familiar.

Evolution is not a sure thing. Evolving from one so-called "species" to the next isn't easy. It takes a lot of focus and hard work. Those who view themselves as successful, continually walk courageously into the uncharted territory of their North Lunar Node time and again. Those who struggle continually avoid being challenged by these uncharted territories. This denial leads to frustration and disillusioned statements such as, "I will never get anywhere" or "I keep doing the same things over and over." Until we can reach some sort of awareness and a willingness to pursue our challenges, we can never really be free in our lifetime.

For example, an individual who is born with their North Node in the seventh house is challenged throughout life to work in partnerships, to develop the skill of compromise, and to learn to give and take in both professional and personal relationships. This individual's South Node will be placed in the first house, which is the house of self-expression, independent identity separate from others, and a self-oriented world.

An easier way for a seventh house North Node person would be to remain separate, to think of self first, because that is what is known, that is what is comfortable. Therein lies their challenge, to bring that sense of individuality into the partnerships they have, to encourage relationship with the development of both of the partners' individual identities.

With this context, it is important that we look at the North Node through the houses, beginning with the Fourth Quadrant (tenth, eleventh and twelfth houses of the horoscope) of Global Community. The Four Quadrants are associated with the four transitional seasons of the year. The Fourth Quadrant represents the Winter Solstice. Winter Solstice is the shortest day of the year and is considered to be the true New Year in the Native American culture. Where there is cold, where there is activity resulting from deprivation, is where the greatest possibility lies. Therefore, the North Node in any of these houses—the twelfth, the eleventh and the tenth, implies a drive that overcomes difficulty. "Picking yourself up by your bootstraps" is the perfect phrase for the North Node placement in any of these houses. An emphasis in these houses pushes the individual to do something in the world. In a word, this quadrant implies selflessness. This is in high contrast to the First Quadrant, which represents the self.

The **twelfth house** holds the last memories of what was going on prior to our birth moment. This house is where all thoughts begin—both conscious and unconscious. It is where we store our attitude toward life. For this reason, the twelfth house is powerful as it acts as the "engine" that drives the personality. If the "engine" is running on positive input, then the personality runs on positive expression. If the twelfth house runs off of negative beliefs and input the personality suffers from the negativity.

When you have the North Node in this house of solitude, of uncharted territory, of recapitulation you can access your prior knowledge. You may have to be alone to sift through those ancient memories, files, skills and abilities. What you believe and experience in the twelfth house is directly related to the amount of success you achieve in your lifetime. Whether success is measured by the amount of money you make or the amount of spiritual knowledge you possess really doesn't matter. In many cases, the twelfth house is the house of the true buried treasure. This is the house of research as well as the inner world of the psyche, intuition, and the agenda of the individual soul. It is in this house where we envision all possibilities or barriers depending on the healthy state of our mind.

In the Vedic system, the twelfth denotes the hidden treasure chest where all conception occurs. The uncharted territory of your business or chosen vocation is to bring information from your "past" incarnations into the present world. This particularly includes your psychic and intuitive abilities to empathize with others. Your great challenge is to be alone with your unconscious, so that its imaginative tools may unfold and assist you in discoveries and bringing forth new solutions. This requires solitude to enable the spirit inside you to re-ignite. The placement of the South Node in the sixth house indicates a remembered ability to serve others in a physical way. You know how to do things, how to organize, how to run those machines and be in the trenches with peers and co-workers to get the job done, but this is not the challenge. It is only some of the abilities you bring to your twelfth house placement of the North Node. **Key Phrase: Master Psychic, Researcher. Alone and liking it.**

The North Node in the **eleventh house** suggests participation within a community, organization, or social circles. Working with community, inspiring groups, forming connections is the challenge here. Socially conscious activities are part of your chosen path. Another challenge is that of making "strangers" your family. This placement suggests political activity in its many forms, but may prove difficult, because this is uncharted territory. An easier placement is the

South Node in the fifth house. Playing and focusing on your individual creative process may be easy, but this asks you to take your abilities in looking at the world through child-like eyes and to bring that to the community at large (eleventh house). It is easier to play with our children and lovers to experience pleasure and joy with the South Node in the fifth, but now we must be less intimate and operate in larger groups (eleventh house).

There is an old saying that says, "It's who we know and not what we know". This is best applied to the North Node placement in the eleventh. The eleventh house is the second from the tenth and represents those acquaintances in the community who may act as assets to your career achievements. All successful businesses survive and prosper through referrals (an eleventh house matter). Anyone who has the North Node in the eleventh is challenged to cultivate acquaintances and associations who can help advance their vocation. By knowing those who know others, you in turn act as a catalyst. **Key Phrase: Community catalyst. Master Networker.**

The **tenth house** placement of the North Node suggests that your uncharted territory is to be out in the world when you prefer privacy with the South Node in the fourth house. Your life may seem as though you live in a fish bowl. Your uncharted territory is to be out there in the world even though you'd rather be hanging out at home with your fourth house South Node. There is a strong foundational memory of your fourth house experiences, good or bad. You draw on the well of family gifts, skills and talents, and/ or, you do something in the world that is a direct result of your fourth house experience. **Key Phrase: Self-made Person. Master of whatever you do.**

Entering the ninth, eighth and the seventh houses puts us in the Third Quadrant or the area of "the other". This Quadrant focuses on being with others. The North Node in any of these houses forces us to learn and study other peoples' values, their beliefs, and learn to share and co-operate with others. We may not be comfortable with that, but the challenge is for us to be in collaboration.

The **ninth house** suggests that your greatest challenge in life is to move into a bigger vision of life and its possibilities. Once achieved, you share that vision with others, as a good teacher inspires their students or as a great writer makes us see beyond our present reality. With the South Node placed in the third house, the tendency may be to stay with measured types of thoughts and communications. Thinking small may be comfortable, but the uncharted territory is to think big. This is the classical mark of someone who wants to be a bookkeeper or secretary and responsible for manageable amounts of data. Their challenge is to move out of this comfort zone and into a bigger way of thinking, like being a marketing director for the company based on their experience of public relations from years behind the counter as a teller. **Key Phrase: Visionary. Master teacher or writer. Expressive.**

The uncharted territories of the **eighth house** are complicated. They suggest that the individual must learn to share their resources, their deepest secrets with others and risk being vulnerable. The North Node placement in this house suggests occupations that deal with other peoples' resources. However, the North Node in the eighth can be frightening because the individual has to learn to trust others enough to work with them. Escaping to the second house is easy, because you just need to worry about taking care of yourself. Your perception may be that there is no help from others, but it is more likely that there is a strong fear or doubt that you won't receive support. It requires tremendous courage to share your deepest secrets, your hard won financial assets and investments as well as your deepest sexuality with others. These are all eighth house or Scorpionic issues. You are usually naturally resourceful, very clear about what you like and desire, perhaps even selfish in this way.

You venture into the terrain of other peoples' resources, which many financial planners, insurance underwriters, conservators do every day. Your challenge is to work with others and not only by yourself. **Key Phrase: Resource collaboration, Master Sharer. Venture capitalists, and money and power brokers.**

The **seventh house** is one of the most important houses of the horoscope because it is the transition house from below the horizon to above the horizon. It is the house we assign to relationships, competition, and litigation. It indicates how we operate in our primary relationships, whether they are personal or professional. It shows how we relate to others over the long term.

The North Node placed in this house forces us to take risks in relationships. With the South Node in the first house it would be easier to be independent and to do our own thing. We know it and we are comfortable with our independence. The uncharted territory is how to create a successful symbiosis with others. Our challenge is to compromise and to give to others as well as ask for what we need from others thereby creating the perfect union. Successful discrimination of what works for us in relationship and what doesn't work for us is the uncharted territory. If something doesn't work it is so much easier to bolt and go. **Key Phrase: Partnerships and connections. Successful litigation. Marriages made in Heaven!**

The Second Quadrant begins with the sixth house and continues with the fifth, and then the fourth house. This is an unusual quadrant, in that it requires us to be somewhat detached and open-handed in our dealings with others. The North Node in any of these houses requires developing a type of cog in the wheel of life mentality. These are all houses of facilitation in some way or another. They are also very private territories, but still require us to mix with those closest to us. The uncharted territory is that of being in your heart, up close and personal. It is much easier to fall back into the South Node placement that may fall anywhere in the tenth, eleventh, or twelfth, where we are closer to strangers than to our most personal alliances and expressions.

With the North Node in this Quadrant, we are encouraged to act as an intermediary or facilitator, and the frustration of this quadrant is that we don't always know that we are doing this, but we are. Ray Merriman terms this quadrant the "Mystic" quadrant. We may walk though life wondering what we are really here for or constantly asking ourselves what do we want? Our connection with other people acts as a catalyst. Sometimes we are apprised of this and sometimes we aren't. Thus, the frustration in wondering about what we are here to do.

Learning to get organized, to help others, to facilitate and problem-solve are the challenges of the North Node in the **sixth house**. This house is similar in some ways to the seventh house in that it requires contact with others, but requires a kind of selflessness to manage details in helping others. Agents, escrow officers, health practitioners, people who work with methods, systems, and act as liaisons in an agency are all occupations related to this house. Taking a great body of information and beginning the task of sorting and then assimilating and processing it into a workable form is what this house is really about. It performs the same activity that the small intestine of the body performs (small intestine is ruled by Virgo) in that it sorts, classifies and assimilates the parts of the greater whole into a workable contract (seventh) or result.

This individual may be comfortable with isolation and not want to tend to the smaller details in others' lives. The interesting thing is that the South Node in the twelfth individual brings to their life a kind of "knowing", a strong sense of intuition in solving sixth house problems. We listen to the situation, we have the skills or methods on hand on how to solve the situation, but then the real ability is to intuitively go to the next level and know what to request and what to do next. This is the power of the sixth house, an under-rated house, whose value lies in the ability to get things in order for successful outcomes as the planets rise to the tenth. This is the challenge of the North Node in this part of our charts. **Key Phrase: Master Facilitator. Problem solving and know how.**

The child within you is your creative center. The North Node in your **fifth house** asks you to be playful like a child. You may have had to be a little adult growing up and are uncomfortable with playing, creating, or trusting in love. Your challenges lie in taking risks, being speculative, creating or relating to children.

Stock speculators and portfolio managers can have their North Node here. This house requires the development of the creative mind. It requires that we trust our creative center and not depend on other peoples' opinions. There is a risk in being rejected by your community or group. It is important when you have the North Node in the fifth house that you repeatedly check-in with your heart and its desires. It is very easy to run away from personal experience or depend too much on other peoples' opinions. Listening to the heart is imperative, but not easy with this placement.

The obvious place to run is to the South Node in the eleventh house where we agree with people in our social group, in our community, with whom we network for our businesses. It is not so easy to stay intimate with ourselves, with the creative being within us. The fifth house is what we desire personally. The eleventh house is what we desire publicly. The challenge of the North Node in the fifth is to identify our creative essence and to express it. **Key Phrase: Master Speculators. Avocations that become vocations.**

The **fourth house** is the most invisible part of the chart and yet, one of the most important as it represents our roots, where we come from and all of our genetic material. The uncharted territory of the North Node in the fourth house is for you to put down roots. This may indicate the possibility of working with the land, the family business, in real estate, building or construction. The easier thing is go to the South Node in the tenth house where you have an easy memory of public life and public reputation and where you have been well received in the past. The North Node in the fourth house suggests that you create a secure environment for your family, your organization, to know the basic structures of existence. It is important to develop your base of operations, building one block on top of another. To use what you have. **Key Phrase: Master builder. Developing formats, structures and systems.**

As we move into the third, then the second, and the first house, we enter the First Quadrant of the horoscope, which is the most independent and self-oriented part of the chart. The First Quadrant is associated with the Spring Equinox, which is the beginning of the growth cycle for the year. It is associated with courage and dedication for many things begin new in the spring. The First Quadrant of the chart is associated with trail-blazing efforts and initiation. The basic challenge for the North Node in any of these houses is to develop the self. To know that others are important, but to primarily develop yourself and your talents. The individual is asked to develop that sense of self that starts things moving in the right directions.

Therefore, when we see the North Node in the **third house**, we are challenged to communicate and to convey to others our ideas and thoughts. We need to learn to communicate effectively about the day-to-day things. It would be easy to philosophize and move out into the ninth house visions, but the uncharted territory is to know how to read and write and do that arithmetic. Bookkeeping, writing letters, journals, articles, commentaries, newsletters, and marketing packages are the challenge. Getting the "ideas" could be easy if you move back to the ninth, but communicating in day-today terms is the challenge. **Key Phrase: Master communicator. Articulating ideas.**

The North Node in the **second house** asks us to define our value for ourselves and to clarify and develop our individual gifts, skills and talents that make us unique. Our uncharted territory is to clarify those values for what we value is what we get back in the form of payment, freedom, and inspiration. The second house defines our emotional spending habits. We need to know what triggers those patterns and we can, through self-awareness, become quite self-sufficient.

North Node in the second invites us to support ourselves first and to then combine our resources with another through the South Node in the eighth house. It asks us to trust our instincts when it comes to spending, developing the different skills we have, to make ourselves more secure. The South Node in the eighth house, however, seduces us into merging with others frequently, but with the North Node in the second, we have to know ourselves first before we can give ourselves away to another. Those who work in industries of comfort, such as food, furnishings and pleasure, in general, can work, negotiate, and sell large commodities, which bring in large revenues. **Key Phrase: Master of Resources and Earning Power.**

The North Node in the **first house** is exactly as it reads. Develop a self, so that you have a self to give away in the seventh house. The memory is that of always being with others, but the uncharted territory is that of the self and the identity. This particular marker, with either North Node in the first or with the North Node in the sign of Aries, suggests an independent worker or someone who works for themselves.

The theme of the person's life may be that they continually find themselves working for others, but leave because there isn't either enough—autonomy, acknowledgement, or that the others move too slowly for their fast paced personality. Bureaucracy and red tape create a level of frustration for the North Node in the first house personality. This continual frustration, ultimately, forces the North Node in the first person to look to themselves as their best counsel. Working with one's body, things that adorn the body as well as image consulting and motivational training. **Key Phrase: Master Trailblazer. Self-employed and liking it.**

Planets Aspecting the Nodal Axis as Career Indicators

Various factors in the horoscope indicate one's career path. The Lunar Nodes are one of the most important factors in generating a primary clue to the vocational direction of the individual. As we delineate the various parts of the horoscope it is imperative to take into consideration the Nodal placements and any planets that are touching this axis by conjunction or by square, as they may be career indicators.

I have observed that natal planets squaring the natal nodal axis may indicate the type of profession or the qualities required for effective performance. The planets as well as Chiron, and, the four major asteroids of Pallas Athena, Juno, Ceres, and Vesta, carry their symbolism over to the successful interpretation of the age old question, "What will I be when I grow up?"

If Mercury is squaring the nodal axis at birth, first examine the placement of the North and the South Node and then look at Mercury. Mercury represents communications and trading among other things (see planets section). This person may struggle with the challenges of Mercury throughout life by wanting to know everything, but perhaps not staying with anything for any length of time. Once they learn to dis-

Illustration 22

Male: *Food Broker, May 7, 1943, 4:30am CWT + 5:00, Winfield, KS, 37°N14'23" 096°W59'43"*

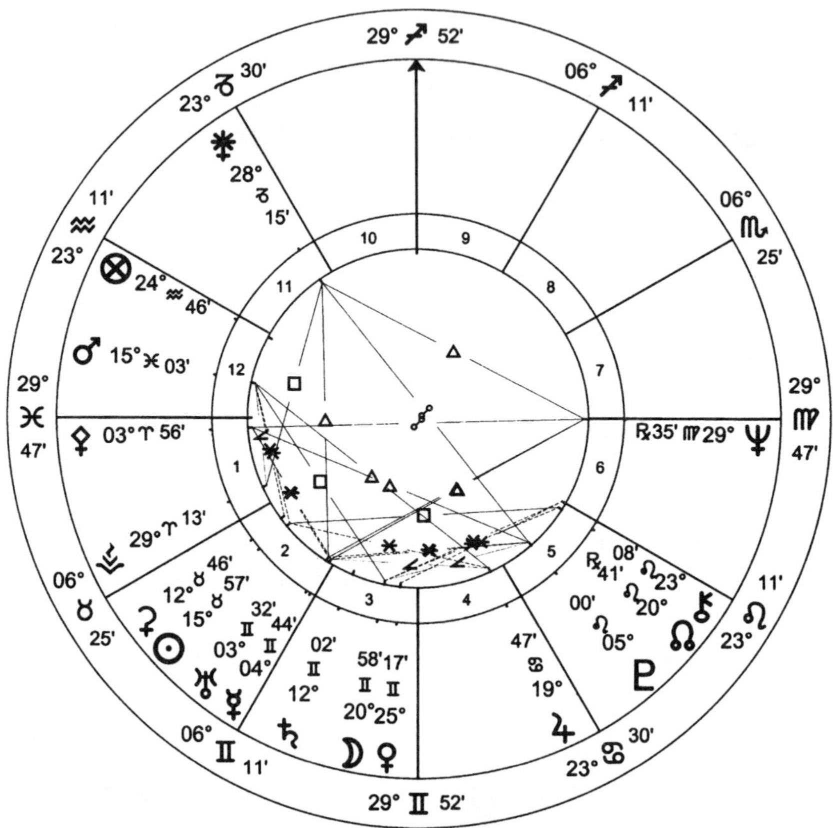

criminate and assess they may find that Mercury related careers would lead them to a proper career choice.

Another example can be seen in the chart calculated for May 7, 1943, Koch Houses (Illustration 22). Notice that the Sun in Taurus is squaring the North and South Node. The Sun also conjuncts Ceres (⚳), which also squares the North and South Node.

Ceres (⚳), like Demeter, in Greek Mythology, is associated with the Goddess of the harvest, the grain or earth Goddess who feeds the people. Note that the Sun in this chart rules the sixth house, which can be associated with restaurant supply or suppliers. Ceres conjunct the Sun and square the Nodal Axis in this case shows a very successful food broker, who at the age of ten started selling his employer's day old fruit on a cart as he walked home from work. This occurred at the time that his father died and left ten children, exemplifying another part of Ceres' myth, a deep loss and descent into the underworld. Each one had to fend for oneself. This evolved into a very successful career as a food broker who worked regionally with a specialty product, mostly Latin American food imports.

Illustration 23

Female: Josephine Baker, Jun. 3, 1906, 11:30am CST + 6:00, St. Louis, MO, 38°N37'38" 090°W11'52" (from Solar Fire)

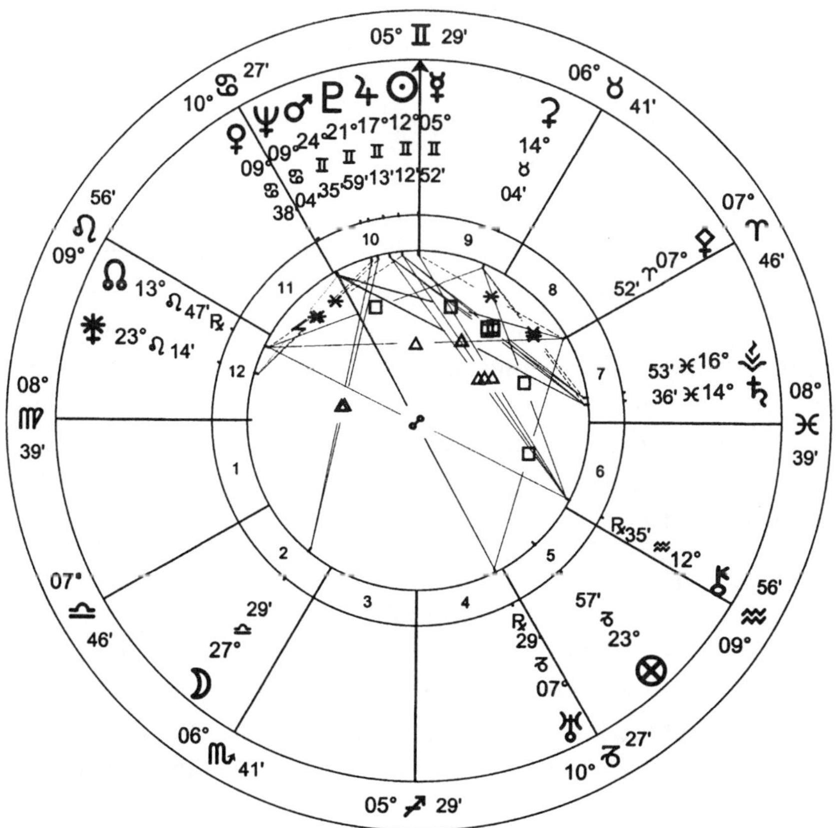

Another example is that of Josephine Baker, a black woman who made a name for herself in Paris. She was an expatriot, who left the United States because of racial bigotry, and was born on June 3, 1906, 11:30 AM, Saint Louis, MO, CST, Koch Houses, (Illustration 23). Note Baker's North Node in the twelfth house. She retreated from her home country and blazed new territories in France. In Vedic Astrology, the twelfth house represents faraway lands. Later in life, Baker adopted twelve children from different races. They were called her Rainbow Tribe. She became a devoted super-mom, much like Ceres who searches the earth looking for her stolen daughter, Persephone. In her chart Ceres squares the North and South Node and is placed in the ninth house of foreign lands.

The above are examples on how to work with the Nodal Axis and career indicators. There are many other factors, but this technique is a simple one that can be used when we don't have a birth time for the individual. Of course, the optimum is to always have the correct time to view the house placements of the Nodes.

Another example is in the following chart of a young woman born on October 13, 1963 (See Illustration 24). We see Pallas Athena (⚴) in a tight square to this individual's nodal axis. In this person's career, she trained at one of the major military academies of the United States, worked for the government in strategic planning, studied law for quite some time, and continued as a consultant throughout her lifetime. These are all qualities that are associated with the energy of Pallas Athena.

Another example is the recent group of candidates for President of the United States in the year 2000. Albert Gore Jr., George W. Bush, Bill Bradley, all had natal Mars squaring their Nodal axes. John McCain does not have this configuration and instead has a natal Mars and Mercury squaring natal Uranus. How fitting that his campaign slogan was about "straight talk".

Illustration 24

Female: Military Trainee, Oct. 13, 1963, 2:15am EDT + 4:00, Buffalo, NY, 42°N53'11" 078°W52'43"

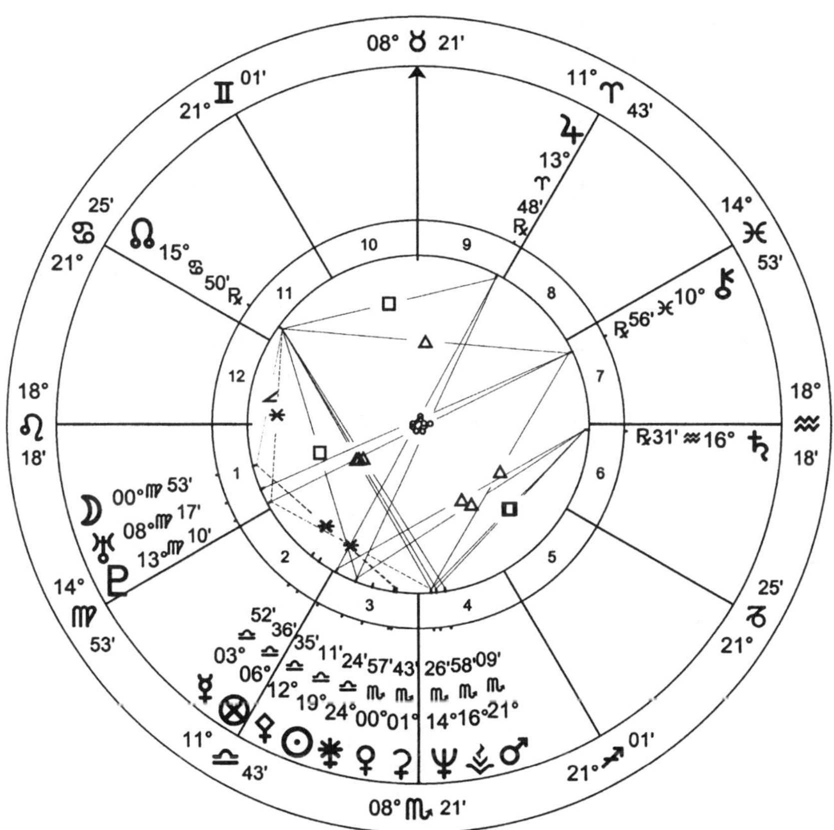

Following the Path of the Nodes and Eclipses

We know that Astrology is a study of cycles. There are many different cycles that dance and inter-react with each other through time. This is why we can sometimes make predictions about business and economic trends and also why we sometimes can't. But there is one cycle that is very clear and fairly predictive in terms of business trends or business and career decisions for an individual. It is the Lunar

Nodal Cycle that runs with the Eclipses.

The Lunar Nodes have an approximate 18.6 year cycle. They spend approximately one and a half years in one sign of the zodiac and then they move retrograde towards the next sign for the next one and a half years. The full cycle runs the same as the more common economic cycles (interest rates, real estate values) have this same approximate cycle length.

The Ancient Chinese believed when the Sun disappeared during a Solar Eclipse that a dragon was eating the Sun (Illustration 25). We know that this is not true, but examining the symbolism is helpful. Why is the dragon eating the Sun? There are many different explanations. The way I explain it to clients is that it needs the Sun for food, for sustenance, and, in order to grow at different times, it needs to shed its skin.

The houses through which the transiting North Node (Dragon's Head) move for approximately one and a half years

Illustration 25

is where you or the company in which you work are "eating the Sun" and "growing"—where opportunity lies and may only show itself through a time of symbolic darkness. Where the corresponding South Node is moving is where you are being asked to let go of old behavior patterns. Like the child's game, Crack the Whip, if you keep hanging on for dear life, you will be thrown off violently!!

About every six months we have a Solar Eclipse (a New Moon) and a Lunar Eclipse (a Full Moon) which, if they exactly conjunct or square a natal planet, will trigger massive changes within three, six, nine or twelve months! This is also based on the eclipse's intensity and whether it is partial, annular, or, the most intense, total. On a larger scale we can examine how this cycle affects business trends. Since the Lunar Nodal axis is the resulting intersection of the Ecliptic and the Moon's orbit, the Lunar Nodes have much to do with public pulse. The Moon indicates the public's response; the Nodal Axis indicates trends. During these cycles, we see major shifts at the very beginning and then again at the very end of the smaller one and one half year cycle as it transits through two opposing signs. As the North Node leaves a sign and completes its last two eclipses in the same signs, we see resolutions of problems associated with those signs and the houses through which they transit.

When the North Node entered Aquarius several years ago in late May of 1989, an Aquarian event arose which affected world politics and history. Aquarius is the sign of human rights and collective thinking. In spring of 1989, we witnessed the student uprising in Beijing, China which ended tragically with the slaughtering of young students and which was the contemporary trigger for the platform on Human Rights! In addition, other cycles such as the synodic cycles of Saturn conjunct Neptune on June 24, 1989, the Saturn/Uranus and Saturn/Jupiter conjunctions, the world is confronting the issue of human rights as a part of political and government priorities.

When the North Node entered Capricorn, we had major depression and recessionary cycles. During this occurance interest rates and real estate values drop, which invite astute buyers to purchase investments. Bernard Baruch, an old-world financier once said when asked the secret of his success once said, "I buy my straw hats in the winter!"

If we read the symbolism of Capricorn, which occurs in the dead of winter when the world in the Northern Hemisphere is its coldest, we see death on the surface, but underneath the cold and icy snow, new life is birthing. The sign of Capricorn is most functional when it is most uncomfortable, and so this Nodal Cycle, though quite difficult, paves the way for the oncoming Nodal Cycle as the North Node enters Sagittarius, which just occurred in early August 1992.

When the North Node was running through Sagittarius a few years ago, the sign, which rules wide-open spaces, truth, religion, publishing, traveling, education. During this time, Native Americans developed new modes of financing through gambling casinos. These developments were highlighted in the news. We saw the fashion industry displaying denim, boots, and backpack-looking purses. We saw major public figures purchasing large bodies of land in Montana and the Dakotas. We saw reclamation by Native Americans of their territories for hunting and fishing purposes, new directions taken to finance educational opportunities from the private sector.

When the North Node began its travel through Sagittarius, travel skyrocketed and new marketing and sales alternatives developed via people ordering over the Internet. More international news, customs, and products merged into our culture and marketplace. Trade and tariffs were the issues of the day as they still are as Pluto transits Sagittarius. Since Sagittarius rules belief systems, philosophies, religions and metaphysics, this represents changes in those areas, too. The blend of the node moving from Capricorn, which is survival oriented, and the move into Sagittarius, which is possibility oriented, provided some new turf upon which practical visions were built.

Alternatives for education occurred in the forms of video and online classes as well as online certifications for the real estate market. New methods were developed to get through the legal system; using paralegals, or information available via computer programs. New job openings in the international sector opened. The need for more and more teachers abroad became part of this growth pattern. Opportunities for teaching foreign languages, skills, and understanding other world customs were only at the tip of the iceberg as the North Node traveled through the sign of Sagittarius. For more clarity as to what was going in business, examine the years of late 1973 through 1974, when the North Node was last in Sagittarius during another 18.6-year cycle? Also examine mid-1955 and all of 1956. What kinds of business cycles were you and the world moving through?

To learn more about the Lunar Nodal cycles, review all of the prior cycles. What trends came forward during the North Node transiting Libra? Best sellers were found in such books on relationships, such as John Gray's, Men are from Mars and Women are from Venus, triggering a booming business on all types of matching services, negotiation classes, new ways of looking at relationships, and new views of relationships. When the Lunar North Node entered Virgo, the holistic health business began entering mainstream medicine. The computer industry prospered with more affordable computers, more user friendly and efficient software.

Now that you have a clearer perception of the planetary meanings you'll need to know how to analyze them within the context of their different field or house placements. For example, an entrance into the horoscope, whether it is an individual or corporate chart, from the Ascendant position will net information that is radically different then if you started with the tenth house of career or the sixth house of service. Standing in each one of these houses looking out into the great circle of the horoscope presents us with a rainbow perspective, so chose a color and let's move forward.

Brain Teaser

See how the transiting North Node affects you when it travels over your second, tenth, or sixth house. How does it affect your company? Where are the Nodes presently transiting your chart? On what dates are the eclipses? After determining this information, while observing either a company or an individual chart, first mark where these nodes are moving, the dates of the accompanying eclipses, and then mark their 3, 6, 9 and 12 month trigger points (90°) after these dates. The activation dates bring some marvelous changes and surprises.

[5] Georgia A. Stathis, "The Other Side of the Paradigm: Man's Personal Equation", Pepperdine University, Faculty of the School of Business and Management, Malibu, California, April, 1978.

[6] Melanie Reinhart, Chiron and The Healing Journey (Middlesex, England: Arkana Publishing, 1989) p. 20.

[7] Joyce Mason, Chiron Authority, Rocklin, California. Email: CHIRONICLE@aol.com.

Chapter 6

A Theory of Houses

Houses are the fields of experience that are contained within the wheel. They help us understand the various aspects of our lives, our companies, or events that we choose to examine. They represent the "land" over which we pass during the course of our lifetimes. Different realms are activated as planets pass through them; those passages force us to examine a deeper side of ourselves whose explanation derives from the meaning of the house.

As the planets pass through the various houses, different experiences emerge. For example, my experience has been that when a planet is sitting on a house cusp, particularly if it is retrograding there or stationing to go direct, the planet and its energy may be lost. It falls into a void and we may be unable to tap into its energy.

This is particularly true for professional objectives. For example, when on the cusp of the tenth house there is a kind of "darkness" that the individual experiences right before a planet finally enters the tenth. The individual experiences a kind of limbo, not knowing in which direction to move. Whereas, when a planet is transiting or positioned natally on the cusp of the second house, there may be trepidation as to whether or not one can manifest their earning power. A time of preparation and incubation may still be necessary before there is a marked change in earnings. And, transits on the sixth house cusp question, the "way" one is working or managing their time.

As a planet is leaving a house, there is a need to wrap things up. The individual may feel compelled to clean up things by throwing things out and get ready to start something new in that area of their life.

Entry Points:

Seeing the Horoscope with New Eyes

Before we go over the general idea of what each house means, we need to first understand how they are very similar in meaning whether we read an individual's chart, a company's chart, or a transaction chart. For example, the identity of the individual is reflected in their first house or by the Ascendant. The same is true for a corporation. The meanings of the houses in corporate charts are further explained in the chapter that covers the delineation of a corporation.

This section will focus primarily on the individual and their work or career. Clearly, the basic meaning of the houses is the same in a vocational chart, but with a different slant.

The horoscope can be viewed from many entry points, not just the entry point of the Ascendant denoted by the moment of birth and the circumstances surrounding that birth. To know more about the different houses and glean a crisper interpretation, we can view the horoscope from a particular house and cast a chart for the house itself.

For example, we can look at the tenth house of the horoscope as the career house or what we came to do in the world. Traditionally, we look at the sixth house as the house that denotes the ways we work, the methods and systems we are best suited to express. The second house part of this important triumvirate when viewing vocational Astrology, is, the house of earning power while its opposite point, the eighth house, denotes our income.

What we usually don't see is the relational quality of the different houses to each other. Using the theory that the horoscope has many entry points, we can look at the individual's tenth house and view it as the entry point for the examination of one's career.

Taking this to the next step, we can turn that tenth house and move it, clockwise, to the position of the Ascendant, or, rising sign. Thus the tenth house now becomes the first house and the original Ascendant now moves down to the fourth house position. In Horary Astrology this is called "turning the wheel".

When we turn the wheel, we also move the planets. By using this technique, we may consider the progressions, eclipses, solar arcs and transits in play.

This can be done for any of the houses, but in the case of business or vocational examination, we focus on the tenth, the second, and the sixth, which are, in sequence, a cardinal, a succedent and a cadent house. This vocational triumvirate is self-contained. These are the houses that correspond to the element of earth, which represents the tangible aspects of life, like vocation and income.

Continuing with the example of the tenth house, which has now been moved to the Ascendant position, the natal eleventh house now becomes the tenth house's second house, the house of the career's values, its skills, its gifts, its spending habits, and its resourcefulness. These are the standard attributes of the natal second house.

In sequence, the natal twelfth house now becomes the career house's third house, which represents the way we do or do not communicate. This is an important skill in business. It also represents our interests, the views we hold and how we focus our thinking process. It represents our innate ability to learn things and of how we open up to new thought patterns such as may be required in vocational training and licensing.

In using the turning the wheel technique, the career's new third house is really the natal twelfth house. The twelfth house is the engine of the horoscope and what drives us to success. Probably one of the least understood, but one of the most important houses in the chart, this is really where everything begins in terms of motivation.

The Importance of the Twelfth House

The twelfth house is the unconscious content of the psyche, which pushes us towards or drives us away from success. It is the pre-birth experience of what we feel right before our descent into this world and how we experience that descent.

In the Vedic system of Astrology, the twelfth house is the house of conception of ideas. I believe it is much more powerful than we realize in the western world, because it also holds all of the experiences that came before, essentially all that has formed us.

It is where we hide long-standing issues which clutter our unconscious minds if we do not occasionally clear and process its toxic waste. I call the twelfth house the "toxic waste management station", because our being successful relies on its clarity. Learning to clear and manage mental clutter is very important for creative energy to flow. Henry James once stated that the outer experience of our world is directly related to the inner realities of our minds.

The truth of this statement is shown by the success of motivational speakers of the past such as Art Linkletter, Earl Nightingale, and Patricia Fripp. In more recent years, the motivational revolution has addressed the role that the unconsciousness plays in not only our career and financial success, but also in terms of our health.

Therefore, the twelfth house needs to be scrutinized carefully when examining an individual's horoscope for career and vocational planning. The sign that we find on the cusp of the twelfth house will give us some indication of an energy that will act as the key to their success. By examining the sign on that house and/or the planet that rules it as well as where that planet is placed, we can gain great insight into helping the client.

A high emphasis in the twelfth indicates a preference as well as the need to be alone, particularly to review your life and your path. Natural born researchers they work well behind the scenes. There is also an affinity to want to help those less fortunate, since this is traditionally the house of institutions such as prisons, hospitals, shelters, or populations that may be autistic or learning disabled. There is an innate healing ability, traditional or less conventional, that can be tapped into.

The First House

The Lens Through Which I See My Life

The first house represents the identity or self-image and the way in which we can best express ourselves in the outer world, our physicality and our physical presentation to the world.

The Second House

What I Value, Where I Cultivate and Where I Am Gifted

Making Money from One's Chart using Planetary Placements:

Earning Power is associated with the second house, which represents the skills, gifts, and values that we have. Look at the second house planets and/or the planet ruling the second house cusp for your natural earning skills and resources.

The Sun in the second or ruling the second: An authority figure, executive status, creating an expression that the rest of the company may follow.

The Moon on the second or ruling the second: Earning power fluctuates. Emotional spending. Skill working with the public. Product development. Industries associated with feeding or housing or comfort, such as chefs, home decorators, antiques, or caretaking occupations.

Mercury in the second or ruling the second: Traders, advertising executives or salespeople. Transportation and communication fields. Problem solving and marketing skills. Analysts, systems managers, and writers.

Venus in the second or ruling the second: Businesses that use design as the base of their operations, such as furnishings, social organizers such as hosts or hostesses, mediation skills, negotiation skills. Any business that provides pleasure, cosmetics and adornments such as jewelry or clothing and textile design.

Mars in the second or ruling the second: Lots of activity around money, easy come and easy go. Risk-taking with money. May be involved in the fitness industry, mechanical industries, tool trades or in a profession that requires the precise use of tools such as surgeons, meat cutters, mechanical engineers, or gem stonecutters. Martial arts, aerobics and any business or industry that includes fitness as well as the individual who works in a manufacturing field. Strategic planning and self-employment.

Jupiter in the second or ruling the second: There is much good fortune with this placement. The individual seems able to accomplish their aims. They may also overspend or overrisk. Some of the professions associated with Jupiter are teaching, professional sales, or marketing and motivational speakers. They may be interested in religion, philosophy and belief systems and may include these ideologies in their profession. This may also imply political positions.

Saturn in the second or ruling the second: Your own perceptions of limitation or fear are the things that get in the way of your cash flow. Excellent organizers, builders, body workers, or chiropractors. Any professions that work with the bones. Government work. Recycling materials or salvage industries. Any business involved in the coffee industry. Working with time management and planning. A "late-bloomer" indicator.

Uranus in the second or ruling the second: You value the unusual, the unique and the progressive. Commission or royalty compensation. Interests range from science, math, electronics, groups, the media, to inventions, flight, and computers. Astrology or any business that awakens people to inner resources.

Neptune in the second or ruling the second: You value the soul. Working with healing and the world of the unconscious, such as in hypnosis and aromatherapy. Professions associated with the sea, fish, the arts (theater, music, dance and photography) and all forms of liquid such as water, oil and wine. The Mystic and the Priest or the individual who works in service for other people's souls.

Pluto in the second or ruling the second: Your interests and abilities lie in transforming the old and outworn into the new and redeveloped. Good therapists, Shamanic work, redevelopment contractors, money brokers, mass production, and working in the area of nuclear energy as well as with any goods or services involving estate management or estate liquidation.

Chiron in the second or ruling the second: Your interests lie in the area of teaching people from your own experience, particularly if it surrounds anything to do with the Holistic Health field. There have been issues that you have had to overcome around your own self-worth. This spills over into your life and the work you do. Remember people who want to lose weight always want to work with those folks who have had the problem and beat it and not with those who know nothing about it!

The Third House

How I Learn and Process Ideas

The way you process thought, the way you communicate that thought and the way you write or present ideas are some of the qualities of the third house. Long known for its processing abilities, if you have a high emphasis in this house, you have the capability to communicate, to facilitate and negotiate with people. It is known as the house of the short writings: poetry; screenplay writing; how-to manuals; business writing, magazine writing, letter writing and, journalism.

The house of licensing and vocational training it represents word processing and bookkeeping. Those of you who have a lot of planets there may also be attracted to internet writing and essays, news releases, news columns and marketing packets that are presented as an adjunct to successful sales presentations.

Look at the cusp of this house. Is the cusp in a water sign (Cancer, Pisces, Scorpio), an earth sign (Taurus, Virgo, or Capricorn), an air sign (Gemini, Libra, or Aquarius) or a fire sign (Aries, Leo, or Sagittarius)? The element denotes the type of thinker you are or the kind of energy that might inspire your thinking. The well from which you draw your inspiration to communicate is expressed through the sign. Your writing may have an emotional base that inspires it. If a water sign rules the cusp or, if you have an air sign on this cusp, you may be inspired by anything that is new and innovative. Practical thinking may be the earmark of earth signs on this cusp or in this house and bright, energetic, trailblazing thought processes may be emphasized whether there is a fire sign on the cusp or many planets posited in this house in fire signs.

This is an important house in terms of early childhood education. Did you have learning disabilities? What areas in school did you struggle with? In what areas did you excel? The third house and its contents indicate the kinds of vocations you choose and how you process the information in order to conduct this vocation.

Since it is the house of vocational training, inevitably when there is a transit, an eclipse, or progressed activity in or on this house, you want to learn new things, or pass that board of certification in order to move forward in your job pursuits.

The Fourth House

Basic Training for Life Purpose: My Genetic Gifts

Continuing with the example of turning the wheel and using the career house as the first house, the Ascendant now becomes the career's fourth house.

Over twenty years of observation have shown me that when transiting Saturn crosses over the natal Ascendant, there is a huge change in consciousness and in the individual's life results include a major career change or move. When Saturn passes through the tenth house, we may make major changes and choices about our careers. However, one of the primary transits is when Saturn transits the fourth house.

The fourth house is the least visible part of the chart, but also one of the most important. It represents our roots, and it is here that we see the true beginnings of a career change. This may come from questioning deep-rooted conditioning from one's family and making changes based on confrontation with one's inner self.

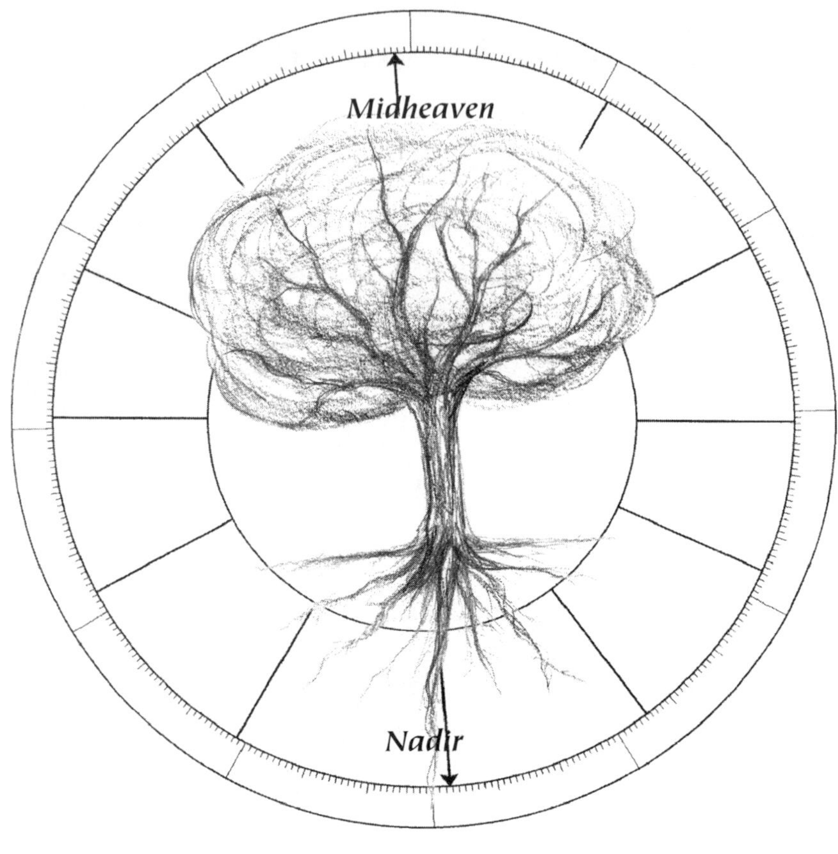

Illustration 26

Many times change comes from a dissatisfaction and desire to be more deeply challenged mentally by the career. (Third house which precedes the fourth). I have observed that in the past the individual may have been perfectly happy with the periphery benefits of their careers, but now they need more.

It is also in the fourth house, which is the root or base of the chart, which shows from where the individual is coming. Another way to put this is that the fourth house encompasses all of the conditions from our family and culture that we carry inside of us. By distilling and separating the positive from the negative qualities—i.e., the unconscious qualities, we glean the best of our heritage and take it with us into the visible tenth house of career. A metaphor would be that the horoscope is like a tree. The vertical axis of the horoscope is its trunk. The roots of the tree are in the fourth house and the foliage of the tree, the tenth, is inter-connected with the trunk.

If a tree's roots have fungus, we still see foliage, but if we treat or eliminate the fungus, we have a much better chance of achieving new growth or those things we desire in the outer world.

By doing this, we can honor the family from which we come, extracting the more positive elements and leaving behind that which our consciousness has outgrown. (Illustration 26)

The Fifth House

Where I Am Willing To Take A Chance, Experience Pleasure and Continue to Create

The fifth house is the place where we take risks. In an ordinary horoscope, we can view this house as the house of children, but from a vocational perspective the creation of "babies of the mind" is how we view this part of the chart, where we speculate on possibilities. It represents our "heart's work", the thing that really gives us joy and pleasure. It is also the house that has to do with hobbies. Ultimately, an avocation for which you hold a tremendous amount of passion can become a vocation.

the Sixth House

the Manner In Which I Organize My Environment In Order to Be Successful In My Outer World Expression

Facilitating events and negotiations are the sixth house's forte. How we handle systems, methods, equipment, and act, as facilitator for different people is a crucial part of the sixth house. It is the house of organization where databases and procedures rule. In the course of a full cycle around the chart, this house is very important, because the more organized you are, the greater the return you receive when the planets transit the tenth house.

This is particularly true of transits of Saturn, because Saturn manages, organizes and prunes. The more you become familiar with new systems and equipment, software and time management, the more you will get it down to a fine science so that you are ready to gain a major return as it transits the tenth.

Signs on the Sixth House Cusp

Aries or Mars: You work independently and much faster than others. Attention to detail may not be your strength, but you excel at offering quick solutions to problems. Watch jumping into some sort of organized system without thinking first.

Taurus or Venus: You are methodical about your approach to systems and organization. Need to feel that you have the resources in order to do the best job possible. Work surroundings need to be comfortable. You know how to make something look good and are very fussy about the aesthetics.

Gemini or Mercury: It is probably better if you aren't in the office that much and that the staff you have is good at taking all of your pieces of information and putting them into some sort of order. Desk and workspace may be cluttered. Problem solving is your forte. You can put together this person with that agent and profit from the connection.

Cancer or Moon: Your role may be that of caretaker of employees. Food service businesses may also be a theme. Workspace needs to feel comfortable and homey. Eating regularly while you process information and organize systems is imperative.

Leo or Sun: You are best in a position of authority rather than an administrative position. Your energy is lively and you have a capacity to inspire others to get the job done and have fun while doing it. You are very creative at knowing who does best at what job. You like your time to be your own. You exhibit pride in the work you do.

Virgo or Mercury: You are most at home in this house, knowing exactly in which order to do things. You learn software and systems quickly and have the capacity to work many hours. Easily taken advantage of by employers, you are a "workaholic". Therefore, be on the lookout as to whether or not you are being rewarded.

Libra, Venus or Pallas Athena: It is important to you that your fellow workers are treated fairly. An astute management ability has you overseeing personnel with finesse. You know how to put together a team of people who will work loyally and selflessly for you. You have a fair mind and willingness to acknowledge the people who work for you. However, you might exhibit the other side of the coin and find it hard to get started. You are strategic and careful about attacking organizational problems.

Scorpio, Mars or Pluto: You have an incredible ability to excavate and re-build the systems and structures in your company. You see the process through from beginning to end always remaining in control. Watch trying to control the team with which you work too much. This need for control may cause some health problems particularly in the colon area, as a proper diet is key to retaining good health.

Sagittarius or Jupiter: Like Gemini you are probably best not being in the office, but on the phone or talking with clients and facilitating projects. You are a natural at teaching employees and can always be called upon to shed a positive light on a new vision for future systems and technological decisions.

Capricorn or Saturn: When no one else can figure it out or inevitably has given up, you come in with the heavy guns, tunnel vision and the capacity to work until you drop. You logically attack each and every phase of the systems and methods that aren't working until you finally figure them out. People with this placement can work for very long hours. Dependable to a fault, they require help because they surely won't ask for it.

Aquarius, Uranus or Saturn: You have an incredible ability to see the bigger picture and look beyond the fixed systems that are blocking the people around you. You are facile with computers, technology, and electronics. You just know the stuff. However, you are unable to work within a fixed 9 to 5 structure, because you need versatility and different challenges when it comes to organization. This is an excellent placement for an independent contractor as well as someone who works with much larger packages, projects and networks.

Pisces, Jupiter or Neptune: Getting organized is tough with this placement. Easily distracted you prefer alone time to think through new methods and systems. Also, since you are so sensitive to others' energies you act as healer for office workers and get drained in the process. Great placement for creative types: artists, designers, healers, and anyone that has to turn a vision into a concrete reality. If they give you a few days to think over a project without bothering you, you will do an even better job because you need to incubate before you operate.

The Seventh House

As Above...So Below...

Vocationally the seventh house suggests your ability to attract people who can assist you and in many ways is an indicator of how others perceive you. In vocational Astrology it can be how your competition perceives you. For example, if you have a transit of Venus in your seventh then a partnership opportunity might present itself. Conversely, as Mars transits this house you may be seen as aggressive, reactionary or on a positive note, pioneering and magnanimous.

Since the seventh house is the first house above the horizon line, whenever planets move up into this house, you become more visible. In the case of Saturn, this denotes that a fifteen-year cycle is about to begin, whereby you are being recognized as an authority figure. You could have been working very hard to establish your career and business over the last fifteen years, but were not noticed until after Saturn crossed over into the Descendant.

Suddenly, Saturn creeps above the line, particularly in the case of *just* entering the seventh and opportunities flood in. Then the lesson is to make sure that you are discriminating in your choices. You have to ask yourself which mountain do you want to climb? This is a question with Capricorn connotations. When the Sun transits this house, you "shine"—you are noticed and project an aura of creativity and optimism, attracting, major opportunities.

Eighth House

Income and the Support You Receive

Robert Jansky once said that the eighth house represents our income and my experience confirms that. Since the eighth house indicates how we share, it also indicates that by sharing we can attract both support and resources. Financial planners, people who work with estates and trusts, and those who work with other long-term investments have an influence in this arena.

The sign on the cusp of the eighth house can indicate a special quality or asset. For example, Aries on the eighth may excel at strategy; Pisces on the eighth house may be a natural psychic, artist, or specialize in drug rehabilitation. It indicates a very intuitive approach to investments and a potential capacity to attract to you what you envision in terms of investment opportunities. It also indicates a need for care and caution when collaborating with others. Asking the right questions is important for success.

The Ninth and the Tenth

What We Believe Is What We Become

The ninth is very important because it is the prelude to the tenth. The zodiac forms a very logical sequence. One house leads to another, which links to the next. The ninth house, known as the house of belief systems and philosophies, is pivotal. What we believe is what we carry into the tenth house of career. When our philosophy changes, often our career direction changes.

The ninth house represents how we project ourselves in the form of public relations, marketing, professional speaking and teaching abilities at their highest level. It is the twelfth house from the tenth house; thus it is the engine that drives the career.

The ninth expresses the visions for the future...the dreams of our youth. Those dreams are important, because in our youth we know what we want to do. We don't usually know how, or why, or when, but in our hearts we feel something. We play at what we want to be. These plays and our dreams, change over time.

An old aunt, who had no children of her own, was very successful in a family business. I heard one day that the young nieces used to go to her house and play "business woman". This was in the early 1980's, a shift from "playing house", which prevailed in the early 1950's!

The signs on the cusp of the Midheaven and planets that rule those signs indicate the type of career or outer world experience we seek. Where they are placed and whether they are directly placed in the tenth house lend some clues to career inclinations.

Aries: Requires a highly personal and individualized career with autonomy and independence. Can be involved in strategic planning, aerobics, martial arts, and self-employment.

Taurus: Expression through the voice and esthetic pursuits. Herbs, leather goods, epicureans, clothing designers, agriculture, animal husbandry, ranching and building.

Gemini: Communications, sales, working with the hands, breath work, two careers that run side by side, commerce, travel, writing and teaching.

Cancer: Family businesses, property, food businesses, catering, nurturing others in their work, films or movies, working with women or women's issues.

Leo: Executive positions, working with the arts and their promotion, involvement with speculative ventures and precious metals.

Virgo: Food service, restaurant supply and any sort of wholesale supply, health fields, both traditional and non-traditional, systems and organizational management, writing and editing, service businesses, engineers and agents.

Libra: Careers that require sociability and tact, legal and paralegal services, businesses that involve social activities, negotiators, clothing, accessories, textiles, jewelry, weavings, negotiations, counseling and mediation.

Scorpio: Financial services such as mortgage brokers, bankers, investors, venture capital funding, psychotherapists, careers that deal with death and renovation, rehabilitation, or reconstruction, redevelopment agencies and gentrification.

Sagittarius: Teachers, trainers, visionaries, international sales, educators, Native American interests, horses, cowboys, philosophers, spiritualists, coaching and wilderness guides.

Capricorn: Builders, real estate, working with the elderly, management, concrete and masonry, chiropractors, orthopedists, dentists, ice and frozen foods, government work and organizations.

Aquarius: Public information, working with groups, social activism, Astrology, computers, large developers, multi-level businesses and franchises, science, math, aviation, futurists, trend setters, radio, television, the Internet and computers.

Pisces: Artists, dancers, actors, wine merchants, painting contractors, gas, oil and petroleum, shipping and fishing industries, healers—both traditional and non-traditional, psychics, alcohol and drug rehabilitation work.

The Eleventh House

Who You Know is Where You Go

The eleventh house is the second from the tenth. Those friends, associates and organizations that provide a network and resources for you in your career pursuits.

The community and the members of its organizations are excellent resources for your career. A strong eleventh house indicates an intuitive connection to a "global pulse". An interest in politics, interest groups and how to connect and integrate them is a special skill. The ability to network with the community and attract resources that enable this integration is a special quality attributed to the eleventh house. Knowing the right people and having the right timing is invaluable. If you need to meet someone or make contact with someone who can assist you in business, help is just a few requests away. Referrals are powerful.

Eclipses
and How They Affect the House or the Rulers of the Houses

Whenever I begin a lecture or discussion on eclipses, I mention one of the more traditional astronomical definitions of eclipses. "There is a temporary loss of light and we see a shadow". We who work with the world of symbols recognize this statement on many levels. Light is associated with the Sun, the symbol of our life and life path. The dark is the shadow associated with Pluto.

Eclipses always accompany the Moon's nodes. Eclipses influence emotional changes. Solar Eclipses, which are New Moons, trigger events or flush out unresolved issues. Lunar Eclipses, which occur on Full Moons, have a strong emotional "breaking out" feeling to them. They act as emotional roto-rooters!

The more precisely a Solar or Lunar Eclipse aspects a planet in your chart, especially by conjunction, square, or opposition, the more "life changing" the event may be in your life. The orbs often used are 2° to 3°.

However, the eclipses aspecting a particular axes of your horoscope such as the first and seventh or the fourth and tenth, can also act as catalysts for change in those areas.

A way of identifying the personal meaning of the cycles is to go back 18.6 years prior, when the eclipses were transiting the same houses in your horoscope.

For example, on August 11, 1999, we had a total Solar Eclipse at 18°21' of Leo. The same eclipse hit on August 11, 1980 at the same degrees, although it wasn't a total eclipse. By examining whether your chart or your company's chart was impacted, you can ascertain what pattern is developing in the cycle.

There may be a correlation between events that evolved

following the year of the 1980 eclipse that are similar to the events that followed the 1999 eclipse.

Once either a lunar eclipse or a solar eclipse hits a key point in your chart, you may experience a major change three, six, nine, or twelve months later. These three-month periods are associated with the New or Full Moons that either square or oppose original Lunar or Solar eclipse degrees.

Quite often Lunar Eclipses stimulate change or crisis within three to six months after they occur, but the effects of the Solar Eclipses seem to have a longer-term effect. This is particularly true when we experience the first in a new series (such as the July 1, 2000 Solar Eclipse at 10° 14' of Cancer, the Total Lunar Eclipse at 24° 19'of Capricorn, on July 16, 2000, as well as the last in the series of Leo, which took place on July 30, 2000 at 8° 12'.)

Two examples of major changes that occur on the "last" hits in the series have been the blow-up of Chernobyl and then the Stock Market crash of 1987.

Other important events to watch are when planets transit over the eclipse degree. For example, if Venus is the first planet to transit over the eclipse point, then the experience of the eclipse might be quite positive. Contrary to that, if Mars transits over that same point first, then the effects may be startling or difficult.

Sometimes the effects of the Solar Eclipse will be felt starting at 90 days or 45 days before the official hit. This is based on the same idea of the quarter cycles or in this case, at the 45° cycles (corresponding to 45 days). These angles cause pressure to be felt and depending how many other planets are aspecting the eclipse, may denote a stressful period.

Always watch which planets of your horoscope eclipses aspect, the house in which that planet falls, and the house that it rules for detailed information. For example, if the Lunar Eclipse of June 4, 1993 at approximately 13° to 14° of

Gemini and Sagittarius occurred on your seventh house axis. This squared your Venus in your tenth house (and Venus is the ruler of your twelfth house). It suggests that there may not only be changes in your personal identity, but opportunities for a new relationship that has a spiritual dimension to it (the twelfth house) which might be an asset in your public and professional life (the tenth house).

Eclipses As They Hit the Houses

If either the Solar or Lunar Eclipse is precisely hitting your **first house** or your first house ruler, then look for a new identity, new confidence, a new look, and independence of thought in the succeeding quarters.

In the **second house** or aspecting its ruler there will be new values, cash flow opportunities, new possibilities for discovering your hidden gifts, skills or talents that will help you and others with their resources. There is a very new view of your personal value as an individual, which changes the scope of how you work effectively in the outer world.

In the **third house** or aspecting the third house ruler the possibility of taking some type of license or credentialing course, as well as writing poetry, articles, essays and lyrics, arises. Becoming aware of new ways in which you listen and communicate is highlighted as well as the need to reorganize books and records.

In the **fourth house** or aspecting the fourth house ruler some type of awakening or change concerning one of the birth parents or the possibility of either moving, remodeling your domain, going into real estate or needing time to withdraw from the world. This allows you to re-group and rebirth when the eclipse moves out of your fourth. Sometimes you begin a new business at home, which develops as the eclipse moves out of the fourth. There is often a need to be at home more and to form a nest, particularly when the transiting North Node is moving through the fourth.

In the **fifth house** or aspecting its ruler, there is a possibility of a new birth—either babies of your body or creative projects of your mind! This, of course, is the more traditional view as well as new possibilities for play and romance, but there is also the possibility of re-acquainting oneself with the child within and moving into a space where one is apt to take risks, which can be of the heart or of speculative ventures.

This house rules speculative ventures and gambles. You become involved in convention planning or special events projects. Avocations can become vocations with an emphasis in this house.

In the **sixth house** or aspecting its ruler the possibility of new systems and methods of work may be implemented. Environmental concerns may come to the fore. New scheduling and time management opportunities may appear. Employees may join or leave your company.

You may give more attention to matters of health by "cleaning up your act". Any health issues that need to be addressed may take up your time during these transits. In your home, you may have to deal with the health or care of smaller, domesticated animals.

In the **seventh house** or aspecting its ruler there are new opportunities in either long-term personal or professional associations. There is a strong desire to partner with others and work on the area of committed relationship. If there is an already existing relationship then the opportunity to renew or redefine it comes. If a partner does not want to work on the relationship then difficulties may arise.

In the **eighth house** or aspecting its ruler there are opportunities for your partner to increase his or her resources, the settlements of lawsuits, dealings with estates or legacies and investing in long-term goals. Liquidation of frozen assets may occur or your company may be offering you an early retirement with an opportunity to cash out on your retirement fund. There is a new view of sexuality as sacred and the re-discovery of your deepest most sensual feelings with a partner who pushes your limits.

In the **ninth house** or aspecting its rulers, opportunities arise to write, teach and help people follow their visions. Long distance relocations may occur, as well as opportunities coming from some distance away.

You could be given opportunities to work in public relations, professional sales training, and consulting as well as the legally related professions. New in-laws, working for in-laws or concerns about in-laws may occur, as well as experiencing the birth of a third child. Direct mail and mail order businesses may be in the offing.

In the **tenth house** or aspecting its ruler, you may receive the recognition for which you have so long worked. Opportunities from other career sources may appear as you may lose a long-time boss or become one yourself.

There may be concerns around one of the birth parents particularly in regard to their health or personal situation.

In the **eleventh house** or aspecting its ruler friends and members of your community may come to your assistance to help you advance your career. You may be looking at contributing to social causes or the community in some way as well as the opportunity for expanding your circle of friends and colleagues.

In the **twelfth house** or aspecting its ruler you may feel a deep need to withdraw and re-group for a while. The Hindus believe that this is the house of conception. The twelfth house is also the "toxic waste management station" where all things must filter through before they begin anew in the first house.

You may find yourself cleaning out closets, letting go of possessions, re-connecting with your psyche through dreams, meditation or hypnotherapy. This is a great time to begin psychotherapy. Your innate creativity may be released and you may find yourself picking up paints, oils, and crayons, to process the past and re-discover your deepest soul needs.

Houses as Dualities

Dualities are important. They are the point/counterpoint of an axis in the horoscope. When we look at one house with its one sign on the cusp, we are doing an injustice to its opposite point if we don't include it in the interpretation of that axis. The opposite point of an axis is actually the shadow side, which you need to embrace to achieve the full power of that axis. (Illustration 27)

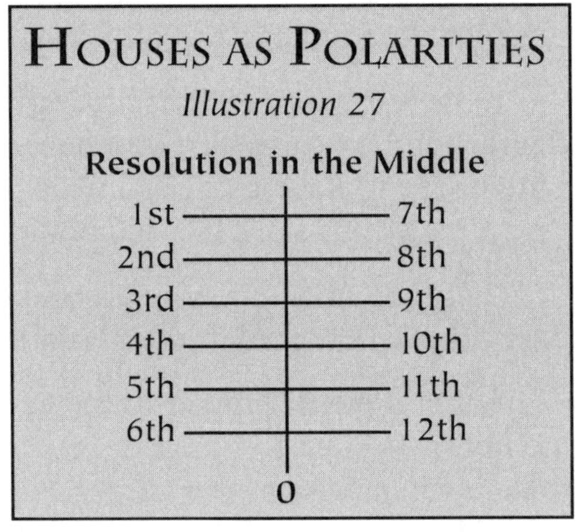

Ignoring the opposite sign of an axis is not giving the interpretation full strength. By including that sign as part of the dynamic, just as we include the planets that are enclosed in those houses, we achieve richer interpretation. These dualities, the axes, act as mirrors that reflect the energy and the presentation of the opposite sign. For example, if we look at the first house of a real estate transaction chart (more information follows) it represents the physical qualities and the presentation of the seller. However, if we don't include the seventh house, representative of the buyer, we are unable to reach a full understanding of the transaction dynamics.

An example might be that if Neptune is on the seventh house of the buyer, the buyer might not be clear about the contract terms. There may be some resistance or ambivalence. This may also have something to do with the seller, the first house, who may really be prepared to sell or part with the property. These subtle distinctions can add a richer delineation and help you, the astrologer, hone in on what may be the underlying issues. In other words, the issue may appear to be concerning one area, or house, of the chart, but in fact, is really coming from the opposite position.

In this last chapter, you have been asked to view the

First House

Real Estate: The first house represents the seller, how they view the transaction and how others view them. It is from the seller's perspective that a transaction is seen from the chart's perspective. The qualities, attributes, identity of the seller are all inclusive in the description of the transaction.

Corporation: Personnel of the corporation, including shareholders, how the shareholders see and identify with the company, the company's morale, company's business objectives, general membership, place of incorporation and its relationship to the public, attitude towards competitors. (Note the ruler of the Ascendant and its house placement.)

Seventh House

Real Estate: The seventh house is simply the buyer of the property. It can also designate legal contracts. What the buyer looks like, what his or her views are about the transaction and what attracted them to this particular transaction are all from the perspective of the seventh house.

Corporation: Relationships with other organizations, sales appeal, how effectively a product is presented to others. This is the house of adjustments, trading volume (stock purchases), public accountings, employee income and payrolls, political or commercial affiliates, women in the organization, trade agreements, mergers, open opposition to growth, lawsuits and legal affairs, competitors and their activities.

First House cont.

Vocational: Self-employment indicator, machinists, aerobics, weight lifters, physical education, artillery, military or militia, adventurers, soldiers of fortune, firemen, policemen; trailblazers, hunters, athletes, bakers, butchers, burglars, diamond cutters, welders, mechanical engineers, tattoo artists, piercing artists, toolmakers and athletes. The visionary leaders of an organization who project the future. They are usually the scouts for an organization who are sent out to seek new business opportunities and strategic alliances. Similar to the soldier ants in an ant colony, they report back to their leaders or managers.

Second House

Real Estate: The second house is the cash on hand and the cash flow. It represents resources that are available in a transaction in terms of property for trade, tangible assets like precious stones, furniture, and refrigerators, which may be used as compensation in a transaction.

Seventh House cont.

Vocational: Negotiators, hosts, people who connect people with people, caterers, counselors, liaisons, partnerships, professional and personal, contract negotiators. Those who work with money and the finances of employees, matchmakers, litigation specialists, mediation and arbitration, public contact, unions, foreign exchange and trade, prosecutors, judges, fine arts and interior designers.

Eighth House

Real Estate: The eighth house represents estates, wills, settlements and business and marriage partnership assets (the second from the seventh). It depicts the joint holdings. In an individual's chart, it indicates whether there is positive or negative financial support from the partner as well as

Second House cont.

Corporation: Liquid assets, revenues, activities in moneymaking, earnings, voluntary expenditures, profits and the disposition of investments.

Yours and ours in the 8th

Eighth House cont.

any inheritance possibilities. It can define the qualities of a mortgage, interest rates and the insurance required. Probate and the escrow itself (including the title search).

Taxes are integral in real estate transactions and this house shows the tax burden. Venus or Jupiter in this house or Libra, Taurus, Sagittarius, or Pisces on this cusp may indicate luck with investments with a partner, inheritances or investments that prosper.

Corporation: Losses or gains through the closing of the business, financial responsibilities, private conferences, the board of directors, credit, dividends, trade secrets, net earnings, insurance, the handling of legacies, nonprofit status, donations to nonprofit organizations, financial conditions involved in partnerships, mergers or lawsuits, financial relations with competitors, competitors' financial conditions, revenues from investments or liquidation of frozen assets, loans and income from sources not under immediate control of the organization and the company treasurer.

Second House cont.

Vocational: Bankers, investors, stock brokers and singers (look at planets in this house and their career significators may indicate professions. For example, Mercury in the second could be someone who works in advertising). Your moneymaking abilities, spending habits and cash flow.

Eighth House cont.

Vocational: Working with other peoples' resources, thusly gaining your own such as a financial planner. Rebirthing work, conservators, morticians, frozen asset management, investigators, insurance underwriters, sex therapists, psychotherapists or hypnotherapists. Any practice that works with the transformation of beliefs.

Third House

Real Estate: The third house represents the signing of a contract and the communication in the transaction. Negatively, it shows the loss of property (the twelfth house from the natal fourth).

Corporation: Contacts with the public, financial and trade publications, financial and trade relations with adjacent states and countries, short-distance travel, neighboring organizations, education, libraries, bulletins and newsletters, magazines, publications, methods of distributing news, literary work, technical publications, rails, telephones and tele-

Ninth House

Real Estate: The ninth house shows the money that comes from an estate or settlement as well as caretaking and any legal situations surrounding the property.

Corporation: Advertising department, shipping, activities abroad, completion of merger contracts, code of ethics and bylaws, audits, contracts with other companies, inter-company communications, company philosophy, publications (same as in third House), any public and foreign relations, long-distance communications, results of mail-order

Third House cont.

graphs, commercial radio, demand for stocks and bonds, trade volume figures, advertising, internal agreements, traffic, transportation and communication departments, interoffice communications and information dissemination within the company.

Vocational: Licensing, vocational training, short writing such as poetry, lyrics, screenplays, press releases, news releases, essays, chapters, journals, bookkeepers, accountants, telecommunications sales, Internet or web masters and vocational trainers.

Ninth House cont.

campaigns, relations with educational institutions and publications, professional consultants, publicity and public relations, officials and all legal affairs.

Vocational: Importing and exporting, professional speakers, consultants, professional sales and marketing directors, public relations, direct mail marketing, publishing and books, international relations, ministers, philosophers, politicians, university professors, teachers, travelers and motivational speakers.

Fourth House

Real Estate: The fourth house represents the property and how one works with it. It indicates vacant property and property damage particularly in regard to plumbing. In corporation charts it represents the warehouses and factories held by a company. As in Horary Astrology, the fourth house can also indicate the outcome of an event.

Tenth House

Real Estate: The tenth house indicates landowners, landlords, land developers, land dealers, and land in general.

Fourth House cont.

A heavily posited fourth house often suggests that real estate might be a suitable choice for your profession or that you could profit from real estate holdings. This is particularly true if natal Pluto is placed here and is well aspected.

Corporation: Real estate investments and holdings, tangible assets of the corporation, hazards involving property, the original home of the organization, investments in land, factory space, office space, the people of the organization as opposed to the president, basic standards, tangible assets, direct competition, power of competitors, roots of a corporation, base of operations or field of activity and the location and condition of factory or office buildings. (Virgo in this position might signify that the organization avoids waste.)

Vocational: Real estate, property, family or family services, building, farming, public housing, rentals, ranches, ranchers, collectors,

Ninth House cont.

Corporation: Supreme or governing authority, president or the chairman of the board, figureheads, national reputation, relations with governments and associations, public image, power, general business conditions as far as its public image and the administrative department. (Look at the ruler of the tenth house and its house placement for insight into the talents or gifts of the CEO.)

Vocational: Managers, coffee industry, public figures, politicians, chiropractors, industrial engineers, comedy business, govern-

Fourth House cont.

home designers and decorators, psychologists, therapists and genealogists are included in this description.

Fifth House

Real Estate: Traditionally the fifth house signifies speculation or taking a gamble on property. It is also an indicator of income from real estate (the second from the fourth house). Sometimes recreational property or income from recreational property is shown here.

Risk & Speculation

Corporation: Executive personnel (except for president or chairman of the board), governing body, attitudes or actions of shareholders or the board of directors in opposition to the president, committees, management teams, advertising success or failure, income from invested capital or re-

Ninth House cont.

ment work, civil engineers, working with the elderly, recycling specialists and industries. These are people who reach the top of their profession.

Eleventh House

Real Estate: The eleventh house designates money that comes from the individual's business or career, the treasury and it may indicate, if negatively aspected, the loss of property (the eleventh house is the ninth from the fourth house and is associated with accumulation as well as loss). Sometimes loss is assigned to the twelfth house since it is the last house before the Ascendant or the first house.

Corporation: Other friendly organizations, friends, acquaintances, political connections, community connections, constitutional policies, resources available through the company head (the second from the tenth), long-range goals of the organization and what it stands for, public relations

Fifth House

sults of speculative ventures, motivation, speculation, the place of deposit of capital such as safes, vaults, and banks, amusements, social affairs, conventions, educational enterprises, workshops, seminars, teaching, examinations, banquets and dramatic or theatrical ventures.

Vocational: Speculative ventures, meeting and convention planning, tourist work, nightclub work, working with young children and people, lottery work, sports professionals, entertainment, professional gaming and golfing. Businesses that involve pleasure and the arts.

Sixth House

Real Estate: The sixth house of the chart reveals the agent, the tenants in a leasing situation, income property and the logistics of the real estate contract.

Eleventh House cont.

through group involvement, intangible assets, indebtedness, mortgages, the treasury, fraternal and club groups providing activities.

Vocational: Community work, group counselors, networks, motivators, trend specialists, club work, civic organizations, legislators, senate, syndication, wish fulfillment facilitators, social and political activists and community relations.

Twelfth House

Real Estate: The twelfth House denotes associations with foreign countries (in the Hindu system, the twelfth is the house of gestation and foreigners). It may indicate what is going on behind the scenes in terms of the seller's circumstances. It may show what has led to the sale of the seller's property. Since it

Sixth House cont.

Corporation: Workers or employees (voluntary or paid), work and equipment, health plans and insurance, work schedules and routines, inventories, lighting and heating bills, performance of workers on the job, cooperation received from employees, assistance received, health policies and attitudes of employees, corporate connections with hotel services, agriculture and agricultural products, fixtures and furnishings, health condition of personnel and the inception of strikes and labor troubles.

Vocational: Time managers, food service businesses, equipment sales, medical supplies, office furniture suppliers, nutrition work, escrow officers, agents, facilitators, recycling and environmental work, efficiency experts, professional servicemen, small animal work, veterinarians, union work and union liaisons.

Twelfth House cont.

is the sixth from the seventh, which represents the buyer, it can indicate the health issues of the buyer, the buyer's real estate agent or escrow agent and the buyer's end of the escrow.

Corporation: Enemies against the organization, sabotage, secret intelligence departments, strikes and labor troubles, behind-the-scenes dissolutions and negotiations; experiments, research and development, trade secrets and formulas, secret assistance, organized and social units, designs for the future relating to past events and the effects of litigation.

Vocational: Welfare work, probation work, foreign work or foreign agents, research and development, dream analysis, hypnosis, biofeedback, writers, musicians, monks, nuns, clergy, working in hospitals or institutions for those less fortunate as in prisons, shelters, schools for the blind, for the autistic, the mentally ill, etc., large animal veterinarians, oil, oil wells, petroleum and the power behind the throne.

houses from many different perspectives. In many ways, you "tried on" many different views of the houses. This is important in that in the next chapter we begin examining the various cycles that contact these houses. Sometimes when we view cyclic activity through one house, we get stuck, because the view is very limiting and the interpretation suffers because of this. In the next section we talk about a very important phenomenon entitled Synodic Cycles. These can occur as quickly as every month to as slowly as every 400 + years. When you work with the Synodics, you experience them in the different houses. By practicing the different "trying on" techniques in this last chapter, your interpretation can expand beyond the boxed structure of viewing the chart from only one perspective.

Chapter 7

Synodic Cycles

Carl Jung once said, "Anything born in that moment in time has the qualities of that moment in time."

Synodic cycles are measured by the interval between two successive conjunctions of any two planets in which they occur. They act as trigger points, providing bursts of activity in their respective houses for the duration of that particular cycle. The fastest synodic cycle is that of the Sun and Moon, with the New Moon (a conjunction of the Sun and Moon) marking the beginning of the monthly cycle. Any two planets can form a synodic cycle. Any conjunction intensifies the energy of the planets involved. The longest of these is the 492-year cycle of the Pluto and Neptune conjunction. My experience indicates that the longer cycles have a very strong influence on events in world history, economics, and belief systems.

In the previous chapter we talked about the planets and their myths and energies. Astrology, particularly when using it as a predictive or planning tool, is similar to the science of chemistry. A planet has a distinct energy. However, when combined with another planet the synergy adds new experiences in whatever portion of the horoscope it occurs. It "brands" the portion of the horoscope for the duration until those two planets come to another conjunction.

The conjunctions reflect the same phases as the

Monthly Lunation Phase Arc Points, which begin at the conjunction (0°), and continue through the First Quarter (90°), the Full Moon (180°), and the Last Quarter (270°).

To understand how the pairs of planets interface lets review some examples. Jupiter and Mars come together once every 2.24 years each time in a different sign. The energy of Jupiter is that of opportunity and expansion. When you add Mars you infuse expansion with motivation, thus providing a very optimistic cycle that encourages growth, spending, and risk. In terms of economic cycles, this particular conjunction encourages more trading on the stock market and more spending in general.

Some of the slower cycles, such as the 126-year conjunction of Pluto and Uranus, occur over a longer period of time affecting entire generations and their consciousness. The Pluto/Uranus conjunction of the mid-1960's stirred revolution and anarchy with student protests, the war in Vietnam, and the awakening of our youth through drugs, sex, and rock and roll!

Individuals born while Uranus conjuncted Pluto in Virgo are the driving force of the technical revolution. The combination of an explosion in consciousness (Uranus) mixed with financial transformation (Pluto) has produced such groundbreaking industries as the Internet, personal computers and wireless communications. This group of individuals experiences transiting Pluto squaring their natal Plutos near the same time they experience their Uranus oppositions signifying a once in a lifetime opportunity of choice, power and resurrection.

Since they were born under this grand Synodic their natal Uranus will also be squared by transiting Pluto symbolizing the need for greater integration. And as Uranus opposes the natal Pluto a breaking down of their power base may mean shared financial concerns and equitable work schemes.

The Pluto/Uranus Synodic cycle opened the doorway to transformational thinking in its last pass in the mid-1960's. In other words, it challenges us to think "outside of the box". Those born with it, both individuals and companies, have as an innate part of their personality, the capacity to change systems, methods, and techniques in the work environment (all Virgo related activities). If these planets are angular in a company or natal chart they are even more powerful as agents of change.

As we move into the future the different elements of living in this world won't be as compartmentalized. Business and living, as well as ecology, creativity, and security are becoming integrated with the advent of new technologies. A greater quality of life combined with longer lifetimes beckons new ways of approaching aging.

There are shorter Synodic cycles, such as the Saturn and Pluto conjunction (a 33-year cycle which last occurred in 1981, the Saturn and Neptune (a 36-year cycle) and the Saturn and Jupiter (a 20-year cycle). These shorter cycles occur more than once in a lifetime allowing us to experience several versions of their conjunctions. They assist us in understanding where we are going and what our life is about. Synodic conjunctions herald new beginnings, much like a New Moon, which always begins the monthly cycle.

(Following is a table of some of the approximate time periods of the synodic cycles contributed by Pat Esclavon-Hardy.)

Synodic/Sidereal Cycle Timetables

These Synodic/Sidereal timetables are the keys to timing. They are the cycles of our Solar System.

1. **A SYNODIC PERIOD** is the time it takes a celestial body to make one complete revolution in its orbit, measured from one conjunction with the Sun to the next revolution, i.e. Sun conjunct the Moon—the New Moon! The following are the planetary SYNODIC PERIODS:

Sun/Moon = 29 days, 12 hours, 44 min., 2.7 sec.

Sun/Mercury = 116 days

Sun/Venus = 1 year, 220 days

Sun/Mars = 2 years, 289 days

Sun/Jupiter = 1 year, 34 days

Sun/Saturn = 1 year, 13 days

Sun/Uranus = 1 year, 4 days

Sun/Neptune = 1 year, 2 days

Sun/Pluto = 1 year, 2 days

2. **A SYNODIC CYCLE** is different in that it is measured by the interval between two successive conjunctions of any two planets, not one planet with the Sun. This cycle is often used in Mundane Astrology to measure important developments in world history. The Synodic Cycles (mean interval of heliocentric conjunctions) are as follows:

Jupiter/Mars = 2.24 years

Jupiter/Neptune = 11.9 years

Jupiter/Pluto = 12.46 years

Jupiter/Uranus = 13.81 years

Jupiter/Saturn = 19.859 years

Saturn/Pluto = 35-36 years

Saturn/Neptune = 36-37 years

Saturn/Uranus = 45.363 years

Uranus/Pluto = 126.95 years

Uranus/Neptune = 171.403 years

Neptune/Pluto = 492.328 years

3. **A SIDEREAL PERIOD** (meaning star period) is the time it takes a celestial body to make one complete revolution in its orbit, to return to a given point in its orbit, measured by its recurrent alignment to a particular star.

Mercury = 88 days

Venus = 224 days

Earth = 365 days

Mars = 1 year, 322 days

Jupiter = 11 years, 315 days

Saturn = 29 years, 167 days

Uranus = 84 years, 5 days

Neptune = 164 years, 290 days

Pluto = 248 years, 157 days

4. **A SUNSPOT CYCLE** is really 22 years due to the shift of the magnetic poles of the Sun reversing every 11 years. Most people are familiar with this 11-year cycle rather than the true 22-year cycle. It takes 22 years of the Sun's poles to come back to their original positions.[8]

In an attempt to capture their essence, I have put together some images that are presented as exercises to captivate your imagination. Next try and build on this imagery with additional themes of your own for each planetary pairing.

Some Synodic Images

Jupiter/Mars = 2.24 years:

Balancing vision and passion. Tribal fertility dance.

Jupiter/Neptune = 11.9 years:

Unification of visions. Slam dancing while others rap in the same hall.

Jupiter/Pluto = 12.46 years:

Metamorphosis of vision. Reluctant caterpillar turns into a butterfly without knowing it.

Jupiter/Uranus = 13.81 years:

Balancing social change and vision. Hula under neon lights.

Jupiter/Saturn = 19.859 years:

Balancing judgment and vision. Professional coaches and trainers. Organizational managers. Quality builders who combine economy and vision. Finding yourself in neutral drive in your car in the middle of the freeway!

Saturn/Pluto = 35 years:

Making a business out of death. Re-writing the rules. Redefining what is considered powerful.

Building new structures using the material from the bones of the ancestors. Practical views of death, grieving and moving on.

Saturn/Neptune = 36-37 years:

Balancing idealism and realism. Harnessing visions. Professional fishermen versus the Exxon Valdez.

Dreamers and artists materializing imagination. Walking on water, being seen, and still not believed!

Saturn/Uranus = 45.363 years:

Merging the traditional with the revolutionary. The corporate rebel. Entrepreneurs.

Plaid socks under navy blue suits. Tango on Acid.

Uranus/Pluto = 126.95 years:

Genetic engineering. Transformation through technology.

Fourth-dimensional thinking. Frankenstein's news. Wireless sex and electronic ecstasy!

Uranus/Neptune = 171.403 years :

Cosmic communications. Star Wars moments. Computer animation and graphics. Morphing. Dissolution of borders and boundaries and massive migrations across the world. The freed imagination. Virtual viruses and wireless worlds transporting transparent currencies.

Neptune/Pluto = 492.328 years:

Mergers between powers. Choosing grand visions and changing Gods! Merging banks and currencies.

Planets join together then separate. They actually begin a developmental cycle that is related to the classic lunation cycle patterns. By working with this cycle, discussed at length in the next chapter, we witness the evolution of one's life, one's career, or corporation. We can use the lunation cycle and the included planning sheet as a guide in understanding as well as strategizing important personal and career moves.

[8] Pat Esclavon-Hardy, Energies, Trends and Cycles, Clearwater, FL; email: patetc@aol.com.

CHAPTER 8

PLANNING AND THE LUNATION CYCLE

Dane Rudhyar described the concept of "Lunation Cycles" for the phases of the Moon within the context of the 28.5-day monthly cycle. At the New Moon there is total darkness and the cycle commences. Traditionally, the old farmers plant their root crops at this time to encourage better growth. The two weeks from the New to Full Moon is the portion of the monthly cycle for growth. It is an excellent time to begin plans, to start projects, and to implement new ideas.

Each month a New Moon falls in some part of the horoscope. This occurs in all horoscopes, be it the chart of an individual, a company or an event. In the course of a month, the development of ideas and concepts associated with the meanings of the house in which the New Moon falls will be highlighted.

There are eight phases of the Moon. The New Moon at 0°, the Crescent Phase at 45°, the First Quarter Moon at 90°, the Gibbous Phase at 135°, and the Full Moon Phase at 180° when the moonlight is its greatest and where the cycle peaks. Following the Full Moon the light wanes and it enters the Disseminating Phase at 225° after the New Moon, then the Last Quarter Phase at 270°, and finally the Balsamic Phase at 315°, just 45° before the beginning of the next New Moon.

Each phase represents a particular form of energy, the most important being at the squares to the New Moon, which fall at the 90°, 180° and 270° angles. These are the critical points of the cycle offering measurable points for timing actions.

Meanings of the Lunar Phases

Lunar Phases are useful for timing the natural flow of a process. You and your company will accomplish a great deal more when you follow the Moon's cycles than if you force things to occur at inappropriate times. (Illustration 28)

Lunar Phases

Illustration 28

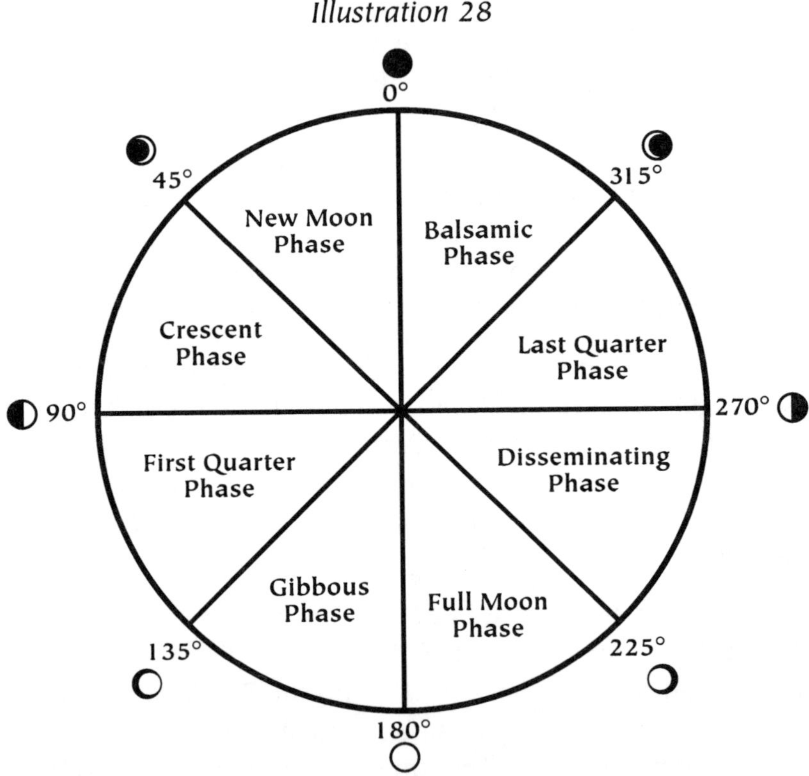

Following are the meanings of the various phases:

New Moon: This is the beginning of the cycle. You see things from your personal perspective and new activities and ideas flow through your body and mind. There is the potential to try a new way of doing things or to have a clear picture of what you would like to do. This is the time to begin new projects and start-ups.

Crescent Phase: This is a time when work presents itself and you become aware of what you have to do to overcome obstacles. You may be handling a lot of red tape, bureaucratic details or juggling various tasks.

First Quarter Phase: This is when you figure out a structure in which to operate, plan and execute your concepts. Managerial concerns occupy your time.

Gibbous Phase: After seeing and executing a structure, you want everyone to know about it. There is a lot of energy directed at this point of the cycle to achieve your goals and be heard.

Full Moon: You've been working very hard and things are coming to a head. However, there is too much to do. It feels as though you are stretched out as far as you can be. Standing back and looking at the activities of the last two weeks (when the New Moon began), you realize you have to let go of something.

Disseminating Phase: It does exactly what it sounds like. You are disseminating information that you have gathered and tested. This is a great time to sell and train.

Last Quarter Phase: This begins the quiet phase of the month. The energy turns inward as you withdraw from the activity of this last phase. There is a sense that something new is coming and intuitively, you begin to study or learn something new to prepare for it. This begins a phase when you clean things out.

Balsamic Phase: This is a very still time. It seems as though nothing is happening; yet much is happening. A seed has been planted and is incubating for the new cycle. A lot of ideas and inspirations are conceived during this time as you allow time for them to germinate and gestate. There is an old saying "still waters run deep". That is the experience of a Balsamic Moon Phase.

How to Use the Monthly Planning Cycle Chart

Following are worksheets—an Arc Lunar Diagram (Illustration 29) and the template for the Quarterly Worksheet (Illustrations 30a-d) to use in planning. You can make a clear overhead of the Arc Lunar Diagram by copying it onto an acetate sheet. Using your horoscope you place the New Moon symbol of the Arc Lunar Diagram onto the house in which the New Moon will occur and center it on the middle of the horoscope wheel. By placing it on your chart in this way, you can approximate and immediately see where the First Quarter phase (90° after the New Moon) falls, which is ap-

Arc Oversheet

Illustration 29

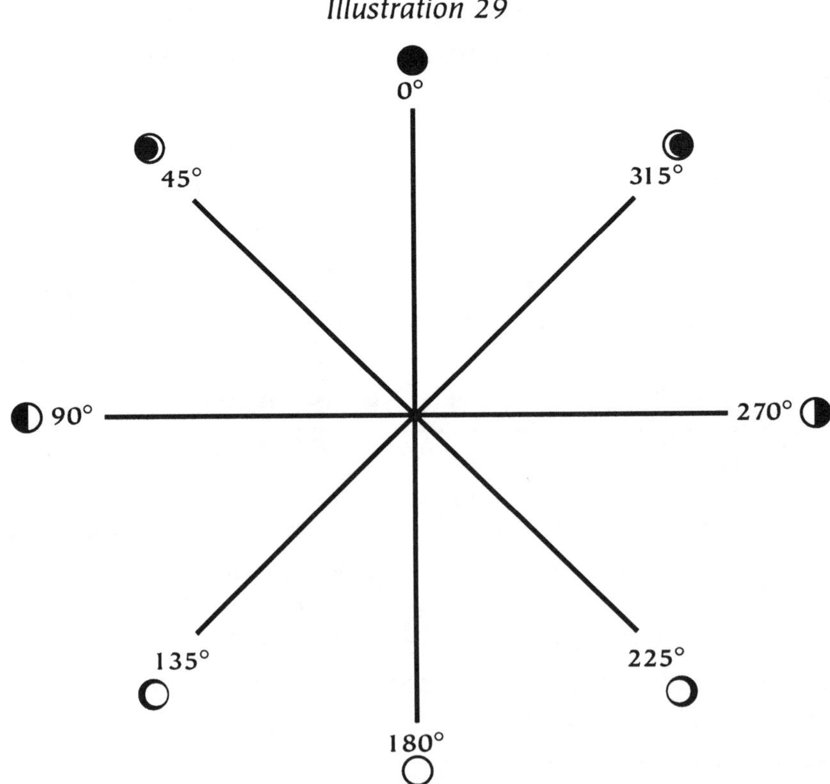

Illustration 30a

Annual Planning Chart for:

First Quarter of the Year

	Date	*House Where Activity Begins*
New Moon Starting Point		
First Quarter Moon		
Full Moon		
Last Quarter Moon		
	Date	***House Where Activity Begins***
New Moon Starting Point		
First Quarter Moon		
Full Moon		
Last Quarter Moon		
	Date	***House Where Activity Begins***
New Moon Starting Point		
First Quarter Moon		
Full Moon		
Last Quarter Moon		

Illustration 30b

ANNUAL PLANNING CHART FOR:

Second Quarter of the Year

	Date	*House Where Activity Begins*
New Moon Starting Point		
First Quarter Moon		
Full Moon		
Last Quarter Moon		
	Date	***House Where Activity Begins***
New Moon Starting Point		
First Quarter Moon		
Full Moon		
Last Quarter Moon		
	Date	***House Where Activity Begins***
New Moon Starting Point		
First Quarter Moon		
Full Moon		
Last Quarter Moon		

Illustration 30c

Annual Planning Chart for:

Third Quarter of the Year

	Date	*House Where Activity Begins*
New Moon Starting Point		
First Quarter Moon		
Full Moon		
Last Quarter Moon		
	Date	***House Where Activity Begins***
New Moon Starting Point		
First Quarter Moon		
Full Moon		
Last Quarter Moon		
	Date	***House Where Activity Begins***
New Moon Starting Point		
First Quarter Moon		
Full Moon		
Last Quarter Moon		

Illustration 30d

Annual Planning Chart for:

Fourth Quarter of the Year

	Date	*House Where Activity Begins*
New Moon Starting Point		
First Quarter Moon		
Full Moon		
Last Quarter Moon		
	Date	*House Where Activity Begins*
New Moon Starting Point		
First Quarter Moon		
Full Moon		
Last Quarter Moon		
	Date	*House Where Activity Begins*
New Moon Starting Point		
First Quarter Moon		
Full Moon		
Last Quarter Moon		

proximately one week after the New Moon. You then move sequentially around the chart to the Full Moon position, two weeks later and finally, the Last Quarter position of that month, which is three weeks after the New Moon. In one more week, a new monthly cycle begins again at the next New Moon.

On the graphed Annual/Quarterly worksheets you enter the dates of these phases by using either the Starcycles Annual Planning Calendar or any other calendars that may have these indicators marked. Each year the New Moon again occurs in the same general area of your horoscope or your company's horoscope around the same time. It moves you to the next levels of planning that have evolved from the previous year's New Moon in roughly the same area of the chart.

More Advanced Uses of the Phase Arc Cycle

A more advanced application of this quarterly phase measurement can be viewed differently. Look at it now as a measurement of the four greater quarters of the year from any given New Moon point. The 90° angle for the First Quarter Phase of the Moon for that month now corresponds to the first three-month period following that point. In other words, if the New Moon were to occur at the Spring Equinox at 0° Aries, then its corresponding First Quarter square for that year then falls at Summer Solstice at 0° Cancer, which is 90° from the 0° Aries point. Sequentially, the 90° distance from the Summer Solstice then falls at the Fall Equinox at 0° Libra and finally follows three months after that at the Winter Solstice at 0° Capricorn. If the First Quarter falls in Libra, then ninety days later the First Quarter square will be somewhere near or around Capricorn and so forth.

At first this may seem complicated, but it provides a detailed delineation that is of great help to your clients or their company, because it gives them a one-year overview. It is an excellent timing technique when working with a company or with a client in evaluating upcoming plans and events.

'Turning the Wheel'

using the Career House (The Tenth House)

In the chapter on "Houses", I mentioned the Horary technique of 'turning the wheel' for more insightful observations into the various areas of life or fields of experience called the houses. For example, if you want to know more about relationships you would move the seventh house (representing close intimate relationships) to the Ascendant position. As a result, the natal eighth house becomes the theoretical second house from the seventh house and represents your partner's earning power or the skills they use to acquire funds or support. The natal eleventh house now becomes the theoretical fifth house of the natal seventh. Your partner's children, his or her ability to speculate, to create and to take risks.

If you are trying to discover more about your client's career or outward purpose in life (his or her tenth house), then you use this same technique. In using the Arc Lunar Diagram and the Planning Cycle Charts, you see things in a fresh way. By entering the horoscope through the doorway of the tenth house and turning the wheel so the tenth house now becomes the Ascendant, you can use the Arc Lunar Diagram and begin measuring the timing on this client's career opportunities for the next year. You execute this maneuver directly from the tenth house position.

Using the following chart for August 26, 1942 (Illustration 31), you can lay out a plan for your client for the course of the year. This client's chart shows an Ascendant of 10° 17'

Illustration 31

Female: Turning the Wheel, Aug. 26, 1942, 9:25am PWT + 7:00, Inglewood, CA, 33°N57'42" 118°W21'08"

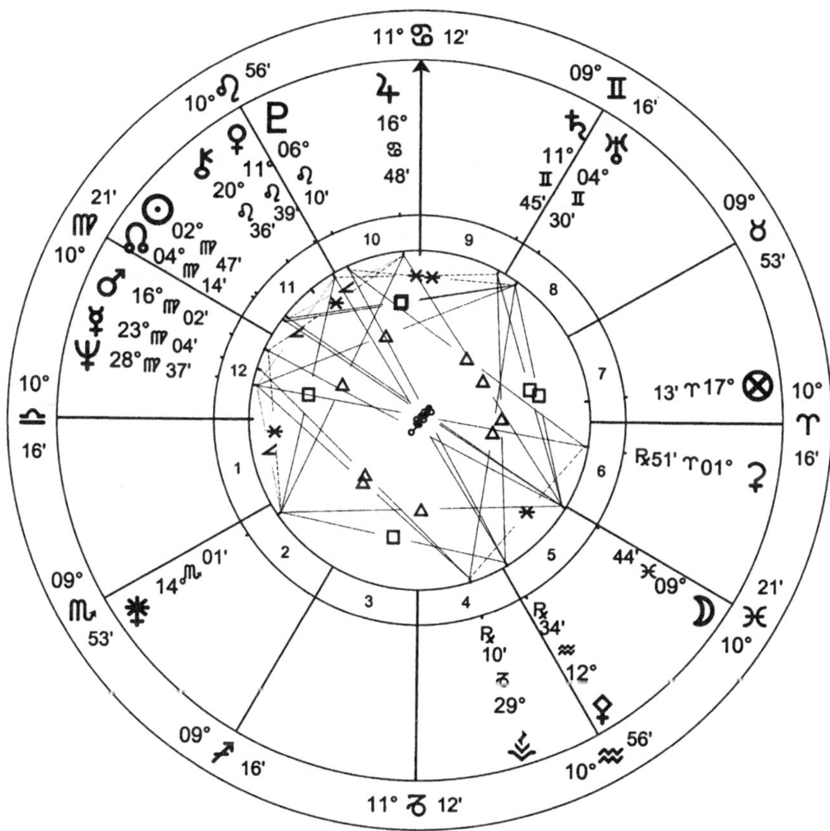

of Libra. Her tenth house is 11°12' of Cancer. You take the tenth house and move it to the Ascendant position, which now holds the tenth house degrees and minutes. You review the year. In this case you are using the year 2000. The New Moon and Solar Eclipse of 10°14' of Cancer occurred on July 1, 2000. This was in her Tenth, which is now turned to the natal Ascendant. This New Moon indicates the possibility of a new beginning in her career as well as an ending, as indicated by the eclipse. Since it occurs here, the push for new beginnings is very strong. The First Quarter Moon that month occurred on July 8, 2000 at 16°39' Libra; the Full Moon and Total Lunar Eclipse occurred at 24°19' Capricorn on July 16, 2000 and the Last Quarter Moon occurred at 1°51' Taurus on July 24, 2000.

The First Quarter Moon, which is the organizing phase of the month, falls at her true natal Ascendant, which, when we turn the wheel, is also the Fourth House from the Tenth house, indicating a possible move in regard to career. The Full Moon position occurred in her natal Fourth House, which is the Seventh House from the Tenth, which might represent a change in partnerships or relationships in regard to her career.

The next New Moon Phase and Solar Eclipse, which occurred on July 30, 2000 at 8°12' Leo in her natal eleventh, was in the house of goals. This house is the second house from the natural tenth; the second house is associated with earning power and values. It is very possible that during this phase, she had an opportunity to increase earnings as well as receiving assistance from her network of friends, represented by the natal eleventh.

An additional use of the planning charts has the New Moon occurring on July 1, 2000 at 10° Cancer which correlates to the New Moon ninety days later on September 27, 2000, at 5° Libra close to this individual's natal Ascendant or the turned career house's fourth. This implies such things as a possible relocation of residence due to a career change. Any idea germinated at the New Moon of July 1 and brought to fruition with the subsequent Full Moon at July 16 will be especially powerful. As will any project embarked upon at the following New Moon on July 30, 2000. These particular dates are even more powerful because of the eclipses. The intensity of their cardinality also encouraged greater changes than usual. Using the planning cycles you can fill in the dates and see the projected career or company development for the year following these eclipses.

In the next chapter, you will learn to examine Saturn and Jupiter, the two planets associated with business Astrology. Since Jupiter is a twelve-year transit cycle, we can view the past patterns of career and vocation and apply those experiences to on-going patterns. This cycle may also be applied to the planning of a corporation. To understand it better, we must first understand the mythology of Saturn and Jupiter.

Chapter 9

The Saturn/Jupiter Career Cycle

The Myth

In Greek, the word Cronos means both time and Father Time. In Greek mythology Cronos was the ruler of the world gods. The mythology prophesized that one day one of his children would overthrow him. When Cronos found out about this prophecy he commanded his wife Rhea to feed him all of their children. Dutifully, she obeyed and fed him the children one by one until she could no longer withstand the sorrow and spirited their son Zeus away for safekeeping in a cave. In his stead, she fed Cronos a rock wrapped in a blanket. Meanwhile, Zeus thrived in the cave fed with milk and honey by Amalthea, the goat.. When grown, Zeus fulfilled the prophecy and battled his father for the position as supreme ruler.

Today we know these Titans as the planets Saturn (Cronos) and Jupiter (Zeus). They are the two largest planets in our solar system. As in the myth, these two have battled for power ever since. Jupiter represents expansion and growth, while Saturn symbolizes limitation and conservatism.

A strong Jupiter in the horoscope implies ease or protection as with Zeus in the story. However, a heavy dose of Jupiter gives a penchant for over-indulgences and secret trysts. Extravagance can be the negative expression of Jupiter in the horoscope, and that is why the balance between these two planets is so crucial.

The battle between the Titans never ends. As we move through life we encounter periods of expansion and restriction. In career or business cycles the ups and downs occur as the Titans play tag with each other in the sky. In business or career development issues of control versus expansion run concurrently. It isn't a linear process as much as a cyclical one. Saturn and Jupiter are key indicators to one's work and one's business ability.

The two major planets to examine for business questions are Saturn and Jupiter. Saturn is the principle of restriction, contraction and structure. Jupiter is the principle of expansion and opening up. If you draw the glyphs for Saturn and Jupiter and then invert them, they are almost identical.

Accordingly, they work very well together in business. Whenever you see successful people, or when people start new businesses or new ventures, often there is a very dynamic aspect happening between Saturn and Jupiter - either by transit in the chart, or by progression. Positive natal aspects between these two in the nativity suggest ease.

Most importantly, we must deeply examine Saturn because Saturn builds new foundations. This is a foundation that requires patience. Liz Green wrote in her book, Saturn: A New Look At An Old Devil. Liz Greene writes,

> *Perhaps what is really asked of us by Saturn, and by our psyches, is that like Parsifal, when he finds himself in the enchanted castle and sees the Grail, we try asking why. It is possible that each delay, disappointment, or fear may be utilized as a means for greater insight into the mysterious mechanisms of the psyche, and that through these experiences we may gradually learn to perceive the meaning of our own lives.*[9]

Wherever Saturn is in your chart requires deep examination. This is where your real work lies, even though that might not be the work that the world sees you as doing. Until you deal with your Saturn, you really can't deal with your work.

The planet Saturn represents restriction, control, discipline, caution and sagely wisdom. By analyzing its position by house placement, the house it rules, its geometric distance from Jupiter, and its general disposition, we can form a clearer picture of the type of work for which an individual might be most suited. Whereas Jupiter represents abundance, optimism, selling, expansion, good fortune and a positive philosophic outlook. It may also represent overindulgence if there are natally challenging aspects.

Both planets are indicators of business and career tendencies. Their movement triggers changes in the career cycle, in the development of a product that has been introduced into the marketplace, and even the developmental cycle of a corporation. Saturn's energy is restrictive, being bound by the cross of matter at the top. It may indicate paternal influence within the horoscope. Saturn shows concrete reality.

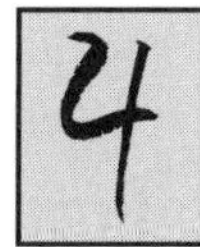

Jupiter's open top and inverted position represents the potential expansiveness of consciousness within structure (Saturn). It is the ever-open vessel, which reaches for greater and larger dreams and possibilities.

Saturn's placement can indicate great stress and hard work and because of this, most people have difficulty welcoming Saturn into their lives. Saturn's nature is tedious when compared to Jupiter's more abundant quality. Jupiter represents the principle of expansion - the luck or fortune of the horoscope. Jupiter's natal position indicates the arena from which Jupiter emerges victorious. Attaining happiness is what Jupiter is all about. The key point here and the point which most do not recognize is that one cannot reach their Jupiter potential until they meet the challenge of their Saturn! Using the metaphor of the gods, it could be interpreted that Saturn, the father, must be paid homage before Jupiter takes his position in equal partnership. And in turn, the challenge of Jupiter is to learn structure and integrate it with possibility thinking. Their greatest success reflects a successful and delicate balance of cooperation.

Saturn-Jupiter Cycles

The normal cycle for Saturn to circle the Sun is approximately 29.5 years. This explains why, at the ages of 28 through 30, and again at 58 through 60, and then finally, as the years unfold and with life extension now a reality, at 88 through 90, an individual comes to major decisions concerning their life's work. For example at 29, you might question whether or not to pursue your current career. If the decision is affirmative, then what actions might you take to make more of an impact upon society? Conversely, at the age of 58 you may begin to contemplate whether or not to consider the possibility of retirement, or, a new challenge or career.

Jupiter takes approximately twelve years to make a complete cycle around the Sun. Its movement is quick because it stays in each sign at the rate of about one-year per sign of the zodiac.

Jupiter-Saturn Conjunctions

Approximately every 20 years, Jupiter and Saturn conjunct and appear as a star in the sky. This conjunction is their synodic cycle. This conjunction is sometimes referred to as "The Conjunction of Kings" as it is believed that this was the true "Star of David" seen at the birth of Jesus of Nazareth. The conjunction of 6 BC occurred in the sign of Pisces, the Fish, [10] which became the traditional symbol for Christianity. The exact time of Christ's nativity is unknown, but it is approximated that it was at about this time the Chaldeans (Wisemen), astrologers in their own right, knew of this conjunction and set out to find their "King of Peace". The birth of this great leader set off major shifts in world belief (Jupiter) and in the world economy (Saturn), something they continue to do every twenty years as these two titans meet (conjunct).

Several great world leaders and prophets are said to have been born near these conjunctions, including such leaders as Buddha and Mohammed. Other historic events include deaths of major public icons and, oddly, rashes in assassinations and assassination attempts.

Saturn-Jupiter Conjunctions Throughout the 20th Century

1901 - SATURN/JUPITER CONJUNCTION IN CAPRICORN represents re-building, expanding boundaries as well as changes in government (i.e. being freed or enslaved by government in a new way). In 1901, U.S. President William McKinley was assassinated and Theodore Roosevelt succeeded him. The Aswan Dam was completed, oil drilling began in the Persian Gulf and J.P. Morgan founded the U.S. Steel Corporation. Massive construction projects were underway worldwide as we entered the 20th Century. Boundaries were being set in a political as well as national way. Borders were redrawn. One of these periods reflected the political aims of the Boxer Rebellion in China and two years later, the first flight of the Wright Brothers made their first flight and opened up an entirely new range of human experience.

1921 - SATURN/JUPITER CONJUNCTION IN VIRGO focused attention on details, technical perceptions, and health and service. The sign of Virgo rules such things as health systems and methods, assimilation, and facilitation. The League of Nations was formed and we embraced the start of Prohibition. Since Virgo is so closely associated with definition, it is appropriate that the true structure of the Milky Way was discovered. Cushing was developing new techniques in the field of brain surgery and the Rorschach Test[11] (inkblot therapy) was developed thereby pioneering new vistas in the field of psychology.

1941 - SATURN/JUPITER CONJUNCTION IN TAURUS focused on values, spending, economy, and building towards a new economic structure. It is interesting to note that the constellation of Taurus is on the opposite end of the pole axis to the sign of Scorpio, the sign that rules birth, death and transmutation. World War II broke out in Germany in 1939, yet the United States did not enter the conflict until 1941. This was the war where an atom bomb was dropped on the Japanese people. This experience ultimately transformed the world as the result of this nuclear experiences. (Wars are not commonly generated by the Saturn-Jupiter conjunction. This is usually triggered by a conjunction or hard angle aspect between Saturn and Uranus, which occurred simultaneously during this particular Saturn-Jupiter conjunction.)

In 1941, the primary political concern in the United States was that of maintaining national security and it was in 1941 that U.S. Savings Bonds were sold for the first time. As we noted the sign of Taurus rules security and this fits in perfectly with the conjunction. As Scorpio, its opposite sign, was also activated. Enrico Fermi split the atom unleashing a power that could continue to threaten world peace through the year 2000 when the conjunction occurred again in Taurus.

1961 - SATURN/JUPITER CONJUNCTION IN CAPRICORN, which is the building and borders theme and presents itself in the form of the Berlin Wall. The United States inaugurated John Kennedy as President and subsequent crises ensued, beginning with the now famous Bay of Pigs incident. The Cold War began to escalate as nations took sides to begin an arms race that would take us into the latter part of the 20th Century. This was a time when the United States was moving away from the perfectionism of the 1950's and the youth of America began challenging old ideas, old philosophies, and old authority figures.

Vietnam began to heat up as this decade unfolded and young people took to the streets, the hopefuls (Jupiter), challenged the authority of the police and government agencies who were fearful (Saturn). The birth of the political Free

Speech movement in Berkeley, California encouraged thousands of people to march for Free Love, Civil Rights, and Nuclear Bans. The government in fear (Saturn) continued to ignore the segregation issues of the South and continued to try to convince us that all of the nuclear tests taking place in the desert were really safe.

The early 60's also witnessed the Thalidomide tragedy, which triggered additional fears and a new awareness about the careless use of pharmaceuticals and medication and drugs in general.

1981 - SATURN/JUPITER CONJUNCTION IN LIBRA focused on fairness in relationships with each other and within the world. In 1981, the cycle shifted. In this century, Jupiter had conjuncted Saturn in Earth signs every 20 years. In 1981, they rendezvoused in the sign, Libra, an air sign and the sign of the peacemaker. An assassin's bullet ended the life of Egyptian President Anwar Sadat. In 1981, assassination attempts were also made on Pope Paul the VI and Ronald Reagan, then President of the United States.

Since Libra is the sign of peace, 1981 addressed concerns in world peace. The United States and China opened their doors to trade. The sign of Libra, which may present the argument that the East will be a major leader in world peace, generally rules the Orient. Libra is the sign of balance, or of the yin and yang, of point and counterpoint, an inherent philosophy in Asian culture.

In 1981, the Physicians for Social Responsibility were founded to raise consciousness about the dangers of nuclear power as a threat to a peaceful balance in the world. Other worldwide groups such as Beyond War also formed to promote world peace.

We can see through this short trip through history that the Jupiter/Saturn conjunctions are pivotal times. It stands to reason that when these vital links occur in our own charts, it heralds change in our lives as well.

Jupiter's Orbit

Jupiter's placement in your chart is where most expansion occurs; it is the indicator of luck. It is the part of your chart to look to for light and enlightenment. Every twelve years, Jupiter returns to its natal position in your chart, giving insight into your creativity and your purpose. Caution must be exercised, so that during your pursuit of happiness you don't become overindulgent or too lazy. Opportunities you might seize at other times could be missed because of a laissez-faire attitude. This is why the relationship that Jupiter has with Saturn should be examined at the outset in the analysis of a chart. Along with the sign Jupiter was in at the time of birth, the house placement must also be examined, that is where you are able to gain insight into innate opportunities.

Jupiter Through the Houses

For instance, Jupiter placed in the **first house** shows that the individual's personal expression is basically expansive and opportunistic. It could indicate a person who is very active or athletic - Jupiter rules sports. Negatively aspected, there can also be overindulgence in some way - either through food or other excesses.

In the **second house**, money and resources may easily appear for this individual as well as the ability to attract people who want to help them in the area of resources. Negatively, this individual could become too dependent on other peoples' resources.

In the **third house**, their greatest gift may be that of gab! Everyday ability to sell, to speak, and to teach are a part of the personality. They may also have clerical or writing ability that is grand and expansive.

In the **fourth house**, these individuals may be lucky at real estate, property, or products that deal with the home. At the very least, they may simply experience great joy with family and home. But they may also overindulge their families by not setting limits.

In the **fifth house**, they love pleasure, taking risks, and they can be quite creative, particularly when working or communicating with young people. They have a basic love of play and enjoy leisure sports. These are people who love kids. Negatively, they may play too much or overindulge their children.

In the **sixth house**, these natives may be master organizers, problem solvers and agents. Their love of detail and efficiency may be of great benefit to them. They may be good at systems, at time management, at health care and health information. They may also spend too much time on details and not enough time on the bigger picture.

In the **seventh house**, they may attract lucky and prosperous partners and actually do better in partnership than on their own. Negatively, they may give too much in the relationship and not receive enough in return.

When Jupiter is posited in the **eighth house**, they work behind the scenes with other peoples' resources, thereby gaining their own. Lucky in legacies and lawsuits and investments, they may have a natural knack for one of these vocations. Negatively aspected, they might be hedonistic or use sex to acquire security.

In the **ninth house**, their greatest gift from Jupiter may be philosophy or writing or marketing or selling. Jupiter here can also indicate dramatic types who may find their expression in the theater, politics or religion. They make excellent teachers and lecturers. Negatively, they can talk or preach too much while trying to convert doubters to their dogma.

In the **tenth house**, they prosper and are viewed positively by the public in regard to their career, which might lead them to teaching, selling, traveling, preaching or selling some type of viewpoint. Negatively, they may talk about all their plans but never act on any of them.

Jupiter's placement in the **eleventh house** has everything to do with the ability to experience abundance in our friendships and the ability to achieve our goals. Acquaintances can be the greatest resource for our profession; they help and support us in our efforts. This could also mark the placement of a good consultant or counselor. Negatively, they can overindulge their friends or conversely, they could be led down the garden path with some big scheme.

And finally, a **twelfth house** Jupiter can bring tremendous inner peace and surety. Their instincts are a great resource. Jupiter offers protection in this placement - a guardian angel may be sitting on their shoulder. They can tap into a tremendously expansive inner world or fantasy life. Negatively, it may be difficult to distinguish fantasy from reality.

Saturn's Orbit

Saturn is nearly Jupiter's opposite. It is restrictive, limiting and responsible. Traditionally, Saturn represents the distinct lessons one must master. Life as well as work present periods where focus ultimately brings success into an individual's life. Approximately every seven years, transiting Saturn will stress its natal placement, thus bringing a shift in focus in the individual's personal, as well as business life. It is around the Saturn return at age 29-30 that the individual begins to reap what has been sown in all previous periods.

Many older references to Saturn and its return to its natal position paint pictures of tragedy, difficulty and unhappiness during these periods. These archaic views frighten people as they enter these cyclical periods. To a certain degree there is truth that Saturn brings delays and barriers, but it is also true that these particular periods are when an individual literally sees the results of all their hard work.

Saturn is not only our karma, but also our work. Work takes on many definitions. Perhaps a better choice of words might be life direction. As Saturn returns to its natal position or stresses it, it redirects our lives. It culls relationships, which we have outgrown. It limits us financially, thus prompting us to finally make long awaited changes. In fact - in its truest form - Saturn brings us minimum resources, which, of course, create (for those who have at least taken on the challenge) maximum creativity! We climb mountains, strive for higher goals and begin to get a clearer picture of our self-worth particularly as the challenge of these periods leave and recognition for our long-awaited efforts finally surfaces.

> *"...we have all, from time to time, been prisoners of one kind or another; we have all, at times, been prisoners to our own assumptions. Because we assume a thing is so, it must be so. And the assumption has always been that the ropes provide a safety factor and serve as a margin of protection for the boxer. But there may be a tragic irony here in that what is perceived primarily as a "protective device", may in reality be itself the cause of serious injury."* Hurricane Carter [12]

Saturn Through the Houses:

Following are some brief insights into how Saturn affects each house by natal placement. This is also a framework that can be used for transits.

In the **first house** it may denote a long, tedious birth process or the individual experiences great responsibility at a very young age - perhaps through the loss or perceived loss of nurturing influences at an early age.

In the **second house** the number one fear may be not having enough security and so the individual compensates by overworking or focusing on lack rather than abundance. As a result, they may become quite wealthy. They may also be in the business of money management, which is one way in which to handle Saturn's placement here.

In the **third house** there may be a fear of lack of knowledge, so the individual either chooses not to study or they overcompensate and develop their writing, listening, and communication skills and develop a highly effective communication style. A desktop publishing or on-line bookkeeping service is an excellent way in which to channel Saturn's stress in this position. Over-involvement in family issues especially with siblings may also occur here.

In the **fourth house** the individual may feel as if they carry the brunt of responsibility at home. They worry about the family not getting enough from them and so pour a great deal of energy whose motivation at times may be from either guilt or fear of the family suffering. An alternative way to use this placement would be to develop a home business in which the Saturn energy is channeled; then home and business achieve balance without guilt. Many real estate or land development individuals have this placement.

In the **fifth house** there may be disappointments in love affairs or delays with children in the first part of life. There may also be responsibilities for other people's children. This is the more traditional definition. Saturn's placement here also denotes an individual of tremendous creativity, and in order to recognize this, they must feel as though their creations have some worth or value. Many times avocations become vocations with this placement, thus successfully combining the idea of work being play and play being work. Disappointments in love keep occurring until the individual is able to successfully integrate their creativity into something tangible. When this occurs, then relationships become easier, because they have resolved the professional dilemma of Saturn in the fifth house.

In the **sixth house** over-compensation in the area of health or time management may occur. This person may be a workaholic. In a positive way it often marks an individual who has mastery over efficiency and organization. For example, someone who conducts time and motion studies as their occupation may find himself or herself able to balance Saturn's stressful energy in this particular area.

In the **seventh house** we find lessons in relationships. In the first half of life it may seem as though the person having this placement must always serve their mate. The issue is not that the individual is doomed to serve, but should be aware of how potential partners might coerce the individual into selfless service. Raising one's self respect greatly improves the manner in which this placement operates. The contrary might also be true. The individual possessing this placement may be selfish and must learn to give to others. Once the individual begins to share out of unconditional love, and they become released from this.

In the **eighth house** Saturn's placement may indicate lessons in the area of sexuality. There may be a fear of intimacy or of being vulnerable. There are deep desires with this placement and balancing the physical with the higher mental and spiritual planes proves challenging. Working as a sex therapist or working in the re-birthing field are some occupational choices associated with this particular placement as it is for many individuals who work in the investment field. Once the individual becomes aware of their power to transform on various levels, then the fear of vulnerability and sexual intimacy lessens.

In the **ninth house** it is an indicator of an interrupted education (this may also occur with this placement in the third). It shows an individual whose greatest challenge is to focus in on the learning process. Writing, speaking, all forms of communication, public relations and marketing are positive occupations through which the individual can express this energy.

In the **tenth house** Saturn is at home and yet can be uncomfortable until mid-life. Anytime Saturn is placed on an angle of a chart the person is a late bloomer as they dutifully search for the answer to 'What am I here for?', and discover the answer later than their peers. Saturn's placement here indicates an individual who has a tremendous need for structure. Management, contracting and building are some of the outlets that utilize the raw talent.

In the **eleventh house** the question that is most often asked is "What is my goal and who are my friends?" Friends are few and far between or are older when Saturn resides here. Trying to find individual fulfillment continues to be a challenge with an eleventh house Saturn. When the individual finally surrenders to the needs of the collective then they receive Saturn's favors. By helping others with their goals and aspirations, the individual finds tremendous satisfaction in their true work. They must continually contribute to friends and organizations. They do well working for community organizations.

In the **twelfth house** Saturn hides so that it can research and develop either creative projects or the soul. This is actually a very comfortable place for Saturn. However, there may be unexplained fears that stem from a difficult childhood with the memory of an absent father or an authority figure who was unavailable emotionally. The unknown must be addressed for the conscious and unconscious mind. Once the unknown is confronted, then a storehouse of wisdom and knowledge pours forth that may be channeled through writing, spiritual or healing work. The veil of fear must part in order for this to occur.

Saturn's Natal Placement in the Signs and How Saturn relates to Career

(If this sign is on the midheaven, then it can also apply)

Saturn in Aries: people work for themselves or are in professions that are on the cutting edge - either literally, such as surgeons and butchers, or figuratively, such as self-made men and women. Headhunters. Scouts working for larger companies in the field of acquisitions for lands and properties. Their work is about coming up with new ideas and new directions.

Saturn in Taurus: people work with finance and monies as well as investments and who help others with their resources. Builders. People in the beauty, clothing, furniture or comfort businesses.

Saturn in Gemini: people work in communications, advertising, or telemarketing, phone work, bookkeeping or accounting. Individuals who are responsible for conveying many pieces of information and have communications as their primary work. Writers, reporters, poets and publicists.

Saturn in Cancer: people may work in the real estate or property business, as well as movies, restaurant and bar businesses. They can be project managers for very large projects and developments. You may also have as your primary market, homes, families, and women.

Saturn in Leo: people are natural leaders and become executives or work in the entertainment, pleasure or marketing businesses. You take great pride in your work and your ego is tied to your many accomplishments. You may conduct or coordinate workshops or convention meetings. Meeting planners, convention bureau coordinators and art directors.

Saturn in Virgo: people can be writers, editors and people in service and/or health or nutrition fields. You may handle details, such as editors, or numbers or facts and have the ability to juggle them all at the same time. You might be excellent with computers as a major tool used in your work. You can work in time management, inventory, environmental protection, restaurants, office supplies, or any type of supply business.

Saturn in Libra: people can be excellent managers, hosts/hostesses, particularly in a business that serves the public in a pleasurable way, such as restaurant or nightclub work. You may be involved in the law or with some aspect of the law, as well as relationship counseling and mediation. Musicians also have Saturn in Libra markers, as do designers.

Saturn in Scorpio: people may work as estate planners, investment counselors or bankers and investors. You may manage large amounts of money or be a major researcher who researches and deduces your findings. You may also be in the field of healing - transformation work, working with people in hospice health care as well as birth or fertility clinics. Community redevelopment workers, power brokers and psychotherapists.

Saturn in Sagittarius: people make excellent teachers, trainers, and salespersons. They may be professional speakers and travelers or those in the travel business. You may work with foreign companies or products or people. You may also work in some type of healing profession, be it non-traditional or traditional. Professional consultants, judges and lawyers.

Saturn in Capricorn: people tend to be late bloomers in their chosen career. You may find success in management and administration, organization, real estate, contracting or building businesses. You seek a high position and high recognition in your career; very ambitious. The other side of this might be difficulty in finding a career because of lack of ambition or fears of judgment. This can be resolved and once done, opens many doors to success in a very short time, because your tremendous ambitions are unleashed.

Saturn in Aquarius people are the big dealers for large commercial developments, and may work on commissions or royalties and on several special projects at a time. Multi-level marketing types, as well as franchisers. Excellent as computer specialists, consultants - those who work and sell information; public relations, advertising and media work. Electronics, aviation, flight work, Astrology or anything that awakens peoples' consciousness is of interests. You are the innovators and architects with your progressive ideas.

Saturn in Pisces people are the musicians, artists and drug and alcohol/rehabilitation counselors. You can be drawn to aquatics, aquaculture, petroleum, paint and shipping. Psychic work, priests, nuns, mystics. Those who work with the disabled, mentally ill or incarcerated. Researchers, writers and anyone that works in the creative arts can be quite successful here with this placement too, but they may require a great deal of privacy in order to achieve their dreams.

The Jupiter/Saturn Cycle

As we compile this information and integrate it into the level of the horoscope to give us information about the individual's career cycle, we must first look and examine the natal relationship between Saturn and Jupiter at birth. This relationship determines the general nature of the type of work that might best suit the individual.

How does one measure the relationship between Jupiter and Saturn? The same measurements, which are used in determining the lunar phase cycle, are the measurements used here.

The Lunation Cycle with Saturn and Jupiter

As I began looking for clues to pinpoint career shifts, Jupiter and Saturn became prominent. Since the Moon represents the public and products, it occurred to me that the phases of the Moon could be used in relation to Jupiter's position to Saturn at birth, and how Jupiter transits during its 12-year cycle. After applying this concept to hundreds of charts a very real pattern began to emerge. As transiting Jupiter conjuncted natal Saturn once every 12 years it created a kind of "New Moon" for one's vocation. As transiting Jupiter continues over the course of the subsequent 12 years, it sets off the lunar phases. Thusly, we see another form of the planning cycle using Dane Rudhyar's theory.

From this structured base I've experimented to see if that theory works on other planetary partnerships as well and I have found that it does. You can use the Lunation Cycle process on the natal outer planets Uranus, Neptune and Pluto. This provides a larger view of your innovative, spiritual, and transformative processes sequentially. You may use transiting Jupiter in the course of its 12-year cycle and apply it to the personal planets, too, such as the Sun, Moon, Mercury, Mars, and Venus and see what you derive. For the sake of this example, however, in examining the Career Cycle we use Saturn and the transits of Jupiter as it aspects Saturn.

To re-iterate, when the Sun and the Moon come together there's a New Moon, which symbolizes the beginning of the lunar cycle - the Moon has a 28-day cycle with each phase providing a differing energy. This same energy will be echoed in the Saturn/Jupiter phases.

This is the first thing to look at when you're examining a chart in terms of business potential. You put Saturn in the place where the Sun would be, and make that 0°, or your start point. Now locate natal Jupiter in the chart. Where it falls in relation to your natal Saturn and the lunar phase it creates, i.e. New Moon, Gibbous Moon, etc., indicates what type of businessperson you'll be, or the way you approach your business. It shows how you motivate yourself and others. As transiting Jupiter moves around the wheel, you can calculate more information. Depending on which phase you are currently in, you can determine what would be the best action to take during that cycle.

THE LUNATION CYCLE

Illustration 32

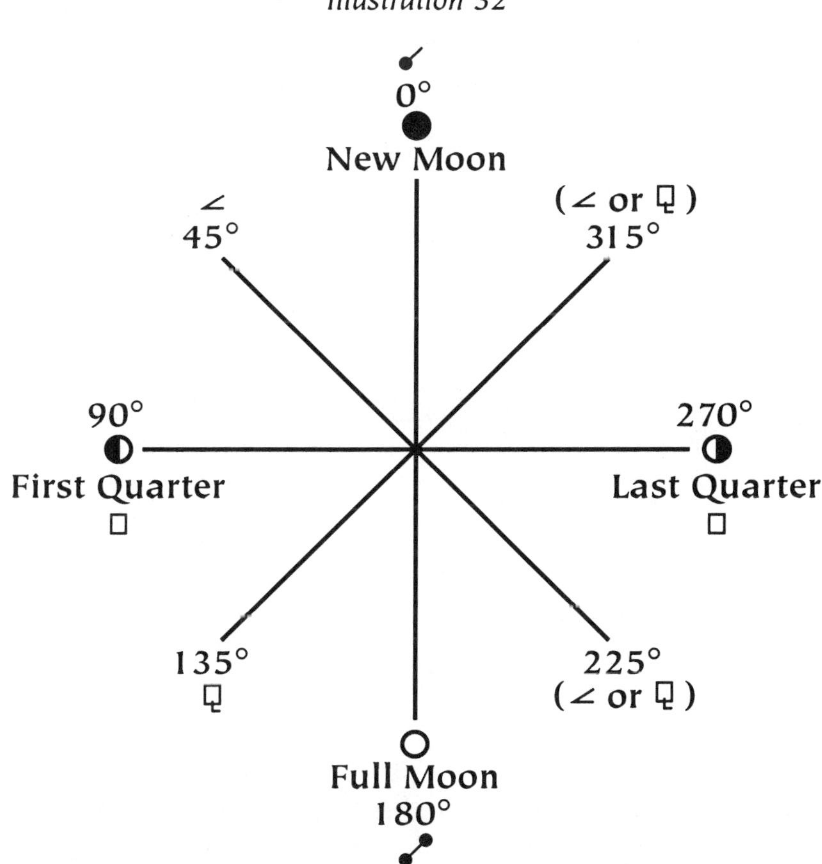

In the lunation cycle (Illustration 32), the Moon forms an ongoing relationship to the Sun as it proceeds along its path. The Moon being the faster planet represents activity, the Sun direction. The Lunation cycle is calculated in 45° increments, with the 90° angles being the most telling. As the Moon moves through the sky in relation to the Sun each month, it makes eight contacts: New Moon, Crescent, First Quarter, Gibbous, Full, Dissemination, Last Quarter, Balsamic and finally a return to the New Moon. These are the basic eight.

Once established in your mind, simply replace the natal Sun with natal Saturn and the transiting Moon with Jupiter. The result is astonishing. As the Moon moves around the earth, it forms various relationships to the natal Sun each month and each person or company's horoscope contains this relationship. So, too, the relationship between natal Jupiter and natal Saturn at birth determines a particular type of career focus, career ability, or person.

The Relationship between Natal Jupiter and Natal Saturn

Illustration 33

(Then watch how transiting Jupiter rotates every twelve years through the Lunar phases, thus triggering off different developments in the career cycle.)

Using the above grid (Illustration 33), review the relationship between natal Saturn and natal Jupiter. For example, if natal Jupiter is up to 45° after natal Saturn at birth, then its relationship to Saturn is in the "New Moon" phase. If it is between 45° and 90° after natal Saturn, then it is in the "Crescent" phase. If it is between 90° and 135° after Saturn, then it is in its "First Quarter" phase to Saturn. If it is between 135° and 180° after natal Saturn, then it is in the "Full Moon" phase. Between 225° and 270°, we move into the "Dissemination" phase. Between 270° and 315° is the "Last Quarter" phase; and finally, between 315° and 360° is the "Balsamic" phase.

These are the measurements for the different lunar/career phases. Now that they have been related to the moon's cycles, how do they act as career indicators in the natal chart?

New Moon Phase (0° - 45°)

The ***New Moon Phase*** is when natal Jupiter is within 45° of natal Saturn but moving away from it. The individual is born during or after Jupiter has passed Saturn in the sky. This is an innovator who likes new things - many operate at an ingenious level! In this phase, we find individuals who use their intuition in response to their work or work environment. There is also a self-centered quality to their personality. Sales people have this placement. They thrive on continuing challenges. The "New Moon" phase means new beginnings, new insights, new ideas and fierce independence.

Particular attention needs to be paid to individuals born at the New Moon phase or conjunction phase of these two planets. John Lennon was a good example of this type. (Illustration 34). [12]

Born in 1940 when Saturn and Jupiter conjuncted in Taurus, a sign associated with the arts and music. John Lennon was assassinated in 1980, at the approaching conjunction

Illustration 34

Male: John Lennon, Oct. 9, 1940, 6:30 BST -1:00, Liverpool, ENG, 53°N25' 002°W55' (From Solar Fire)

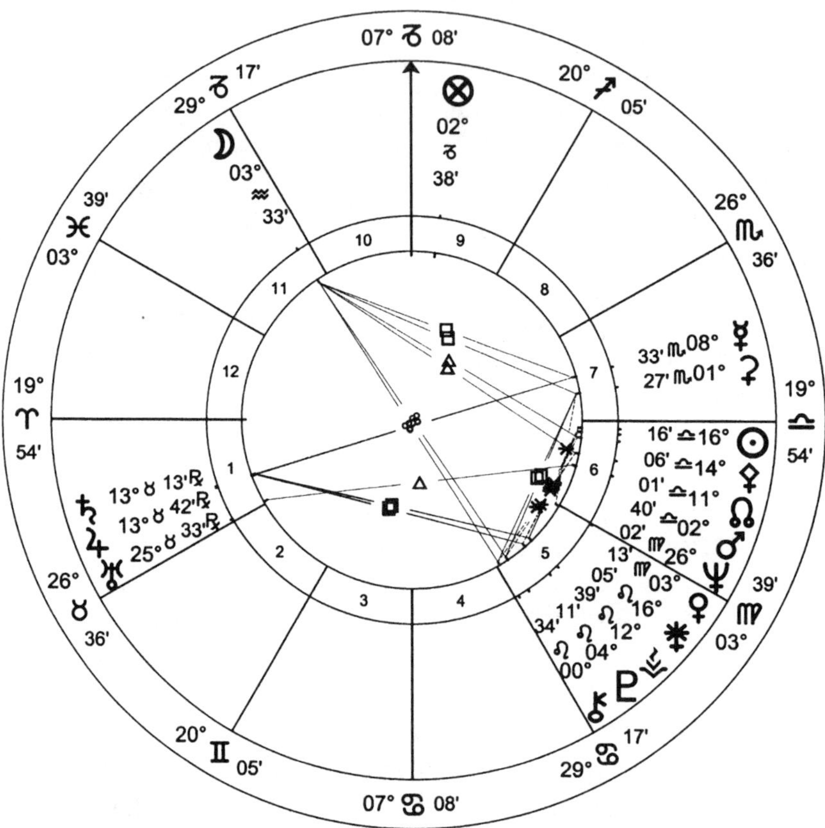

of Jupiter and Saturn in the sign of Libra, the sign of the peacemaker; the synchronicity is striking. This, of course, does not imply that everyone born during Saturn and Jupiter conjunctions will die by an assassin's hand. However, historically it does mark new beginnings in industries and economies and is a period when the major players of the world begin or end their "tenure".

As a transit, this part of the cycle brings in new freedom and a release from the restrictions, burdens, and judgments of the past. It paves the way for new ways of doing things starting with a clean slate.

Crescent Phase (45° - 90°)

A person born in the ***Crescent Phase*** has natal Jupiter between 45° to 90° past natal Saturn. Their work is comprised of obstacles they are consistently required to overcome. A good example might be someone who works in government offices where there is a lot of red tape and paperwork required just to get the job done. There is tenacity inherent in the personality. New territories must be established. Someone working for the Welfare Department or Social Services might have this placement.

Illustration 35

Female: Eleanor Roosevelt, Oct. 11, 1884 NS, 11:00am EST +5:00, New York, NY, 40°N42'51" 074°W00'23" (From Solar Fire)

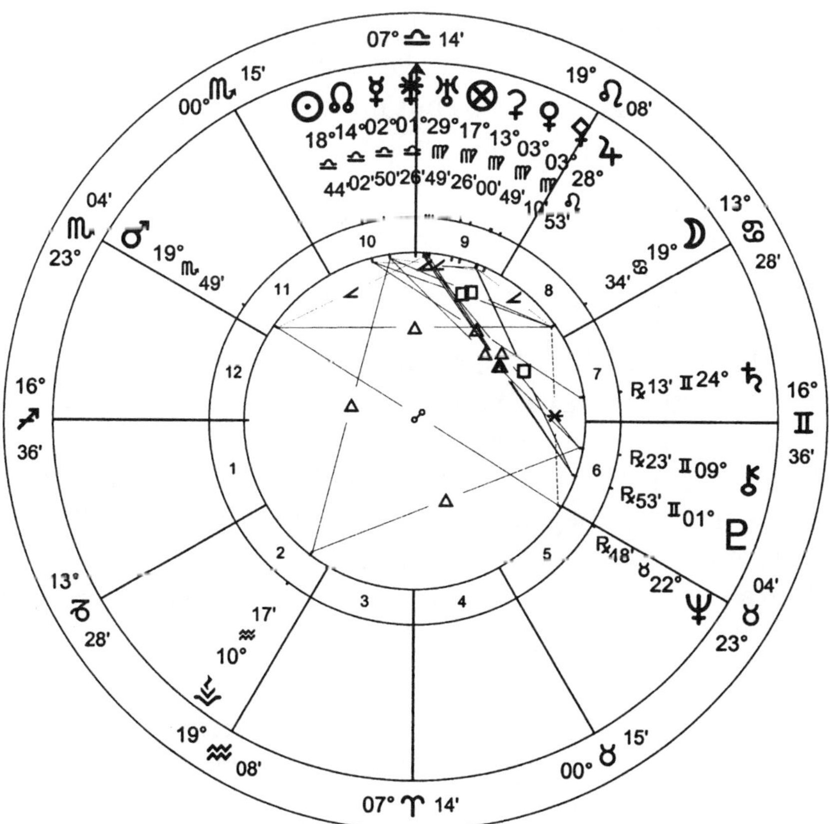

I have found that many of the people who have this configuration are people who create obstacles so they can overcome them. Similar to Libra who might sometimes throw a monkey wrench into the works, just so they can fight or struggle to get things placed back into balance.

Eleanor Roosevelt who had natal Jupiter in crescent phase to natal Saturn virtually took over the Oval Office when her husband, Franklin Delano Roosevelt, was stricken with Polio. She was his emissary during his years of illness at a time when women were not in politics. During this time major world issues needed attention. She met the challenge brilliantly. Her chart is seen in Illustration 35. As a transit, the Crescent Phase finds you confronting issues such as funding, processing papers, coordinating meetings, or whether or not to adapt or introduce certain routines and procedures into your organization. The amount of details involved and the blockage that is common in the workplace can be overwhelming and may require good assistants. This is the person who wears many hats, but none of them for too long a time, because they are also on the go a lot.

First Quarter Phase (90° - 135°)

The ***First Quarter Phase*** usually is an indicator of managerial ability. It implies someone who works with or creates structures and frameworks where they work. They are good at defining and executing structure. This is the type of personality who has a game plan and sticks to it. The work style tends to be structured and targeted. The push of this First Quarter energy has, as its base, motivation to get things done even though these very actions can create crisis and resistance from others.

Following is the chart of Richard Carpenter, surviving sibling of the famed brother-sister team known as the Carpenters. Richard Carpenter formed and founded the band with his sister Karen. Not only did he found and form the Carpenters, but he also wrote many of the songs with John Bettis, his writing partner. Note the highlighted third house where one of the planets is Jupiter. Also note that Saturn in the twelfth house is conjuncting Pluto, the ruler of his fourth house of Scorpio, implying managing family members. The loaded third could also imply working with siblings or, since Pluto also rules a portion of the third, the managing of siblings.

As Jupiter transits around the horoscope over its twelve-year cycle, and moves through this First Quarter cycle, you

Illustration 36

Male: *Richard Carpenter. Oct. 15, 1946, 0:53am EST + 5:00, New Haven, CT, 41 °N18'29" 072°W55'43" (From Solar Fire)*

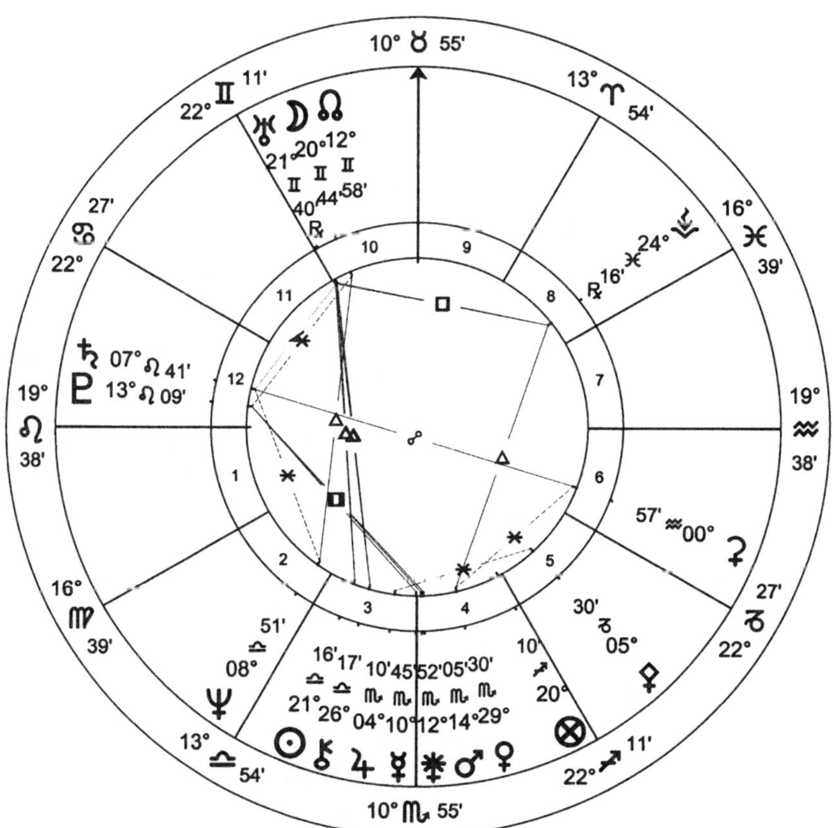

find yourself in a position of re-inventing the wheel. There are a lot of hours spent in this building process. Though difficult, it is a crucial part of the cycle from which solid foundations are built. (See Illustration 36).

Gibbous Phase (135° - 180°)

If natal Jupiter is in the ***Gibbous Phase*** to natal Saturn, the individual needs to feel as if their work affects a great num-

Illustration 37

Female: Aimee Semple McPherson, Oct. 9, 1890 NS, 5:00pm LMT + 5:23:20, Salford, CAN, 43°N00' 080°W50' (From Lois Rodden's Profile of Women)

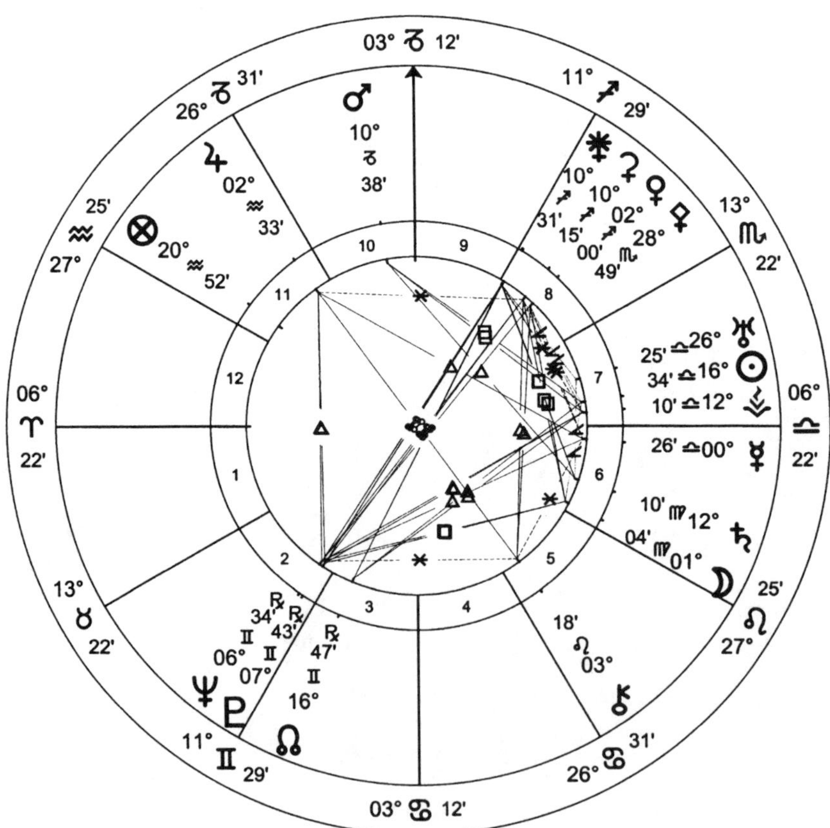

Another View of the Lunation Phases Using Hard Aspects and the Number 9

Illustration 14

Using the principal of numerology, the number 9 represents the "end" of a cycle, or, a transitionary number, which begins again at the number 1. The number 9 is the number of release. The number 9 represents the last of a cycle, leading to a new territory of experience.

Square aspects (90 degrees) and their derivatives, the semi-square (45 degrees), the sesquiquadrate (135 degrees), all can be linked to the lunation cycle and the number 9. Each one of these aspect degrees totals to the number 9. For example, the semisquare, which represents the Crescent Phase and Balsamic phase, measures 45-degrees. Taking the number 4 and adding it to the number 5, we arrive at the number 9. The number 4 is associated with hard work and possible obstacles. The five represents learning. Using the sesquiquadrate measurement, which relates to the Gibbous Phase and the Disseminating Phases of 135- degrees, we add the 1, the 3, and the 5 and arrive again at a total of 9. The 1 represents a fresh new look or identity, the 3 represents communication, and the 5 represents learning. Adding the 9 and the 0 in the 90-degrees gives us a 9.

As we move from the 45-degree semisquare, to the 90-degree square, and then to the 135-degree sesquiquadrate, we experience a shift of experience. This is the basis of the phase arc transitions I use in the Career Cycle for transitions in careers and in companies.

The number 9 in the Tarot is the Hermit, or, the Monk, who lights the way and invites the viewer to follow. When the Hermit is drawn from a Tarot deck, the reader often remarks on how something is ending and senses that there is really also beginning, but something not yet visible.

The 180-degree opposition is another aspect that totals to 9. In an opposition, we have two points that are as far away as possible within the context of a 360-degree circle. The numbers involved are that of 1, which represents individualism and the number 8, which requires us to release something (8 is associated with the sign of Scorpio) in order to begin again. The opposition is when two points are as far from each other as possible, inviting an objective perspective where one separates from what no longer works, or finds a way of unifying opposites.

ber of people. Aimee Semple McPherson, the American evangelist who founded the International Church of the Foursquare Gospel had this phase between her natal Saturn and natal Jupiter. She was a revivalist who played to over 5,000 patrons in her temple. In Lois Rodden's, Profiles of Women[1], she states, "McPherson was a worker and go-getter. She set up four hundred churches and two hundred missions, a Bible college, and a radio station...a flamboyant (perfect for a Gibbous phase) evangelist McPherson was known as the "Barnum of Religion"..." [13] (See Illustration 37).

The Gibbous individual's work involves some higher purpose or inspiration. Their work must take a philosophical stand in some way. The Gibbous phase is very similar to the number "9" in Numerology, which represents as part of its definition cause, purpose and selflessness. It is also similar to the energy of the ninth house in the horoscope. It is between the Gibbous phase and the subsequent Full and Disseminating phases that follow that the creative spirit unfolds and the career sprouts a new direction or purpose, which is the result of the vision of the Gibbous phase. It acts the same as a transit in that you are fired up about what you are doing and want to tell anyone who will listen.

Full Moon Phase (180° - 225°)

The ***Full Moon Phase*** is the phase in which the individual is in a constant state of stress in their work. Their work might involve heavy risk-taking, danger, and action. The individual views their work as an all-or-nothing proposition. In fact, the very nature of risk in their work as it is the juice that spurs them on.

This is the classic placement for people whose middle name is career risk. Like the firefighters who parachute out of planes into the heart of the forest fire, they cannot live without this risk, or they feel dead. These "Full Moon" indi-

Illustration 38

Male: James Earl Jones, Jan. 17, 1931, 6:05am CST +6:00, Arkabutla, MS, 34°N41'56" 090°W07'20" (From Solar Fire)

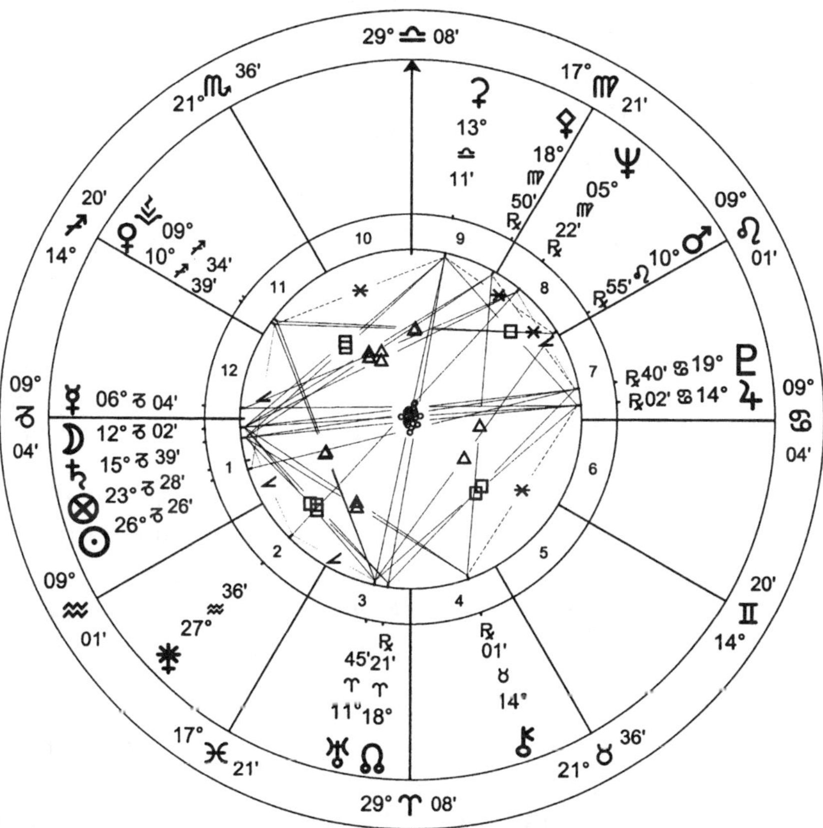

viduals are visible in their work. Therefore, the problems might involve not having enough time to focus in on specifics. Their work may also take on a social nature or social reform nature. They might even be extremists. James Earl Jones, the well-known actor has this placement, whose work (Illustration 38) includes the groundbreaking television series "Roots" and the voice of Darth Vader in the Star Wars film trilogy grew up with the challenge of stuttering. At some point in his youth he was mute. He became highly successful and ironically, is most recognized by the quality of his deep, rich voice.

The Full Moon position of Jupiter and Saturn is also seen,

however, in extremists' charts such as Marshall Applewhite and the Reverend Jim Jones. Both of these men are remembered for not only taking their own lives, but also for the deaths of their followers for the purpose of some higher ideal and belief system that went haywire.

As a transit, this may feel as though a rubber band is being stretched as far as it is going to be stretched and something has to give. If it doesn't, the rubber band breaks. If you realize that something has to be released when you are in this phase then as you let go you open yourself to greater challenges.

Dissemination Phase (225° - 270°)

In the ***Dissemination Phase,*** an individual shares lots of information. Teachers, consultants, writers, and transportation specialists, public information jobs - all are occupations that are perfect for this placement. They are naturals at finding the right information and distributing it at just the right time.

As a transit, it is a time when you get in touch with what is valuable to you, and a desire to get that information to those who can benefit from it. It can be a time when your vision is shared, and you are valued because people can see the full scope of your ability. In your zeal however, you may come on too strong or be perceived as pushy.

Last Quarter Phase (270° - 315°)

Perhaps the most difficult phase to define is when Jupiter is in the ***Last Quarter Phase*** to natal Saturn. The individual finds that work is always presenting new challenges. This in itself can be stimulating, but here it is accompanied by the need to learn new skills constantly in order to survive. The steady pressure of preparation hounds people with this placement and either they meet the challenge or find themselves eternally frustrated. Their work may involve the breaking down of old structures. Persons in social reform or a business that has to do with releasing and re-appropriating, such as the liquidation business, might have this "Last Quarter" phase emphasized in the chart.

Josephine Baker (Illustration 39), the expatriate performer, whose chart we viewed earlier in this book as well as Woody Allen (Illustration 40), the offbeat playwright and actor, have the Last Quarter phase of Jupiter to Saturn in their charts.

Illustration 39

Female: Josephine Baker, Jun. 3, 1906, 11:30am CST + 6:00, St. Louis, MO, 38°N37'38" 090°W11'52" (From Solar Fire)

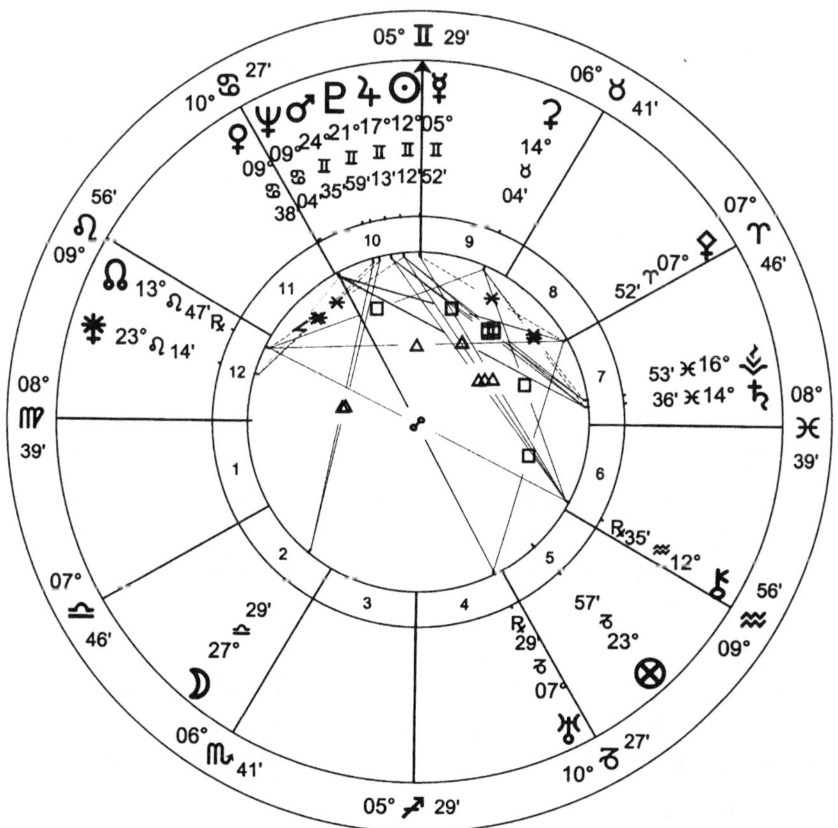

Illustration 40

Male: Woody Allen, Dec. 1, 1935, 10:55pm EST + 5:00, Brooklyn, NY, 40°N38' 073°W56' (From Solar Fire)

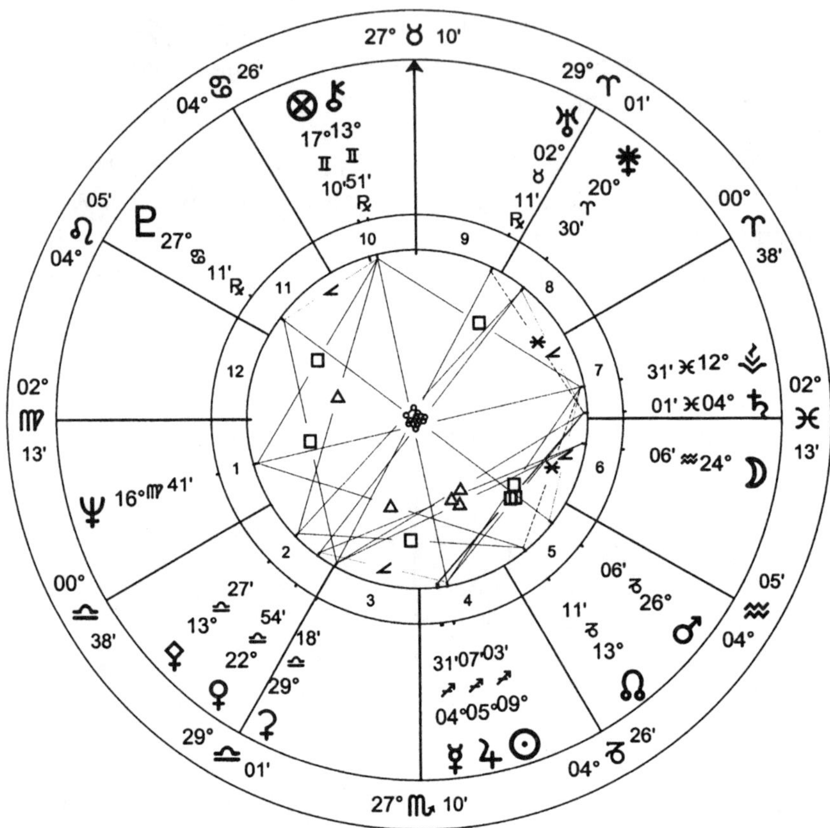

Someone who has Jupiter in the Last Quarter phase is a person who might have difficulty with focus. As their mind is in this continual state of tearing down while re-building it exacerbates this inability to focus. If their chart shows a predominance of fixed energy then they may have difficulties with their diffuse thinking, but those with a lot of mutable energy may better handle the flexible thinking patterns and harness the process for creative output. In this the Last Quarter phase, the Jupiter just before the Saturn - the light and inspiration of the career cycle is dimming and making way for something new.

Ernest Hemingway (Illustration 41), the well-known author, wrote incredible literary pieces, but he struggled with meaning in his life asking himself the question of what is this all about. His natal Jupiter is at the tail end of this Last Quarter phase at the brink of the Balsamic phase which follows.

As a transit, these people may decide to learn something new, which adds value to their future work. They also perceive that down the road, they may want to begin something new and need to let go of their current situation. They may find themselves totally dissatisfied with what they are doing; though others believe that they have a lot of useful information.

Illustration 41

Male: *Ernest Hemingway, Jul. 21, 1899 NS, 8:00am CST +6:00, Oak Park, IL, 41°N53'06" 087°W47'04" (From Solar Fire)*

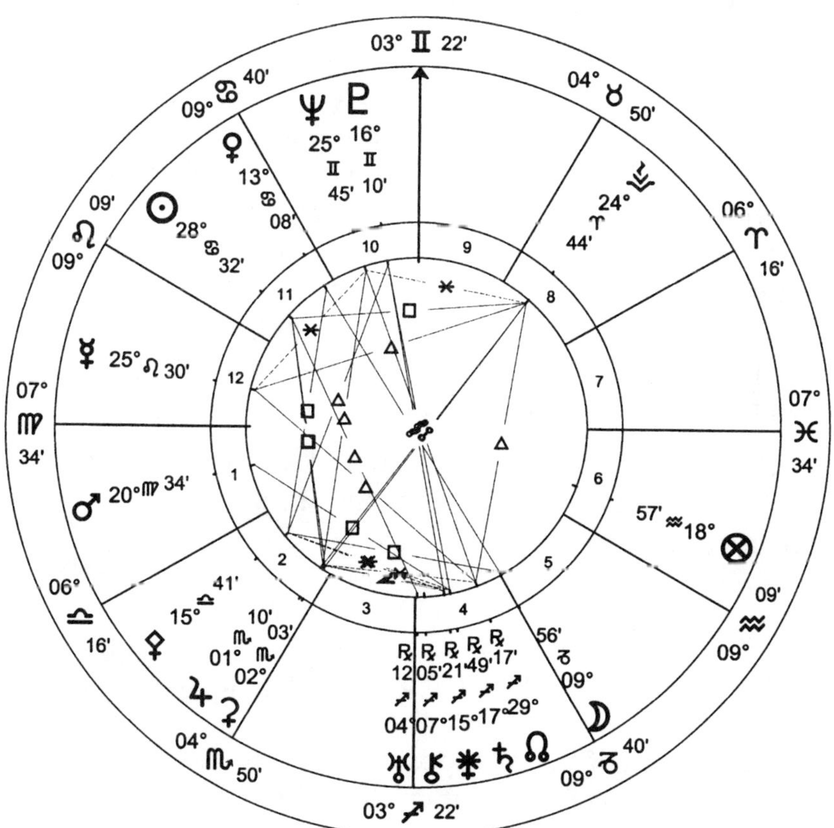

Balsamic Phase (315° - 360°)

The ***Balsamic Phase*** is the final phase in the cycle of the relationship between natal Jupiter to natal Saturn. Individuals who have the balsamic phase natally require a great deal of privacy in order to do their work. They work behind-the-scenes, comfortably, without having a strong need to be in front of the public. Their retreat enables and stimulates creativity and for this reason their jobs might involve some type of artistry. This artistry may provide a "seed" of new thought for the next generation of artists or thinkers, which can also be seen in the chart of Ernest Hemingway (Illustration 41, above), whose life also exhibited these qualities. His natal Jupiter bordered between a Last Quarter Relationship and a Balsamic Relationship to Natal Jupiter. There is something about the Balsamic phase, which though appearing silent is actually prescient. In their silence they intuitively sense what the future holds.

Always at the brink of the future, but still cautious, as is exhibited in the above example, the Balsamic type operates from instinct, lighting the way for others and all the time not knowing if what they are thinking or doing is relevant or holds the correct information. These people find themselves in coaching positions, research posts and in positions working behind the scenes where their insightful skills assist others. They might also be the people who are recognized and acknowledged after their death for a body of original work.

As a transit, they may want to pull away from people for a while to re-think their direction and sit quietly allowing new ideas to emerge.

20-Year Jupiter/Saturn Cycle

Regardless of the relationship between natal Saturn and natal Jupiter, it is important to note where their twenty-year conjunction cycle transits an individual or company's horoscope. Wherever it occurs, it shows the area of life where the individual will experience growth, discipline, and philosophic expansion during the course of the next 20 years. For example, if it occurs in the seventh house, then marriage and legal/business partnerships - how one relates to others, and how others relate to oneself, become the major thrust of the ensuing twenty-year cycle and perhaps the base for the evolution of the individual's work.

Once the relationship between these two planets is established, then we must look at the individual placements of both Saturn and Jupiter at birth. We do not necessarily look at the signs at this particular point. It's interesting to see where those Saturn/Jupiter conjunctions take place in your chart every 20 years, because that will trigger a 20-year change in your business direction. For those who were not around in 1921 or 1941, that's okay, but check 1961 and 1981 as well as the recent 2000 alignment. Every 60 years those two planets come together in the same sign. In 1901 and 1961 it was in Capricorn. In 1921 it was in late Virgo, almost Libra and 60 years later in 1981 it was in early Libra. In 1941 it was in Taurus and repeated in 2,000 at 23° Taurus. Where did the most recent conjunction occur in your chart? Where did the Saturn/Jupiter conjunction before that fall in your chart?

Saturn

The house in which Saturn is found natally gives us insight into either the type of work or the methods the individual uses in their work. For example, if natal Saturn is found in the fourth the individual might work at home or in real estate or both. Saturn placed natally in the twelfth may indicate an individual who requires privacy or who works in the health, hypnotherapy or music field.

Looking at the house which Saturn rules may provide further insight into the type of work we're naturally adept at. Saturn rules Capricorn, but the old rulership for Saturn was also Aquarius. Therefore, both houses having these signs on the cusp and the houses into which they overlap can give us clues.

Jupiter

When you examine Jupiter, you see the potential for fun, luck, travel, enlightenment and enjoyment. As noted earlier, Jupiter might also indicate indulgence. For example, if Jupiter is in the fifth house, you might love romance, children and play! You might also benefit financially through speculation or overextend yourself in these areas. Once Saturn is given its due attention, then you can enjoy Jupiter and reap its promised reward!

Jupiter in the ancient myths was Zeus, King of the sky, and he experienced life to its fullest. With his thunderbolts, he awoke people. Jupiter is the gift of the horoscope. It suggests the path of least resistance as far as talent or knowledge or ability.

Look at the houses that Jupiter rules. Since Jupiter is the ruler of Sagittarius and Pisces, both houses, which have these signs on the cusps or are intercepted, should be examined. The energies of those houses must be brought into the house in which you find Jupiter in order for a fuller interpretation. Jupiter has a kind of guardian angel feel to it. The house in which you find it is where you may feel protected, and perhaps, indeed might be. It is the antidote to Saturn's heavy energy.

Career Cycle

After the natal relationship is established between Saturn and Jupiter along with the individual examination of natal Saturn and Jupiter's placement within the horoscope, then we are prepared to ascertain the individual career cycle. We do this by observing the movement of transiting Jupiter as it sets off various phase arc measurements to its constant - natal Saturn. This career cycle is approximately twelve years, the same time it takes Jupiter to transit the zodiac. Transiting Jupiter moves in counterclockwise fashion to natal Saturn and sets off the lunation cycles that were mentioned earlier; it triggers different phases during its twelve-year period.

Setting up the Transiting Career Cycles: A Case Study

By following Illustration 33 (p. 204), you can set up the basic structure for the career cycle. This framework may be applied to various charts. Following is a chart that you can use to work with to sample this theory. The chart we are using is for a man, born June 19, 1941 (Illustration 42).

He is a real estate broker, the result of a career that began in real estate in the late 1970s. He acts as his own broker in a small, pared down format which he has chosen and which suits his independent personality. He works from home, has no employees, and specializes in listing and selling distressed properties.

First, a brief overview of the real estate influences in his chart. Indicators are a strong concentration in the fourth house anchored by Saturn, which is placed there. Both Saturn and Uranus are co-rulers of this chart, which has later degrees of Capricorn rising and has Aquarius in the first house. Everytime a transit hits Saturn; it also hits Uranus, which brings unexpected turns of fate, ultimately contributing to his consistently enlightened views. His personality is a unique combination of both Saturnine and Uranian energies. Often those who have Uranus on any of the angles, or highly

Illustration 42

Male: Case Study for Saturn/Jupiter, Jun. 19, 1941

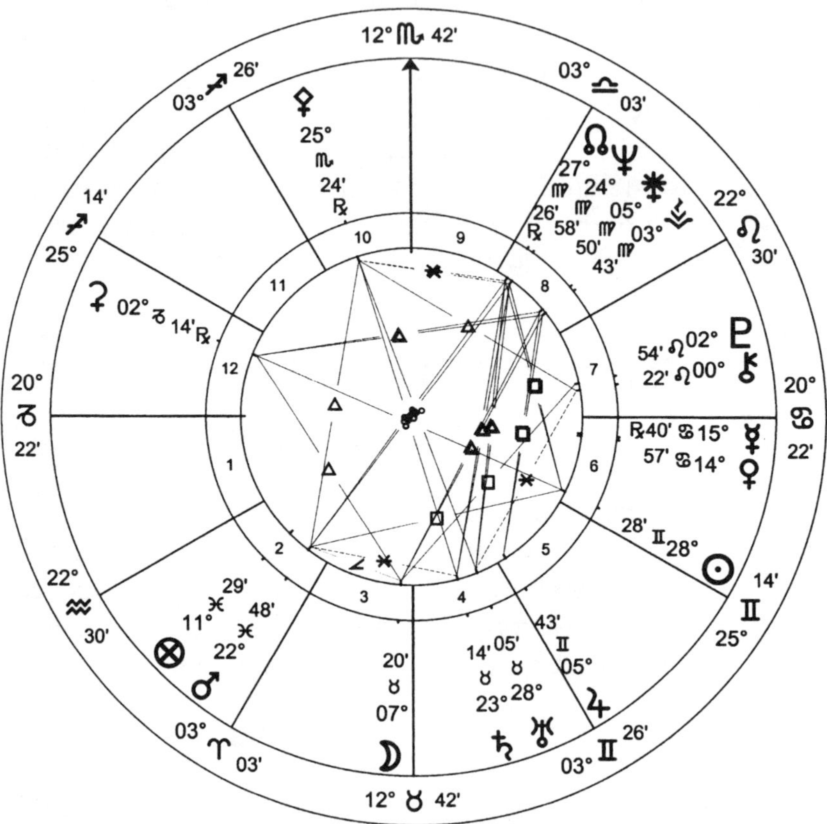

aspected, are considered Uranian types. They cannot be pigeonholed and they may have many job changes or careers in their lifetimes that seem somewhat unrelated, but in fact as they mature, serve them. The work finds them due to their unique mix of knowledge and experience. Their pattern is such that they move through their lives in six to eight year (approximately 7 years) increments. When these occur, they may suddenly bolt and change directions.

This man was originally trained as a teacher, but upon graduating could not find suitable employment and in the spring of 1965, as transiting Jupiter conjuncted his natal Saturn, began a career in sales in the commercial foods business. His family background and work experience had been in the food business and so it seemed like a good fit. Also note that his natal Ceres, one of the signatures of the food business, is just past an exact square to his natal Lunar Nodes.

Subsequently, as transiting Jupiter passed over the conjunction to his natal Saturn and hit his Uranus, he suddenly found a position teaching while still in the New Moon phase. He continued to teach until sometime around February 1974 as transiting Jupiter entered the Last Quarter Phase to his natal Saturn. He began to become discouraged with teaching. His training was in math and science and he was teaching elementary school at the time. As transiting Jupiter continued and moved into the Balsamic Phase, the school suddenly told him to change his curriculum and teach new subjects that he was not only unprepared for, but was not trained in either. He had little time to prepare and he was now moving into teaching High School students. He also had a severe learning disability that he would not become aware of until close to his 45th year, which impaired his ability to adapt to his school's new requirements.

During this particular Last Quarter Phase in 1974, there were many difficulties in U.S. high schools. Students would leave narcotics on his desk at the end of the Health Education sessions. He would attempt to talk to parents, who were going through their own psychological epiphanies (not uncommon in the 1970s) and it resulted in disinterested and uncaring parents. The types of frustrations mounted and led to graver disappointments with an overall feeling of being ineffectual.

As Jupiter traveled through this phase, he felt that he had to get out of this mode of teaching and go back and finish his counseling credentials, which he had previously set aside. The completion of this credentialing afforded him some freedom and creativity, which could ultimately translate into an increased income. He returned to school to complete his counseling credentials, one of the choices that people commonly make during the Last Quarter Phase

However, as does occur when Uranus is thrown into the mix, just as he was completing his training, the schools ran out of money for counselors! So, he continued to teach the unrelated subjects many of which he found difficult as he entered the next Balsamic Phase. The schools then went on strike in the fall of 1976. He believed in teaching the students regardless of politics and ever being the maverick, he broke through strike lines to teach, enduring name-calling as well as the threat of physical violence. The school finally went off strike right before the Christmas break of 1976. One day in the middle of teaching, he put down his chalk, stopped teaching right in the middle of a class, put his papers down and walked out of teaching, forever!

Seeing that he had a family to support consisting of a wife and two young babies. By January of that next year 1977, as transiting Jupiter completed the old career cycle, he began to work in sales again. He enjoyed his new career and found himself to be gifted both in problem solving and negotiations. He started by selling copy machine equipment (note the placement of his Sun in the sixth house of food supplies and office equipment). As Jupiter transited his natal Uranus, another "fateful" turn in the road, he had a severe accident that injured his back and left him bedridden for two years! In fact, for one entire year, he was in a body cast unable to do anything physical and a dark depression set in.

During this time he experienced severe discomfort along with a serious determination to get well and succeed, professionally. The sign of Capricorn is ruled by Saturn, which rules the bones and the skeletal system. Since these individuals are known for their incredible ability to endure difficulty and discomfort, it inevitably is the discomfort that motivates them to make changes. He had always considered real estate as a potential profession. He enjoyed homes, the promise of freedom and high income and independence. One day, a friend of his (Uranus rules friends), remarked to him that while he was laid up with his back injury, he might study for his real estate license. He was still in the New Moon Phase of the career cycle and the thought of a new and burgeoning career intrigued and excited him.

He studied and received his license around February of 1978. He was still in bed with pain during his studies and as May 1978 approached, the Crescent Phase of the career cycle began and he initiated several real estate transactions with the aid of the same friend who suggested he study for his license. He conducted his business from his sickbed.

By now his Uranus opposition had begun. This can trigger a mid-life crisis. In April of 1979, his wife presented him with divorce papers and another round of overcoming obstacles began. There were now inordinate amounts of physical pain, exacerbated by mental pain and this particular crossroads was the trigger for a life-long bout with depression, which he finally began to overcome in his late fifties.

In August of 1979, he entered the First Quarter Phase of his career cycle and finally his life flourished. He experienced a great deal of success and support in his newly chosen profession and improvement in his health. He was walking and able to drive in limited trips between his office and home. During this First Quarter Phase between August of 1979 and December of 1980, the manager of his company, who had also become a close friend and had aided him during his illness, began to include him in her managerial decisions. He learned about management through her and became comfortable with the concept of management, an offshoot of First Quarter Phases.

As Jupiter entered the Gibbous Phase of the career cycle in December 1980, he was offered a management position at another company—again, through a friend. The friend was the owner of the new company. With his Uranus very closely conjunct Saturn friends figure prominently. He felt he was on a mission during this managerial phase of his career, because the office he managed had been the lowest producing of all of the company offices that were owned by his friend.

As his income was dependent upon his own sales and a small salary, but mostly on the overrides that are paid to the manager via the salespeople's income, he was motivated to improve the fiscal activity of this office. Ultimately he managed to raise the production of the salespeople in his to become the top producing office in the chain. Finally he prospered.

However, as transiting Jupiter approached the Full Moon Phase of the career cycle in Fall 1982, a severe recession cycle began in real estate. Interest rates were high. The lease on the office he managed ran out just as trends in the California real estate industry forced office consolidations to survive the recession. The owner of his company notified him of the change and he was relieved of his duties as a manager and returned to the sales floor as a salesperson in another office in which several offices had consolidated.

He had subsequently remarried since his divorce in 1979, during which time he had another child. In addition, he gained custody of his other two children from his previous marriage. His financial responsibilities increased as the real estate industry was experiencing a downturn. As the Full Moon Phase of his career cycle began in November of 1982, and real estate activity had markedly dropped, he suddenly decided to take a job with a stable income and became a salesperson for a wholesale meat company. He continued a few real estate transactions here and there, but he was stretched.

Full Moon Phases of the career cycle imply a different mindset that includes occasional chaos, unexpected events, and epiphanies. During this Phase, in August of 1983, he attended a workshop whereby he "walked on fire" literally. Of all the attendees, just a few chose this action and he was one of them. This was an out of the ordinary response for someone usually so conservative, but he did it. During the incident transiting Pluto was stationing direct at about 27 Libra trine his Sun and transit Mars was squaring his Uranus! I believe that transiting Mars triggered this action, which occurred so suddenly.

He states that it was in this moment that he decided, "if he could walk on fire, he could do anything". This action offered him the belief that regardless of the economy, he could be successful in real estate. The following Monday after the event, he quit the wholesale meat job and returned to real estate full-time. This sudden decision happened at the Full Moon phase. The rubber band had snapped and provided an inspiration towards a new consciousness that helped birth his career direction.

As Jupiter continued into the Disseminating Phase of the career cycle in October 1984, another child was born. Amore mature wisdom was birthed, too. He became more conscious of "how" he was doing business. He employed his former teaching techniques and began disseminating a lot of information. He hired a secretary to help him with a monthly news bulletins, information letters and sales letters. He began to actively network past acquaintances, always sharing his information with potential clients as well as his peers.

In the Last Quarter Phase of the cycle, he seriously began considering working towards his Broker's license and developing some family property. He attained his Broker's license and gained success until the early 1990's when the real estate market went into a steeper recession. He suffered a great deal of illness and depression as the market declined. The combination of the fall in the economy as well as moving through a kind of male menopause set him back markedly. He was unable to continue with the challenges of family life. His recuperation began when he began simplifying his lifestyle, learning to work on a computer and cutting his overhead by moving into a smaller home and starting an office from home.

He had completed his second Saturn return, which was accompanied by the year 2000 Saturn Jupiter conjunction in late Taurus, where they were around the time of his birth in the early 1940's. Saturn and Jupiter have completed their 60-year cycle and he is successfully buying his own properties and investing for himself thereby creating a new way of doing business. Through the use of the Internet he is selling government housing and amassing a lucrative cash flow with little stress or physical effort. He is again creating a new career direction. His life, now more in balance between family and career, has helped alleviate the stress of his lifelong bout with the depression and his health continues to improve as he guards it more carefully. He not only specializes in low-income government housing, but also began to put investor groups (Uranus) into equity share investments. This is a perfect marriage of his traditional (Saturn) and his non-traditional (Uranus) approaches to real estate and supports the innovative aspects of his personality.

Applying This Cycle Theory to the Other Outer Planets

The above theory can be applied to the reversal of transiting Saturn aspecting natal Jupiter or any of the planets, particularly the outer planets Uranus, Neptune and Pluto. This alternative cycle can also be applied to any combination of the two slower moving planets or asteroids. You can even reverse the transiting Jupiter hitting the natal Saturn cycle and use transiting Saturn and watch its relationship to natal Jupiter as it travels through its 29.5 year cycle around the Sun. It constricts and molds Jupiter. It can either feel repressive or bring a welcome discipline to large, undeveloped visionary ideas.

We can also take transiting Saturn and apply it to natal Uranus. Unlike Jupiter, Saturn has a more controlled and repressive effect on Uranus. However, since they sit next to each other in the solar system and since in mythology, Saturn (Cronos) slays his father Uranus, the God of chaos, separation and fusion, their relationship creates a tension that generally affects economies and fixed perceptions of reality, particularly in business.

Using the planet Uranus as the anchor point, you can take transiting Jupiter and apply the above lunar phases to it to interpret the opportunities that may arise. What may also emerge is out of the box thinking that is the result of Jupiter's transit around the natal chart of the individual or company. Note where Uranus is in the individual or company's chart. What house or houses does it rule in the birth map? In which sign do we find it? What are the natal aspects to it? Using the many symbols and stories of this slower planet (refer to Planets chapter), what information can you glean from its placement? Transiting Jupiter conjuncting natal Uranus breaks open new possibilities that may seem as though they came out of the blue. It can bring windfalls, extraordinary insights, community associations, and put you in the right place at the right time with the right attitude, which knows not to reject change.

Every time transiting Jupiter hits the position of natal Uranus in your chart, you break open your old realities and opportunities present themselves. Being ready for change is the best thing we can do during these times. If you are ready for change, remarkable events and opportunities present themselves in an almost magical fluidity. Unfortunately, many people resist the change that Uranus demands. Resisting changes can result in sudden losses such as company consolidations and mergers. This may happen on the surface quite suddenly leaving the individual distraught, but, in fact, is something they have been wanting for a long time. Their fear (Saturn) prevents them from making a change but Uranus clears the air (which it rules) and makes us start over.

Therefore, the reputation that Uranus carries, of being troublesome and unpredictable, is based on the level of resistance exhibited by individuals, companies, countries and economies. Uranus' energy gyrates long enough to throw us out of our comfort zones. When Uranus comes we are dancing the Hula under neon lights and we don't know what hit us. Some people will experience this type of change as pleasantly remarkable, while others will exhibit aberrational behavior. Trying to harness unbridled energies always presents challenges. Using another set of images, we can say that Uranus rules electricity and Saturn is the frozen ice cube being thrown onto the electric current. As that ice cube makes contact with the electricity, sparks fly and combustion occurs. In our economic cycles, we see a great deal of chaos when transiting Saturn is creating hard aspects to transiting Uranus, something which occurred in the year 2000 as the NASDAQ dropped markedly over the course of a few months. It is during these periods that wars, revolutions and general anxiety and unrest are active. This particular combination precipitates states of revolutionary thought and problem solving, which are the result of technical breakdowns and discoveries. The impending energy crisis and the fall of the dot.com companies are good examples of the above.

Ultimately, this combination, once blended creates unusual models from traditional structures. It creates hybrid solutions, which result from the mediation of Chiron who joins these two planets via its orbit and fuses ideas.

One Example of the Lunation Cycle on a Larger Scale:

The Economy and the Last Quarter Phase of Jupiter and Saturn

Examining the 1996 election, we can observed aspects between Saturn and Jupiter at that time, thereby gaining insight. There are various phases between Saturn and Jupiter that continually shift and push the economy into its cyclic highs and lows. Their great cycle is their conjunction, which occurs once every twenty years, the last two cycles occurring in 1981 and again in 2000. The greater Saturn/Jupiter cycle is that of approximately every sixty years, when Saturn and Jupiter conjunct close to the same sign and degree, triggering an even larger economic shift, the last one of which occurred in 2000 in Taurus, and previously in 1941.

The twenty-year conjunction of Saturn and Jupiter can be compared to a New Moon, which represents new beginnings. The quarterly and oppositional cycles between Saturn and Jupiter continue to create energies that are similar to the energy of the moon at its first quarter, full moon, and last quarter positions, but the effects are more far-reaching.

As mentioned, one of these conjunctions occurred in 1981, in the early degrees of Libra, the Yuppie era of chrome and steel furniture, which cast us into one of the most overwhelming bull and bear markets in history. It continued through the spring of 2000, when the new Saturn Jupiter conjunction occurred in Taurus, triggering a volatile stock market and corrections, particularly with the NASDAQ. Historically, as Jupiter and Saturn aspect each other, we have economic shifts, the most stressful of which are at the squares and oppositions. When these occur, people become more conservative.

In my writing about the Saturn and Jupiter Career cycle, I have discovered that each quarterly position is related to a certain kind of event. For example, the opposition between Saturn and Jupiter always accompanies an economic crisis, similar to the one in 1930 and more recently in late 1990 and early 1991, when the U.S. entered one of the deepest recessions in its history. Spending stopped, prices fell, and business activity declined.

Earlier I mentioned the greater cycle when Saturn and Jupiter conjunct in approximately the same place in the sky as they did approximately sixty years prior. For example, Saturn and Jupiter conjuncted in the sign of Taurus between 1940 and 1941, just as the United States was about to enter World War II. This same conjunction took place in May 2000 as the U.S. was about to elect a new president. The irony of this type of conjunction is that it doesn't matter which party claims the presidency, the stage is set for an economic shift and the party that claims the title will not have much control over what happens economically. Expect a shift occurring from 2003 through 2006, as the squares take effect and as Pluto squares the Nodes.

When we are in the last Phase of the greater sixty-year cycle, we are in the Last Quarter to Balsamic Phase of the cycle. These phases are the breaking down of the cycle. This is what happened in early Spring of 2000. It is when Saturn and Jupiter's planetary energies appear to be "dying on the vine". Though this period appears to be a breaking down cycle, which triggers all types of confusion in directional choices, it also implies new possibilities for growth, one in which education or rather re-education is a significant factor and an important focus.

These Phases may indicate tight economic sanctions. However, it does not imply that there is no possibility for growth. In order for economic growth to occur, there must be a breaking down of old forms and structures. The way to move forward is through re-education. As re-education occurs, we enter a transition state where many ideas are planted and nurtured, making them ready for new growth.

Since the Jupiter/Saturn opposition of 1990 to 1991 there has been an inordinate amount of takeovers and job layoffs. As a result greater numbers of people are moving away from traditional forms of work. The Internet has made its mark by allowing people to work at home, work from a distance, and invent new jobs. An individual moving through the Last Quarter or Balsamic Phase of their own personal career cycle finds that one of the best ways to move forward is to learn new skills. They get training and prepare for new fields.

There is an old saying that "necessity is the mother of invention". We were in the Balsamic Phase of the cycle as Saturn traveled through the sign of Aquarius between 1991 and 1994, creating a final square prior to the year 2000.

That administration found itself in the midst of this "breaking down" cycle. One of the challenges they faced was of restructuring the educational system.

On a lesser scale, at the end of 1995 and through the end of 1996, Jupiter and Saturn were finishing a ninety-degree square to each other, again forcing us to look at the economy. The housing industry was depressed during this period of time, but as this smaller square released, we saw rising prices, increased real estate activity and renewed activity in the marketplace.

The key is to look at Saturn, the planet of perceived limitation in a new way. The combination of Jupiter, the principle of expansion coupled with Saturn, the planet of reserve and form are healthy checks for one another.

How interesting that the Democratic Party is ruled by Saturn and the Republican by Jupiter. There is an old rule that I teach students... that the slower planets always win. Why? Because they stay longer in one place, forcing us to look seriously at their rulership issues.

[9] Liz Greene, Saturn: A New Look At An Old Devil, (New York: Samuel Weiser, Inc., 1976.

[10] Neil Michelsen, Tables of Planetary Phenomenon, ACS Publications, Inc., San Diego, California, 1990, p. 91.

[11] Funk and Wagnall's Standard Dictionary, New American Library, New York, New York, 1980, p. 698.

[12] James S. Hirsch, Hurricane-The Miraculous Journey of Rubin Carter, (Boston-New York: Houghton Mifflin Company, 1999), p. 223.

[12A] Source of charts of famous persons is Solar Fire software available through Astrolabe and designed by Esoteric Technologies-See resource page in back of book.

[13] Lois Rodden, Profiles of Women, (Tempe, AZ: The American Federation of Astrologers), 1979, p. 202.

Chapter 10

Delineating the Corporation

If we can assign a birth chart to every living entity (based on its birth date, time, and place), as well as set up birth charts for events in history, then it is appropriate that we should assign a birth chart to a corporation. The most commonly used birth time for a company is Noon. An accurate incorporation time is very difficult to come by unless the incorporation papers were time stamped. Another time determinant for an unincorporated firm is when it opens its doors for business. The most commonly used time is either when the business or company takes in its first dollar or consults with its first client. Calculate for Noon if this other information is not available.

There will be times when a business partnership will ask the astrologer about the planning phases of their business and offer the time they first had the idea, when they agreed, when they met for the first time, etc. These are all very important dates, but the most important is when the contract of business is SET INTO MOTION. This is considered the birth moment and the legal time that the business begins. Incorporation dates are always changing, particularly as larger companies are gobbling up smaller ones in mergers; there will be frequent changes in incorporation dates and charts. The standard rule of thumb is to use the most current incorporation date, using the city in which it was recorded as the birthplace of the company.

Several companies on the New York Stock Exchange are

incorporated in either Wilmington or Dover, Delaware, so these cities are used as their places of birth. Multinationals have branch offices throughout the nations of the world. The original incorporation date of the parent company is always used, but it is also important to examine the date, time and place of birth (the opening date) of the branch office, particularly if an individual is considering employment at that particular branch of the corporation or business.

A good source for incorporation dates is *Moody's Investor Services* in New York. Each quarter they publish an updated manual, which lists all of the companies currently offering stock on the NYSE, along with their history, products, a value line showing the activity of the company in recent years, and other useful information. If a company has been re-incorporated, the manual will reflect the change.

Another way to find out the incorporation date of a company is to call the head office's librarian or reference department. Since incorporation dates are a matter of public record, they are obliged to give you that information, although it has been my experience that sometimes the data given by the librarian is incongruent with the published data, or, they only give you the month and year, without the specific date.

Falling back to using a Noon hour as a default time elevates the Sun, which represents the chief operating officer or president of a company. They are the figurehead for the organization and so are symbolically placed at the apex of the chart. The tenth house or Midheaven represents what the public perceives, as well as the reputation of the company.

Setting Up a Corporation Chart

If a corporation has been formed, use that date, time and place for the business chart, but if you are fortunate enough to be able to plan your company chart, a few factors need to be taken into consideration. Keep in mind that probably there will always be areas that present stress or unforeseen difficulty when erecting the chart. Stress is not necessarily a bad thing to have in a company chart because squares and oppositions motivate and stimulate growth.

As in planting, it is a good idea to set up a company between the New and Full Moon cycle, but not during a void-of-course Moon. It is not wise to use a void-of-course Moon because the Moon rules employees and how the public sees the company. If the Moon is void of course, a vague quality may emerge and the identity of the company is never

Illustration 43

Event: *Holding Company, May 3, 1983, 12:00pm PDT + 7:00, Concord, CA, 37°N58'41" 122°W01'48"*

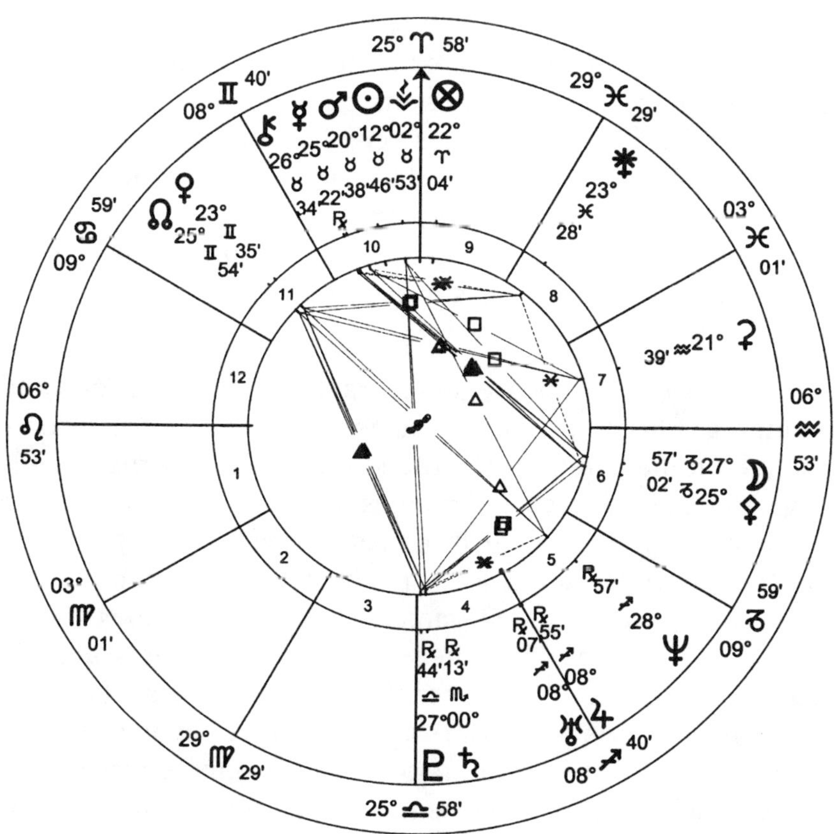

really established in the eyes of the public. Since the first quarter Moon can indicate structure and management, this phase should be considered.

There are exceptions to this, such as a holding company (one that has no purpose but to act as a structure that holds a company until its structure is defined). Illustration 43 shows a company formed as a holding company for a major international cosmetic and skin care manufacturer and distributor. Subsidiaries have been formed as they pass through this company's possession. Note the Sun in Taurus ruled by Venus, the ruler of cosmetics and skin care products. The void-of-course Moon in Capricorn is in the sixth house of employees and many employees move through this company quickly. People have been hired and assigned jobs in conjunction with their varied talents.

When establishing a company, note which planets are retrograde and which are direct. There will almost always be some retrograde planet since the outer planets usually retrograde for a few months each year, but Mercury, Venus and Mars should not be retrograde. Mercury retrogrades three times a year for approximately three weeks at a time. Venus retrogrades about once in 18 months for approximately 40 days and Mars retrogrades every two years for about three months.

Since Mercury rules legal contracts, communications and planning, particularly in a business chart, it is not recommended to have retrograde Mercury. Venus governs spending, talents, resources and monies. A retrograde Venus could indicate a company which makes inappropriate choices in partnerships or purchases, or which may develop an uncomfortable working environment. Mars, the old rule of Scorpio (banks and profit), when retrograde, suggests a company that may never quite reach its projected goals because it is easily sidetracked. Mars is the planet of action and aggression and if it is retrograde in a company chart it may indicate a lack of assertive action. Also, when Mars is retrograde by transit, it has been noted that business slows down and the market can be depressed.

A predominance of cardinal signs in a chart is good, suggesting a pioneering spirit and the ability to adjust to changing times. It is also important to have some fixed energy in the chart for follow-through and accomplishment, as well as mutability for a smooth flow of affairs. Too much cardinality can indicate a company, which excels at developing new ideas but is not strong in following through on their visions.

The Moon in an Earth sign is positive because it suggests practicality and tangibility. Saturn should be strongly placed. A retrograde Saturn may actually be an asset. Saturn rules karma in spiritual Astrology, but in a business chart it represents organization and career direction. If the business has to do with building materials and contracting, then Saturn may be even more prominently placed since it rules concrete and construction. However, an angular Saturn is not beneficial for most business charts.

A prominent (possibly angular) and well-aspected Jupiter is always an excellent placement since Jupiter rules sales and marketing. Jupiter placed in either the second or eighth house of resources or forming a positive aspect to the rulers of the second and eighth indicates ease in financing and cash flow.

The planets ruling the second, sixth, and tenth houses should be direct, and the signs on these houses are indicators of the type of business represented by the chart. The planets ruling the second and eighth should be well aspected for the business to be financially successful. Following is an example of a planned company chart (Illustration 44). The business had been in existence for five years prior to the date of this writing, but a new chart was set up for the opening of this individual's first office (a new venture). This chart was erected for the time the first clients were seen at the new office.

Illustration 44

Event: *Planned Corporation, Nov. 1, 1982, 11:00am PST +8:00, Pleasant Hill, CA, 37°N56'53" 122°W03'35"*

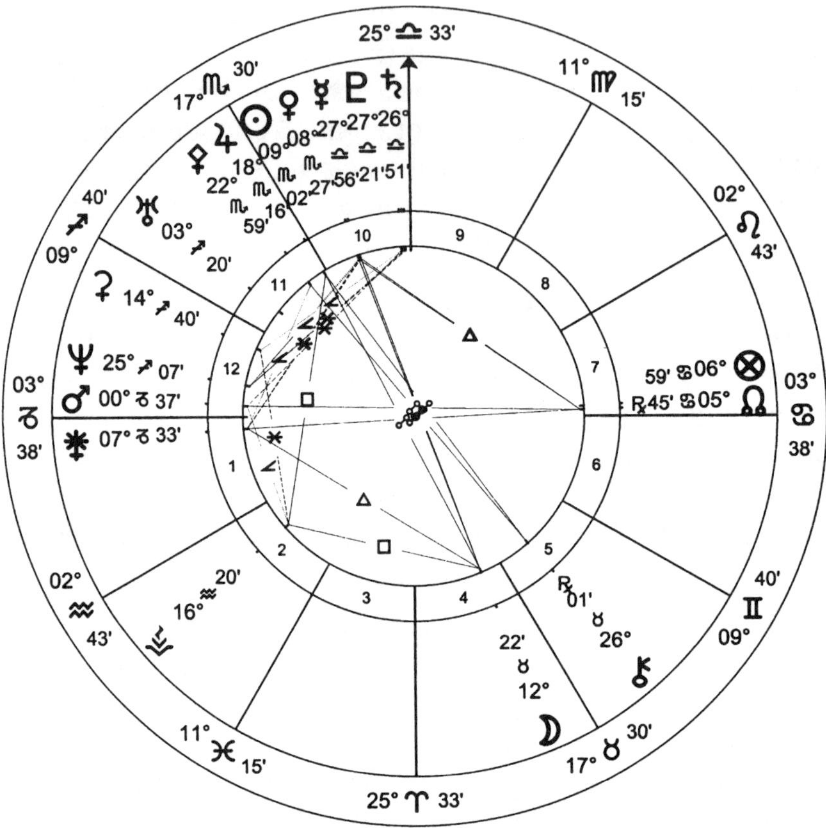

The business is a sole proprietorship and primarily consults with people about their career and business direction. The product is information, which requires detailed analysis. The clients are presented with alternative options as well as timing and forecasting for their businesses. Note the Scorpio Sun in the tenth house. Scorpio is the sign of transformation. The consultant also speaks and presents her ideas to large groups of people. Mercury in the tenth house is an excellent placement for this type of chart. The primary source of new clients comes from referrals. Uranus rules the second house and is in the eleventh house of groups and friends who act as resources for the business and help to achieve its goals.

Prior to opening the office the owner worked out of her home. The Moon in Taurus in the fourth house indicates an ability to work from home. The fourth house of a corporation chart signifies its roots. A good portion of her business comes from real estate and loan agents as she was in real estate and investment prior to opening this business. The fourth house also indicates real estate and property. The Moon rules employees and in this case all of her employees continue to work out of her home.

Note the balance in cardinal, fixed and mutable signs. The business continues to be strong and balanced. As transiting Saturn and Uranus move over the Ascendant of the corporation chart into the first house, the company's business objectives are changing. Information researched over the last three years (transits through the twelfth house of research and development) is starting to reach a larger market through writing and training workshops.

Pluto (the ruler of mass production) conjuncts the chart ruler Saturn in the tenth house. This new information creates controversy and wakes people up. The chart has the hallmarks of being a late bloomer with the Capricorn rising and the strong tenth house emphasis. Since there are a high percentage of planets in the fourth quadrant, particularly in the tenth house, this company will grow as it matures.

The Planets in a Corporate Chart

In order to proceed with corporate chart delineation it is important to provide meanings for the planets in a corporate chart. The following compilation of definitions may also be applied to transits through the horoscope for any business.

Sun: The life force drive; the company identit; its founder, chairman of the board or corporate head; the owner or top management. The Sun may represent government and administrators, authority figures; gold and speculation; or the theater as the primary business. If eclipsed, it can send the company into a completely new direction.

The Sun brings attention and success to whatever part of the chart it is moving. It can also promote recognition and success if positively aspected.

Moon: The Moon symbolizes the employees or "family" of the company and their involvement in the company. It is the public image, how the public responds to the services or products of the company; women in the company in general; the "home" office and its functions; the company's ability to nurture its products, services and popular ideas to which the public responds. The crowds or masses, which respond to the product; harvests of crops; the ocean or water products in general are all represented by the Moon. A stressfully aspected Moon may indicate a poor public image. If heavily aspected by Saturn, Neptune or Pluto, it may indicate some type of hazardous situation around employees.

As a transit, the Moon may temporarily increase the price of stock if it positively aspects the Sun, Venus or Jupiter. A temporary decrease in stock price may result from a difficult aspect to such planets as Saturn or Pluto.

Mercury: Mercury represents the sales, service and the communication facilities of the company. The commercial or scientific/analytic abilities demonstrated by management, the work force; literature and printing are symbols of the Mercury. Information distributed, health and environmental concerns of the work force, company books, secretaries and clerical staff, telephone operators, software, training facilities, advertising, food product or food supply services, small animals and veterinary, the media, trade and commerce, short trips, doctors, publishing and printing are all Mercury ruled.

As a transit, it can bring out news or information that changes the attitudes of the employees or the public and the company investors.

Venus: The company's general assets and its appeal for partnering or merger possibilities; its popularity; public's approval or acceptance of product lines; credit. A well-placed Venus indicates a pleasing work environment; architectural beauty; aesthetics like art, fashion, music, cosmetics; and recreation and pleasure perks. Venus retrograde is uncommon in corporate charts and should be avoided.

As a transit, Venus brings things to the attention of the public by making them popular or appealing to investors. When Venus is well aspected people are more content. Transiting through the second or eighth house Venus may bring a successful sale or purchase.

Mars: Indicates stock activity, new beginnings and the company's ability to act; the urge to pioneer, to be aggressive; its motivation and drive; its competitive spirit; and the desire to be the best. Negatively aspected, Mars can bring accidents, violence, epidemics, and explosions. It rules such things as the military, athletics, surgery, war, iron, steel, diamonds, explosives, machinery and equipment, munitions, and tobacco. (Note that the Mars/Jupiter midpoint is a point of prosperity and positive results from strategic action providing a key to the company's success).

As a transit, Mars indicates activity and volume in the markets. It may bring a general atmosphere of anxiety and action and can trigger sudden negative activities in a company. When retrograde, Mars often curtails activity.

Jupiter: this planet represents the entire urge to grow, expand and be successful, as well as the company's moneymaking abilities. Jupiter enhances foreign concerns, education and philosophy, publishing possibilities and optimism. It rules bankers, brokers, courts, churches, public relations, the horse racing industry and direct mail.

As a transit Jupiter is an excellent sell signal increasing prices or value. It brings promise and hope. If negatively transiting, a company can overindulge, over-expand, or take a downward turn because of overly zealous actions.

Saturn: The administrative or management ability of a company; the corporation in general, its structure, the governing body (usually the board of directors), the authority or policy-making branch. Saturn rules the company's stability, conservatism and ability to consolidate and limit in a practical ways. This is where the corporation may adhere to traditional expression and paternal relations toward its employees and shareholders. Saturn represents labor or laboring places; land as in farms, real estate, grains, mines, mountains; and the elderly.

As a transit, a well-aspected Saturn may indicate a buy signal. It can decrease a stock price, limit or depress the market, restrict and create worry and concern with the company, or bring delays in progress.

Uranus: Uranus rules the innovative ability of the company, its progressive thinking and any new inventions. It encourages the company to be unique. It provides a future orientation. The company may be heavily invested in electronics, computers, high-tech developments, railways, strikes, radio waves, utilities, airlines, and air carrier production or public information. Negatively aspected, Uranus may bring sudden shocks or changes within the company or bring acts of God such as tornadoes and hurricanes, earthquakes and explosions.

When positively aspected as a transit, Uranus may herald news of stock splits as well as new and unique efforts. The company may depart from the conventional way of doing things through some crisis. It could indicate a breakup as in the AT&T trust bust. It could bring revolutionary breakthroughs, expansion and branching out or franchising.

Jeff Green, in his book Uranus: Freedom from the Known (Llewellyn Publications) states that when heavy Uranus aspects are operating sometimes there may be paralysis and then a healing. This concept can also be applied to a corporation chart.

Neptune: Represents the ability for a company to seduce its public into purchasing its product via a specific image it creates for a targeted market. Neptune indicates the vision held by management; illusion or dissolution. As mentioned earlier, it shows its seduction potential created by successful advertising campaigns; the potential for rumor or sabotage or behind-the-scenes problems. It may indicate a company which deals with acting, movies, beverages, hospitals or hospital development, narcotics and pharmaceuticals, oil, shipping, photography, political idealism, or inspiration from research. It can bring a redistribution of monies and create altruism and virtue in a company or the polar opposite as with drug and alcohol problems, confusion, and obfuscation and deliberate hiding of assets.

As a transit, Neptune can make a company ripe for a merger. It can be inflationary and expansive in a Bull Market, but deflationary in a Bear Market; lead to uncertainty and confusion within the company; and, dissolve a portion of the business in preparation for a new way of doing things. It shows the ability to take what is already there, reprocess it and create something better. It may indicate toxic and waste management, literally.

Pluto: This is the power behind the company. Every good company has a strong Pluto, showing the potential and ability to regenerate itself. It depicts the hidden treasure or assets of a company, its resources and its ability to research, develop, and successfully mass-produce, manufacture and distribute. It rules plumbing, sewers, rackets, plutonium, radiation, cancer research, atomic research, genetic engineering, life extension, redevelopment and urban renewal. Negatively, it indicates the potential to wipe out, to go bankrupt, to sabotage; dealings with the underworld of crime and corruption; internal dictatorships; and compulsive behavior patterns like unknown gambling debts. Pluto may indicate power struggles within the company.

As a transit, Pluto may purge the company or even threaten to eliminate it, but it can also rebuild the corporation after a devastating period. It can indicate crisis and group movements within a company that are accompanied by mass hysteria. A heavy transit of Pluto may cause major changes in the structure of the company. It this is positive it is successful particularly in large ventures; if negative it can bring on bankruptcy.

A strong Pluto transit brings the need to reorganize or restructure to eliminate and get down to basics. It may be a factor in precipitating mergers, but my experience has indicated Neptune to be the primary planet for this action.

If a strong Pluto transit is occurring and a company has large outstanding debts, then it may be a time to cut spending and reduce cash flow. The opposite may also be true: they decide to take greater financial risks by spending to improve systems and equipment in order to penetrate a wider market. Either way, it requires caution on the part of the company. If Pluto is well aspected and the company has few debts then a period of long-term growth is just beginning.

North Node: This point indicates contact with the outer world and the public's perception of the company. Transits to the Nodes bring the company attention.

THE HOUSES OF A CORPORATE CHART

Each house of the horoscope represents a different area. The houses of the corporation chart are similar yet different from those in a regular natal chart. For example, the first house of a corporation chart represents the shareholders of the company and the company's business objectives, while a regular chart reflects and individual's body and personal direction. The following are the assigned meanings of the houses in a corporate chart.

First House: Personnel of the corporation, including shareholders; how the shareholders view the company; company morale; company's business objectives; general membership; place of incorporation and its relationship to the public; and, its attitude towards competitors. (Note the ruler of the Ascendant and its house placement.)

Second House: Liquid assets; revenues; activities in money-making; earnings; voluntary expenditures; ability to earn profits; disposition toward investments.

Third House: Contacts with the public; financial and trade publications; financial and trade relations with adjacent countries and states; short-distance travel; neighboring organizations; education; library, publications of all kinds (bulletins and newsletters, magazines), methods of distributing news, literary work; technical publications; rails, telephones and telegraphs; commercial radio; demand for stocks and bonds; trade volume figures; advertising; internal agreements; traffic, transportation and communication departments; interoffice communications; in-house information dissemination, in-house policies and platforms.

Fourth House: Real estate investments and holdings including raw land; tangible assets of the corporation; hazards involving property; the original home of the company; direct competition; power of competitors; roots of corporation; base of operations or field of activity; location and condition of the factory, warehouse or office buildings.

Fifth House: Executive personnel (except for the president or chairman of the board); governing body; attitudes or actions of shareholders or the board of directors in opposition to the president; committees; management teams; advertising success or failure; income from invested capital or results of speculative ventures; speculation; the place of deposit of capital such as safes, vaults, and banks; amusements, social affairs, conventions; educational enterprises, workshops, seminars, teaching; banquets; and, dramatic or theatrical ventures.

Sixth House: Workers or employees (voluntary or paid); type of work and equipment; health policies and insurance; work schedules and work routines; inventories; lighting and heating bills; performance of workers on the job; employee cooperation; assistance received fellow employees; attitudes of employees; corporations connected with hostelries (inns or hotels); agriculture and agricultural products; business fixtures and furnishings; health condition of personnel; and, the inception of employee strikes and labor troubles.

Seventh House: Relationship to other organizations; sales appeal; how effectively a product is put across; house of adjustments; trading volume (how much stock is being bought); public accountings; employee income and payrolls; relationships with others (supportive or hostile); political or commercial affiliates; trade agreements; mergers; open opposition to growth; lawsuits and legal affairs; and, competitors and their activities.

Eighth House: Losses or gains through the closing of the corporation; financial responsibilities; private conferences; board of directors; credit, dividends; trade secrets; net earnings; insurances; handling of legacies; nonprofit status; donations to nonprofit organizations; financial conditions involving partnerships, mergers or lawsuits; financial relations with competitors; competitor's financial condition; revenue from investments or liquidation of frozen assets; loans and income from sources not under immediate control of the organization; and, the company treasurer.

Ninth House: Advertising department; shipping; activities abroad; completion of merger contracts; code of ethics and bylaws; audits; contracts with other companies; intercompany communication; philosophy of company; publications (same as in third house); any public and foreign relations; long-distance communications; results of mail-order campaigns; relations with educational institutions and publications; professional consultants; publicity and public relations; officials; and, all legal affairs.

Tenth House: Supreme or governing authority; president or the chairman of the board; figureheads; national reputation; relations with governments and associations; public image; power; general business conditions as presented to the public; administrative department. (Look at the ruler of the tenth house and its house placement for insight into the talents or gifts of the CEO.)

Eleventh House: Allied organizations; colleagues, friends; acquaintances; political connections; community connections; constitutional policies; resources available through the company head (the second from the tenth); long-range goals of the organization and what it stands for; public relations through group involvement; intangible assets (knowing people who know people to get things done); its indebtedness; mortgages; the treasury; and, fraternal and club groups.

Twelfth House: Enemies and secret organizations against the organization; sabotage; secret intelligence department; strikes and labor troubles; dissolutions and negotiations. The list also includes behind-the-scenes research and development; trade secrets and formulas; secret assistance; designs for the future; and, the effects of litigation.

(Refer to the Appendix for a keyword sheet on corporate house meanings.)

Hemispheric Influences

Before any statement is made about hemispheric influence, it must be noted that charts calculated for Noon will always have several planets in either the third or fourth quadrant. If a relatively accurate time is available then the following may be of interest.

If there is a strong influence in the right or Western Hemisphere, much of the company experiences may be subjective. Certain choices may present themselves and the challenges may be in the choosing. Accordingly, when there is a strong influence in the left or Eastern Hemisphere, the company has more control. Of course, in having control, it must also take responsibility for the consequences of its choices. An Eastern influence may tend to perpetuate an aggressive company, but this also depends on other factors, such as the type of company or the product.

Illustration 45

Event: Zweig Mutual Funds, Oct. 1, 1986, 12:00pm EDT + 4:00, Baltimore, MD, 39°N17'25" 076°W36'45"

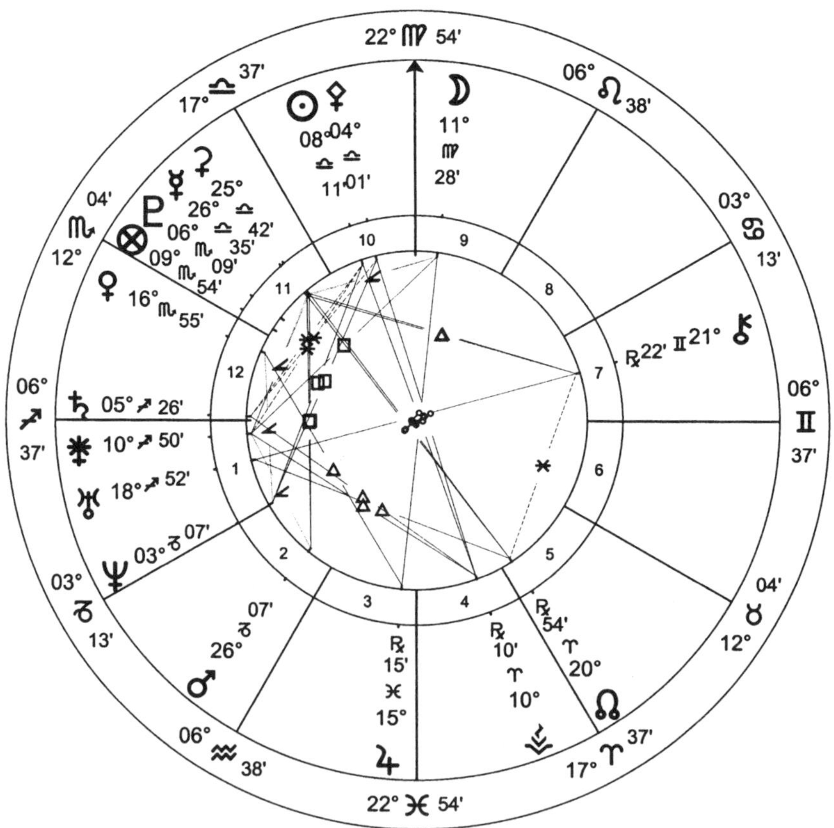

Since the Midheaven usually indicates the leadership of the company, the ruling planet of the Midheaven and where it is placed has a lot to do with the leader's interests. For example, in the case for the original Zweig Mutual Funds (Illustration 45), Marty Zweig, the founder of this fund was known for his conservatism, his writing, and his large investments in his own company treasury (Mercury, the ruler of the tenth, in the eleventh house). The company has Sagittarius rising, and the Ascendant conjuncts natal Saturn (conservatism). Its ruling planet, Jupiter, is in the third house of communications, and the newsletter is indeed a moneymaker for this company. Jupiter, the chart ruler, in Pisces (intuition, perception) implies that the company operates on hunches. Just before the crash in October 1987, Zweig pulled his company out of the markets, thus saving the company's treasury (eleventh house).

Aspects in a Corporate Chart

The following is an example of how aspects can be interpreted when looking at a corporate chart. The chart example (Illustration 46) was a graphic arts company, which included photography and typesetting as part of its company's services and which was in business several years before it legally incorporated on September 24, 1987, at 11:22 AM in San Ramon, California. The Midheaven is Virgo, ruled by Mercury, which governs advertising and graphics. At the time of this writing, the company was about to be re-incorporated as it added a business manager and new branches. This company went through extreme changes while it was still a functioning company and is indicated by the fact that it was established very close to the Solar Eclipse at 29° Virgo 34' on September 22, 1987.

To briefly explore aspects we will discuss those of Mercury in this chart as well as the heavily aspected Moon (the

Illustration 46

Event: Graphics Business, Sep. 24, 1987, 11:22am PDT + 7:00, San Ramon, CA, 37°N46'48" 121°W58'37"

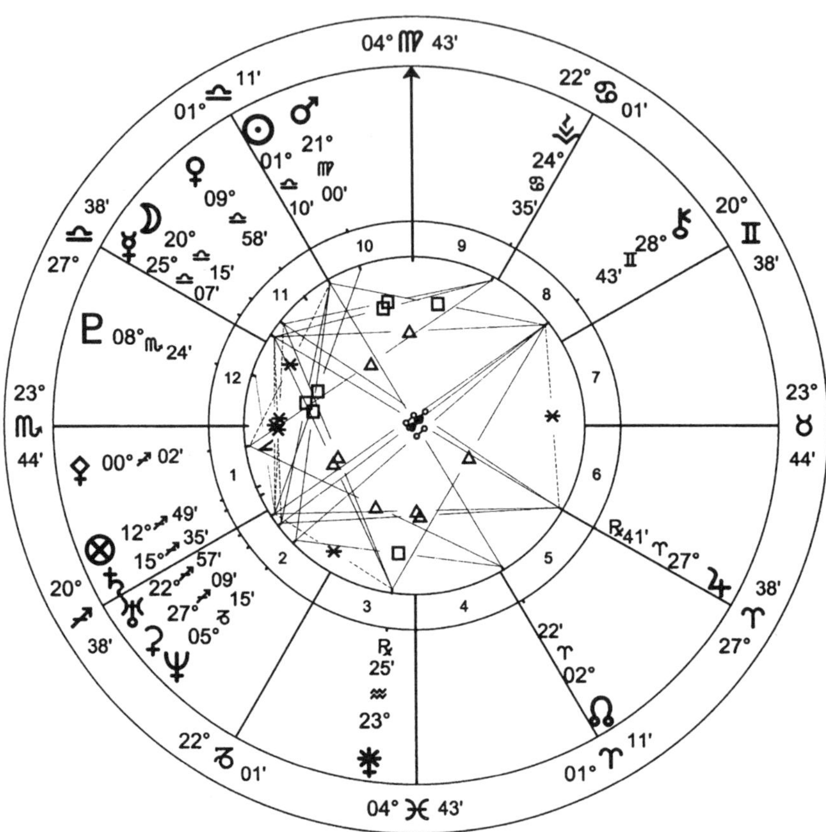

ruler of the employees). Mercury is conjunct the Moon in Libra and close to Venus in Libra in the eleventh house of the treasury, goals, friends and acquaintances. Mercury generally rules the clerical staff. A high percentage of their staff is female (Mercury conjunct the Moon), as are the primary contributors to the treasury. Clerical assistants have contributed their portion of profits to own the company as a collective. There are however, two major corporate holders.

This has had a positive as well as a negative effect on how the company does business. Positively, there is a great deal of support from the community, the New Age organizations they belong to, and friends, but everyone has something to say about how things should be run, which sometimes gets in the way of production. With so many opinions and a stellium in Libra, there is a lot of vacillation about decisions. There is, however, an incredible sense of fairness about decisions in the organization. Mercury conjunct the Moon suggests that many decisions had been emotional ones and often changed based on the latest input.

Mercury, the ruler of the eighth, and Jupiter, the ruler of the second, oppose each other. This illustrates a struggle between having enough revenue and taking an ethical stand about which contracts they choose. In other words, the issue is similar to investment choices people make. Do they want to purchase stocks from firms that are socially responsible? Or do they simply seek a secure high rate of return? Mercury sextiles Uranus and this is an excellent aspect for a company that produces graphics with computers and whose concepts require innovative perspectives.

When transiting Jupiter entered Gemini in March of 1989, it transited the company's seventh and eighth houses while trining its Sun, Venus, Moon and Mercury (ruler of the eighth and tenth houses) and sextiling natal Jupiter (ruler of the second and fourth houses). They re-incorporated and restructured (transiting Saturn and Uranus squared its Sun) to immediately realize a profit (good aspects to the planets that rule the business and Mercury, as well as the second and eighth house rulers).

THE NODES AND ECLIPSES

The North and South Node, both natally placed and transiting, play an important part in delineating a corporate chart. Since the Lunar Nodes are created by the intersection of the orbital paths of the Earth and the Moon they indicate the public's response. Where the transiting North Node is moving is where the company is experiencing gain, and where the South Node is transiting is where the company needs to let go of its enterprises or objectives. The transiting Nodes are connected with eclipses and create opportunities for major change.

The natal Nodes and the last Solar Eclipse occurring prior to or within a few days of incorporation of the company (the pre-natal eclipse) are sensitive points, which when aspected by transit or progression, will put the company in the news. Following are several examples.

Illustration 47

Event: R.J. Reynolds, Mar. 4, 1970, 12:00pm EST +5:00, Dover, DE, 39°N09'29" 075°W31'29"

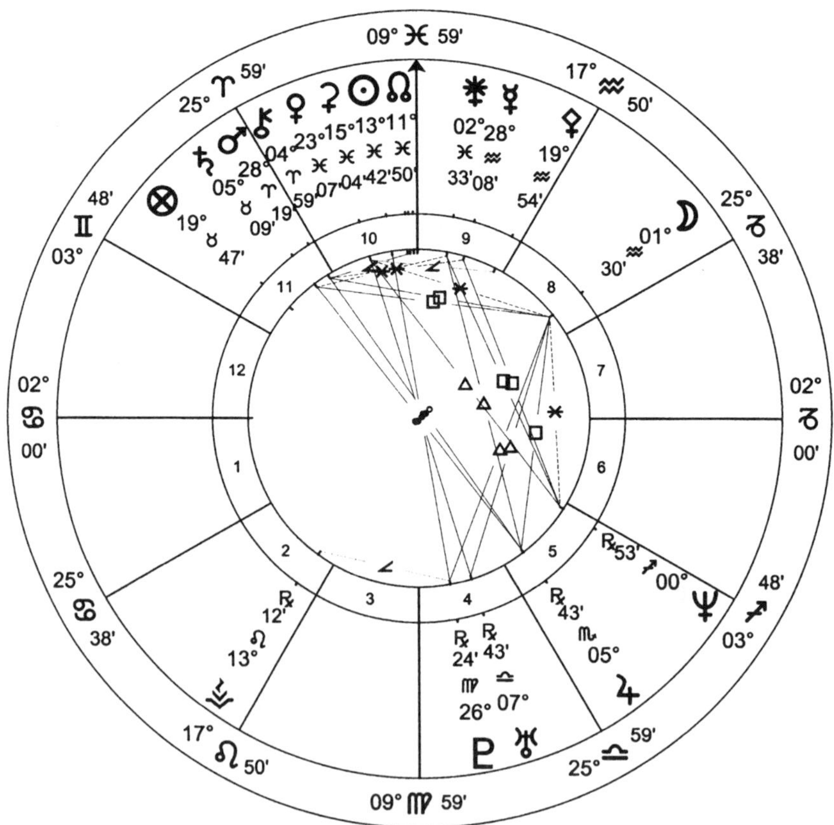

R.J. Reynolds (RJR) (Illustration 47) was incorporated on March 4, 1970, in Dover, Delaware. Its original chart was a Pisces company established with its pre-natal eclipse at 16° of Pisces conjuncting the company's North Node in the tenth house at 12° of Pisces. During September, October, and November of 1988, RJR had been in the news because of its development of an "ashless" cigarette and a proposed buyout by Kohlberg, Kravitz, Roberts and Company. Transiting North Node had returned to the natal position of the North Node (at 12° of Pisces) during the above months and the newspapers were full of stories.

As the Solar Eclipse of September 10, 1988, at 18° of Virgo neared the company's Pluto in the fourth house, although not conjunct it, it brought news of a possible change or restructuring of the company's foundation. The transiting South Node in Virgo in the company's fourth house, its roots, indicated a need to let go of some of the old ways and structures on which the company was founded.

Safeway Stores' original incorporation on March 24, 1926, in Baltimore, Maryland (Illustration 48) shows a pre-natal Solar Eclipse at 23° of Capricorn in the seventh house of competitors. In July 1986, the Haft Corporation took over Safeway, creating a new incorporation chart for August 29, 1986, in Dover, Delaware (Illustration 49).

At the time of the takeover, the transiting North Node was in Aries exactly square the pre-natal Solar Eclipse in the original company's chart and square the original natal Nodes at 21° of Cancer/Capricorn in the first and seventh houses. At the same time, transiting Neptune was at 3° Capricorn exactly square the company's natal Sun at 3° Aries a frequent signature of takeovers and mergers.

The new Safeway chart has its pre-natal eclipse near the North Node at 19° of Aries in the sixth house of labor strikes and labor troubles. Whereas the original chart appeared to show a competitive company, now the company found itself in the media mostly due to labor disputes and environmental concerns. As an interesting aside, when the huge Safeway warehouse fire happened on July 11, 1988 transiting Pluto was exactly conjunct the Pluto/Ascendant midpoint.

A series of eclipses in Pisces and Virgo transiting the company's fourth/tenth house axis coincided with changes in their facilities. As the South Node transited the tenth house during the last Virgo eclipses, managers who were figureheads were laid off for various reasons. Information surfaced about improperly graded meat, reportedly of inferior quality,

Illustration 48

Event: *Safeway Stores, Mar. 24, 1926, 12:00pm EST +5:00, Baltimore, MD, 39°N17'25" 076°W36'45"*

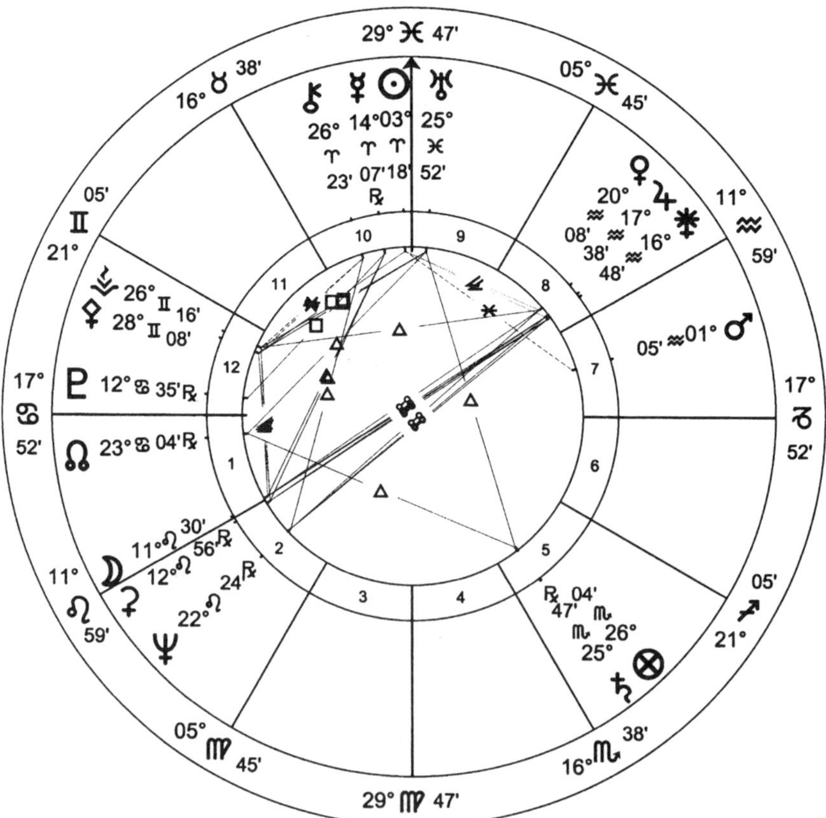

Illustration 49

Event: Safeway Stores, Buyout, Aug. 29, 1986, 12:00pm EDT + 4:00, Dover, DE, 39°N09'29" 075°W31'29"

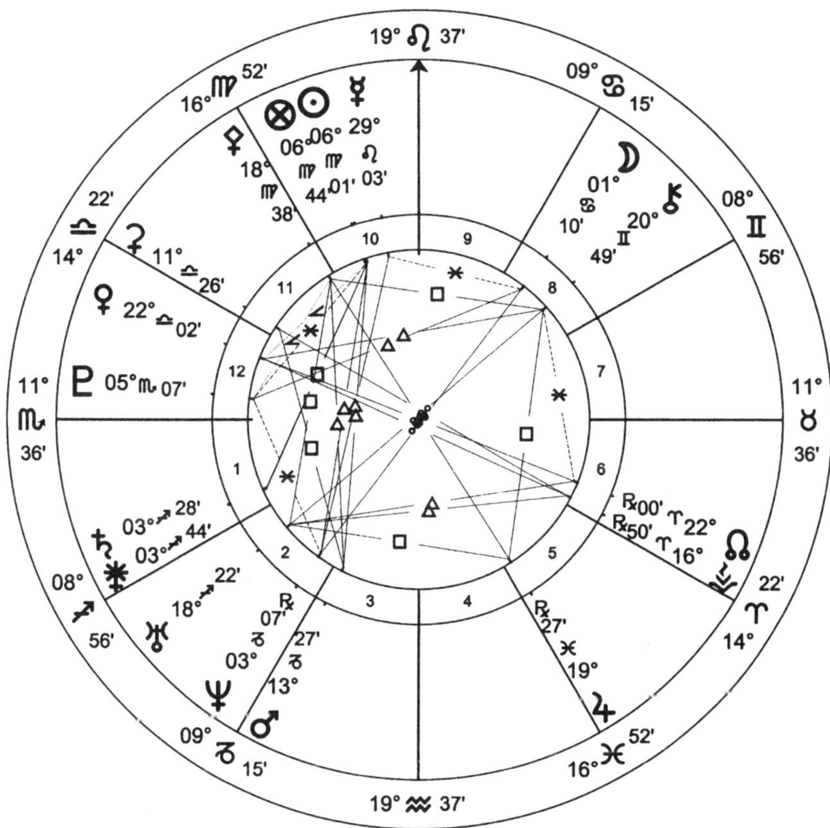

found in some of the stores. Quickly thereafter several executives were discharged as the transiting South Node (letting go) in Virgo was in the tenth house of people in charge!

Merger Mania

Since transiting Neptune entered Capricorn in 1984, there have been increasing numbers of buyouts and mergers. As Pluto finished its run in the sign of Scorpio in 1995, these mergers set off tremendous stock market activity. Both events dramatically turned the corporate business upside down as it struggled to incorporate the new with the old.

These two planets both may indicate an impending merger. Neptune dissolves and reforms and in the process can add a great deal of confusion to the situation while Pluto transforms and regenerates a situation into a new more workable solution. Pluto sextiling Neptune combines the opportunity for major change for individuals as well as corporations.

Other merger indicators can be angular Solar and Lunar Eclipses, which take place on or near a company's Sun. As in a natal chart, an eclipse that hits the Sun will temporarily cut out the "light" so that the corporation can get in touch with its "shadow" side and make a life change.

Several examples of mergers have been mentioned— the typesetting and graphics company, R.J. Reynolds Company, and both charts for Safeway Stores. Another example is that of Continental Illinois Bank (Illustration 50), originally incorporated on October 15, 1932. With its Sun in late Libra, the Federal Government in the summer of 1984 bailed out Continental Illinois. The long-time failing big bank had had transiting Pluto on its Midheaven. Transiting Pluto had moved to 29° of Libra and was retrograding back across Continental Bank's Midheaven at 28° of Libra, restructuring it and its public image.

In 1984, when Neptune and Jupiter conjuncted Continental's early Capricorn Ascendant, the shareholders were asked to dissolve their investment in a protective move towards the company. This bail out had profound ramifications. Continental Illinois had been one of the leading banks in the world and its demise heralded the beginning of the additional bank failures that followed.

As mentioned earlier, the graphics company was incorporated after a Solar Eclipse and was reincorporated as transiting Saturn, Uranus and Neptune squared its Sun in early

Illustration 50

Event: Continental Illinois Bank, Oct. 15, 1932, 12:00pm CST + 6:00, Chicago, IL, 41°N51' 087°W39'

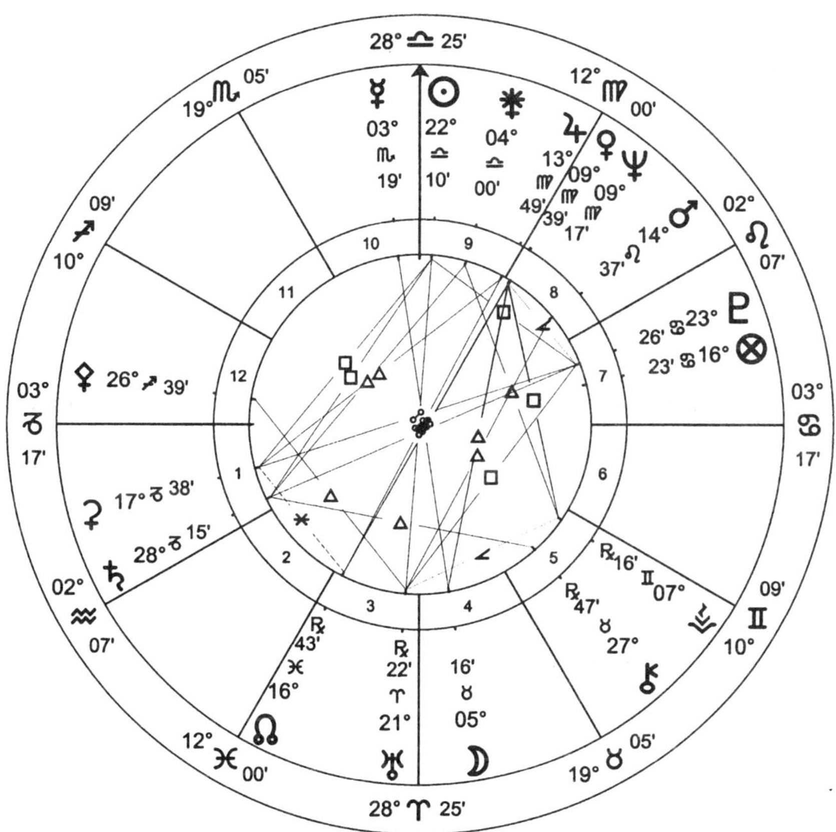

Libra. Its North and South Nodes square the second house Neptune at 5° of Capricorn, further illustrating the power of transits in corporate delineation.

On October 20, 1988, RJR management announced a private company buy-out as transiting Mercury turned direct at 11° Libra, conjunct natal Uranus in the fourth house. Transiting Mars was also stationing direct at 29° of Pisces in the tenth house, square the first/seventh house axis, (representative of shareholders and competition). Transiting Saturn and Uranus had conjuncted for the last time on the seventh house on October 18, 1988 and were quickly heading to the early degrees of Capricorn conjunct the seventh house of competitors, indicating a sudden change in trade volume.

As it turned out, the public was outraged because Shearson, Lehman had been selling bonds for RJR and was now part of the proposed in-house buyout. People were furious because they felt that Shearson, Lehman lowered the bond prices for the purpose of RJR's buyout. The plan was that if RJR privately bought out, it would sell the food division while holding the tobacco division. Perhaps this decision was made in the hopes that the new smokeless cigarette named "Premier" would revolutionize the industry. However, another company, Kohlberg, Kravitz, Roberts and Company ended up making the final buy-out offer. This came after yet another offer from the Theodore Forstmann Company. The original intent of KKR was to sell the tobacco division and keep the food division.

In the process of this entire transaction corporate bond markets were devastated, but the shareholders (the first house) benefited. Transiting Jupiter was trine RJR's natal Moon at 1° of Aquarius, the ruler of the first house. The last Solar Eclipse at 17° of Pisces occurred on March 7, 1989, and will not return for 19 years.

For the Safeway Stores buyout in July 1986 and the new incorporation on August 29, 1986, transiting Neptune was at 3° of Capricorn squaring the original company's chart Sun at 3° of Aries. Transiting Pluto was coming up to a square to the original chart's Moon in Leo in the first house. Transiting Mars, the company's ruler, was squaring the company's natal Mercury in the tenth house at 14° of Aries. Witness that Mercury rules the company's natal fourth house of its origins and its entire foundation was being uprooted!

The last Solar Eclipse had hit that same Mercury (legal agreements, contracts) within 5° at 19° of Aries on April 9, 1986, shortly after Safeway's birthday on March 24. Again, we see an example of eclipses hitting near a company's Sun sign (its life and its path) and how it unexpectedly changes its face forever.

There are obviously many factors that create a merger, but Neptune or Pluto or a series of eclipses on the company's Sun seem to trigger overt directional change and are factors that should definitely be taken into consideration as part of the delineation.

A Corporation in Crisis

On February 10, 1986, at 3:07 PM in New Brunswick, New Jersey, David Clare of Johnson and Johnson Pharmaceuticals (J&J), the maker of Tylenol, received a phone call that poison had been found in Tylenol capsules and had killed several people. This was not the first time that this had happened to Johnson and Johnson. On September 29, 1982, in Chicago, Illinois there had been other Tylenol poisonings. On February 11, 1986, all packages of Tylenol capsules were removed from market shelves. When the Chicago poisonings happened in 1982, J&J had removed all Tylenol packages from the shelves and revolutionized the over-the-counter drug market with the now common safety seals. As the second poisonings occurred and all capsules were removed from the shelves, J&J again revolutionized the industry by designing caplets. At what price?

How can we foresee a crisis or a possible area of concern happening to a corporation? First examine the natal chart and the progressions to that chart, particularly the solar arc directions, since their slow movement activates a natal chart when within one degree of orb. We also can look at the solar return for the year of the corporation, as well as the placement of the prenatal eclipse and the effect of the current cycles of eclipses on the corporate natal chart.

J&J incorporated on November 10, 1887, close to noon in a former wallpaper factory in New Brunswick, New Jersey (Illustration 51). Its first products were medicinal plasters mixed with adhesive, but it soon developed highly absorbent cotton gauze dressing, which was mass-produced and shipped to hospitals. In the late 1800s, they (there were three brothers) began work on the development of the now-famous Band-Aid. As the years continued, the company moved into first-aid supplies, contraceptives, shampoos, disposable diapers and over-the-counter headache remedies. It was the famous Tylenol, the non-aspirin headache remedy, that

Illustration 51

Event: Johnson & Johnson, Nov. 10, 1887 NS, 12:00pm EST +5:00, Brunswick, NJ, 40°N29' 074°W27'

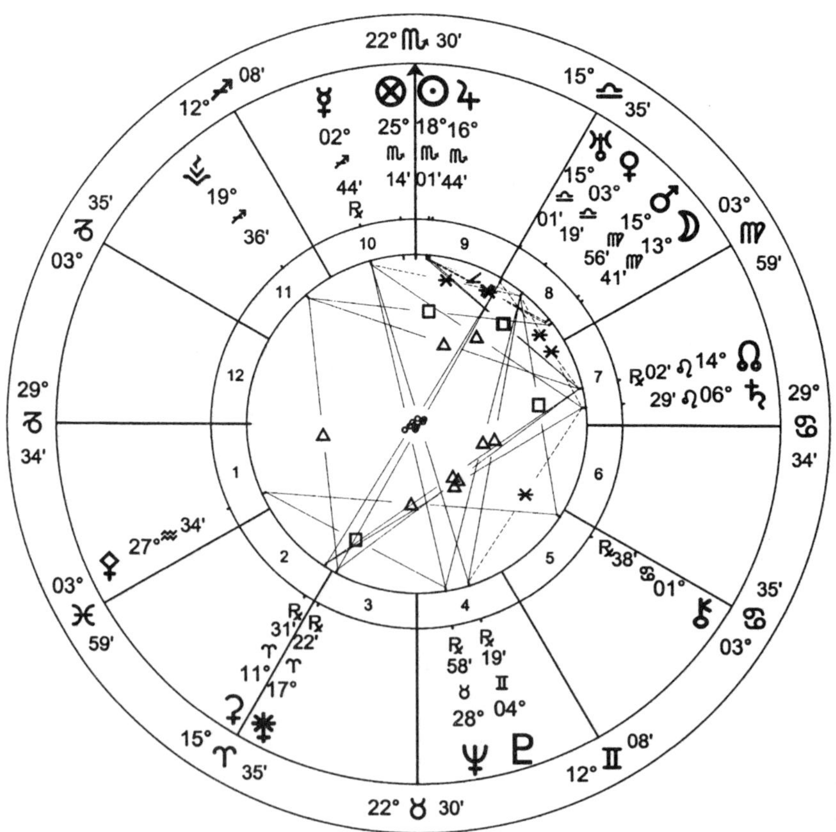

Illustration 52

Event: Johnson & Johnson (Precessed Solar Return), Nov. 11, 1985, 3:01:25pm EST + 5:00, New Brunswick, NJ, 40°N29'10" 074°W27'08"

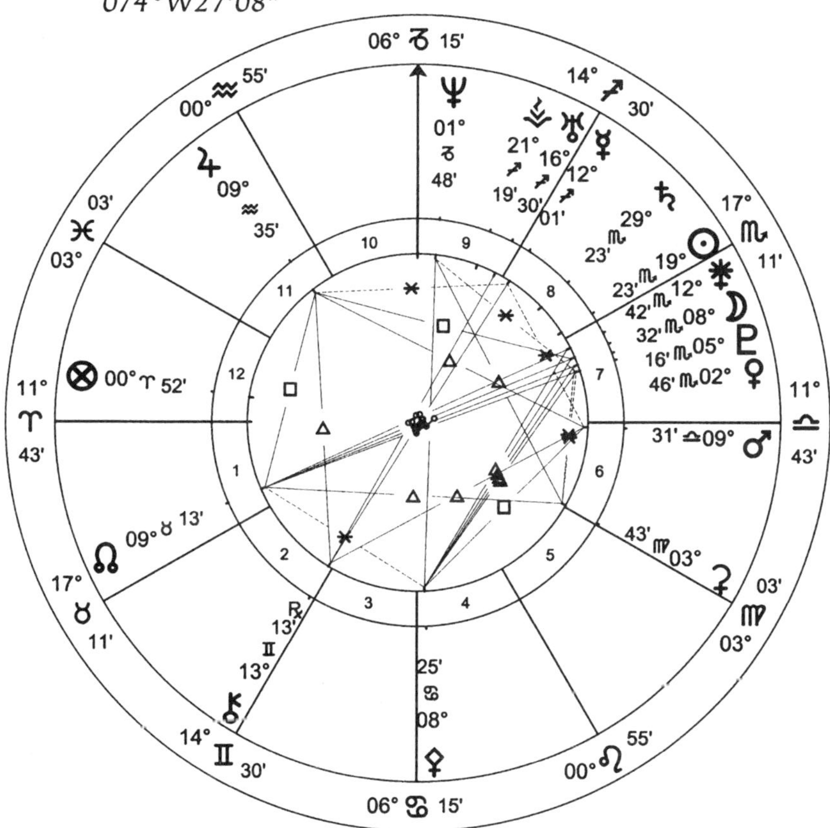

turned the company into one of the largest and wealthiest in the world and it was this development that brought it the most grief.

An important aspect of this entire chart is that the prenatal eclipse before its incorporation was in Leo at 26° near the North Node at 14° of Leo in the seventh house of lawsuits, legal affairs, competition, and trading volume. In (Illustration 52), the November 1985 solar return for J&J occurred on November 11th, one day before a Solar Eclipse of 20° of Scorpio on the company's Sun, squaring the pre-natal eclipse at 26° Leo. As mentioned earlier, any eclipse on a company's Sun will trigger vast changes for the company, depending on the aspects at the time of the eclipse. Another rule is that one should watch exactly 87 days later or at the next New Moon that squares the eclipse point, for a change will be triggered by the square to the eclipse point. This date fell on February 10, 1986, the fateful day David Clare received the phone call that there had been poisonings!

J&J's corporate chart shows 29° of Capricorn on the Ascendant, ruled by Saturn and Uranus (Aquarius is intercepted in the first house). This Saturn/Uranus shared rulership implies changes for this company that may come quite suddenly as a result of an unexpected event.

This energy is similar to 1988 and the Saturn/Uranus conjunction, which brought a great deal of tumultuous change, but which brought people to a new awareness. With Capricorn rising, this company will have its setbacks but use the Capricorn fortitude to do its best work when managing crises.

The company was established with the Sun in Scorpio. Pluto, the ruler of Scorpio, falls in the company's fourth house of foundations and roots. This Plutonian energy provides the company with extra gumption, but can also imply that, like the Phoenix, it re-emerges from tragedy stronger each time.

The company's Moon is in Virgo, a good sign for health products, and is placed in the eighth house conjunct Mars in Virgo. The eighth house indicates losses or gains through death and in this case, it is particularly profound. The public and the company have experienced a loss, and from this loss there has been a gain for the company. Since the Moon rules the public and is conjunct Mars, the God of War, there have been lawsuits as a result of these poisonings. Insurance claims have also been paid as a result of the loss in life. These are all eighth house matters.

The 1985 precessed solar return has Aries, ruled by Mars, on the Descendant. Transiting Mars was at 9° of Libra in the sixth house and was just completing a square to transiting Neptune (drugs and potential sabotage) in the ninth. It was also on the midpoint of natal Venus/Uranus, indicating an unexpected event (Uranus) that would cost money (Venus). Natal Mars at 15° of Virgo was being squared by transiting Mercury while transiting Uranus was square the natal Mars, a sure indicator that something was afire. Mars square Uranus aspects indicate accidents and tragedy.

The Solar Eclipse of November 12, 1985 was at 20° of Scorpio in the eighth house of the solar return chart. It activated the midpoint between solar return Saturn at 29° Scorpio and the Sun at 19° of Scorpio, again suggesting possible death and loss. Transiting Pluto at 5° of Scorpio activated the Venus/Moon midpoint in the seventh house of how other people viewed the company, and it also squared solar return Jupiter at 6° Aquarius in the eleventh house of unexpected events. Pluto squared natal Saturn at 6° Leo, forming a T-square (natal Saturn, solar return Pluto and Jupiter). Pluto rules sabotage and death, and squaring the ruler of the company, Saturn. It almost "killed" the company in the eyes of the public.

In Illustration 53, we see the solar arc directions for February 1, 1986, (calculating the distance the Sun travels in one day and adding that increment to the rest of the planets determine the solar arc.) When the solar arc directed planet is within one degree of aspecting the natal planet, it indicates possible significant changes approaching over the course of the next year and a precise change at the precise aspect. Note how many stressful aspects there were to Neptune (drugs, sabotage, dissolution and creativity) and to Pluto (sabotage, wipe out and transformation).

At the time of the crisis, the solar arc Sun at 27° Aquarius and solar arc Jupiter at 26° Aquarius were opposing the pre-natal eclipse point and squaring natal Neptune at 28° Taurus in the fourth house. They also widely squared the eclipse point of November 12, 1985, at 20° Scorpio in the ninth. Since the Sun co-rules the intercepted

Illustration 53

Event: Johnson & Johnson Solar Arc, Feb. 1, 1986, 0:00pm EST + 5:00, New Brunswick, NJ, 40°N40' 074°W27'

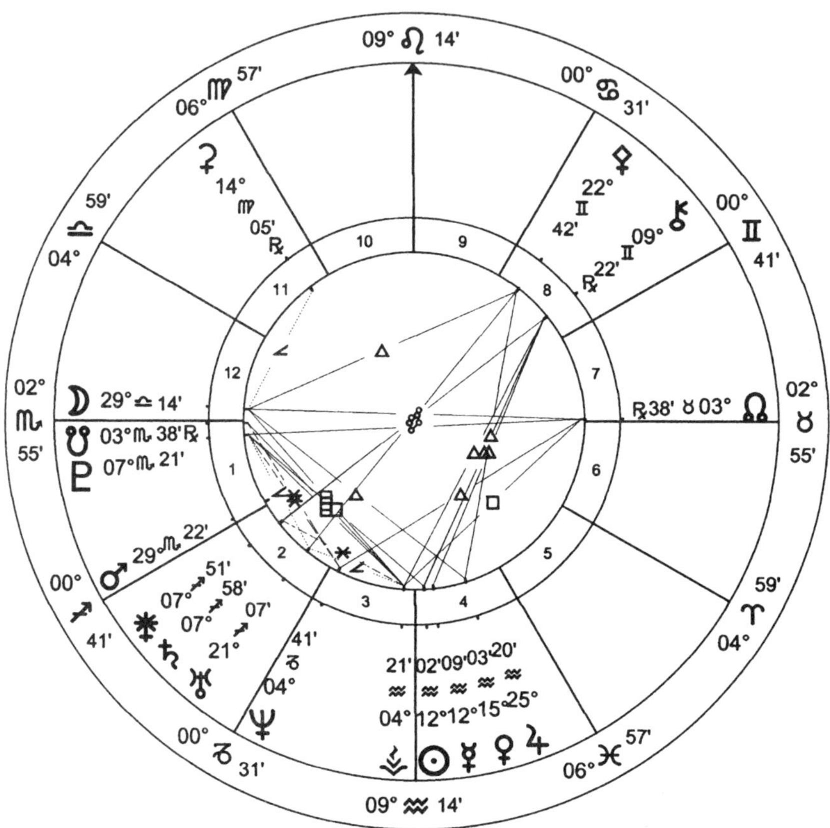

natal seventh house and Jupiter rules the natal eleventh and second houses, J&J's seventh house trade volume was affected, resulting in depletion in the eleventh house treasury and the second house of moneymaking activities. Neptune was also involved in the square. Neptune, like Dionysus, dismembers and separates as well as dissolves the current form.

Solar arc Saturn was at 16° Scorpio, conjunct natal Jupiter at 16° Scorpio and very close to a conjunction of the natal Sun at 18° of Scorpio in the ninth. The solar arc North Node was at 23° Scorpio on the natal Midheaven (public reputation) at 22° Scorpio, again squaring the pre-natal eclipse of 26° Leo and closely conjunct the Solar Eclipse of 1985 at 20° Scorpio bringing the company before the public eye.

Solar arc Venus moving through the natal twelfth house of unseen activity did not lend itself to popularity, but since it was in the twelfth, which is associated with research and development, the square to Uranus over that next year signified a creative (Venus) solution to the tragedy, the now well-known caplets. In the ensuing months, J&J had placed gel capsules on the market during the time that transiting

Illustration 54

Event: David Clare Phone Call, Feb. 10, 1986, 3:07pm EST + 5:00, New Brunswick, NJ, 40°N29'10" 074°W27'08"

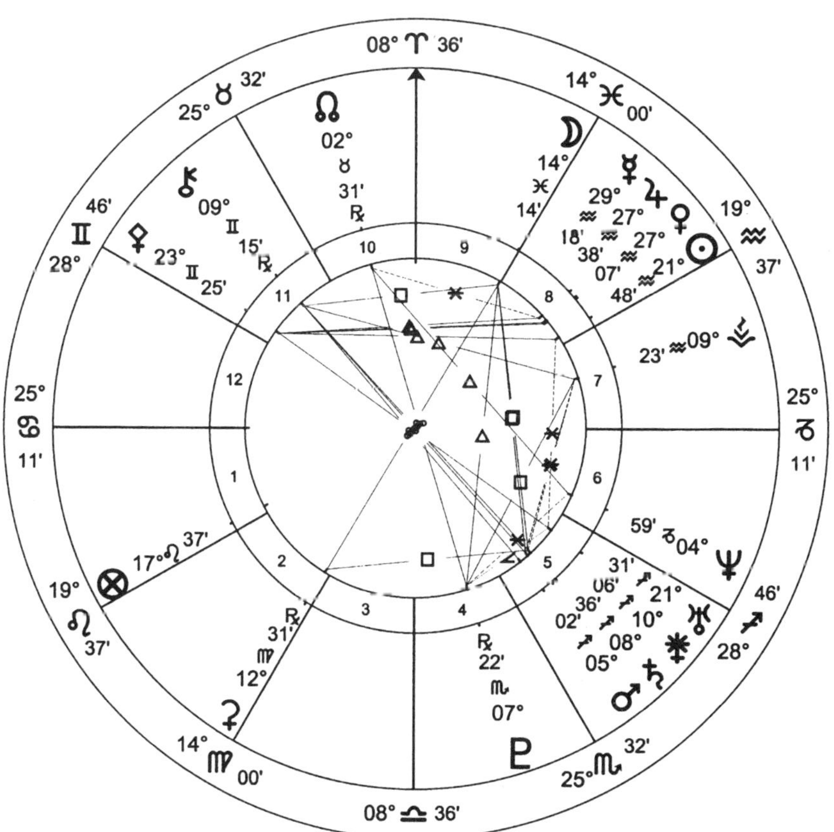

Jupiter was in early degrees of Gemini trining J & J's natal Venus in the eighth at 3° of Libra.

Solar arc Uranus was at 24° Capricorn, which may imply an earlier incorporation time. If the incorporation Ascendant were approximately 24° of Capricorn, then progressed Uranus on the natal Ascendant could indicate a sudden awakening to all concerned. Again reviewing the David Clare phone call chart (Illustration 54), the last chart to look at in this drama as the poisonings were being reported. This event chart can also be used as a transit chart to the natal. 25° Cancer Ascendant is almost the exact opposite of the natal chart's Ascendant at approximately 29° of Capricorn, indicating a mirror image or reflection of what J&J was about to experience.

The event chart Sun (the co-ruler of the intercepted natal seventh) was at 21° of Aquarius. This opposed the pre-natal eclipse in the seventh and squared natal Jupiter at 16° Scorpio, forming a very challenging T-square to natal Sun, Neptune, and the pre-natal eclipse point at 26° of Leo. This combined with the former aspects to form a Grand Cross!

The event Moon was at 14° Pisces opposing the natal Moon in the eighth house at 13° Virgo and natal Mars at 15° Virgo. It was also squaring the solar return Mercury/Uranus conjunction in the middle degrees of Sagittarius.

Transiting Venus was at 27° of Aquarius, again opposing the pre-natal eclipse and square natal Neptune (drugs/sabotage) at 28° Taurus while widely squaring the natal Sun at 18° Scorpio. The same squares to Neptune and the Sun and the opposition to the pre-natal eclipse at 26 ° Leo were activated by transiting Jupiter at 27° Aquarius and transiting Mercury at 29° Aquarius. Transiting Neptune was at 4° Capricorn, just past a square to natal Venus at 3° Libra in the eighth. Again, and again, and again, Neptune is disturbingly involved.

Pluto also played in with some stress aspects. From the time of the company's solar return in 1985 to the February

1986 event, transiting Saturn had moved from 29° Scorpio to 8° Sagittarius, opposing natal Pluto at 4° Gemini in the fourth house. This indicated a need for the company to transform itself by careful research for the future. Meanwhile, transiting Pluto at 7° Scorpio was squaring natal Saturn at 6° Leo in the seventh house.

In fact, Pluto had just stationed retrograde at this degree on February 8, 1986! It is the experience of this author that when Pluto retrogrades or goes direct, Plutonian events (tragedies, abandonment, deaths) are prominent in the news. The transit of Pluto squaring Saturn, the natal ruler of this chart, indicates loss or literally a killing off of the established order.

Since Mars tends to be the trigger for events it wasn't surprising to find transiting Mars at 5° Sagittarius having just opposed natal Pluto at 4° Gemini in the fourth house. This was the very same position of transiting Mars at the time of the first Tylenol poisonings in Chicago on September 29, 1982! 5° of Sagittarius has its solstice point at 25° of Capricorn, the approximate degree of the company's Ascendant.

When a company chart is strongly activated by stressful aspects in the solar return, the transits and the solar arcs to the natal, caution needs to be exercised. Of course, the converse is true. When all of the above have positive aspects, it can indicate a major company expansion. The corporation chart is a living entity that can be read as accurately and specifically as a natal chart.

Using a Midnight Time

We can use a midnight time to work with incorporation charts. In several states, the corporation legally begins on midnight of the day of incorporation. We still use the legal place of incorporation, but approaching it from the midnight perspective provides us with additional analysis opportunities. This will invariably place the Sun in the fourth house.

When we use the Noon birth time the Sun is at the Midheaven position, placing the symbol for the CEO, the Sun, at the apex of the chart and thus, the activities of the corporation through the eyes of the company's leader. Each Astrological analyst uses what works for him or her in terms of the time. It is important to try both techniques. However, it is always preferred that we have the exact time of incorporation as mentioned earlier in this chapter. The incorporation chart is the chart that explains the activities both seen and unseen of the company.

First Trade Charts

The First Trade chart gives us yet another perspective of how to read the trading activity of the company. Bill Meridian, who has written an excellent book on the subject entitled Planetary Stock Trading, first published in 1994, and revised in 1998, has done extensive research.

First trade charts are calculated for when the CEO of a company buys the first public offerings of the stock. Up until September 1985, the New York Stock Exchange opened trading at 10:00 AM, but after September 1985, trading began at 9:30 AM. [14]

Incorporation Dates & Times

Grace K. Morris, a well-known business astrologer from Oak Lawn, Illinois, who specializes in incorporation work, states that you can call the State of Delaware at (302) 739-3073. Press 0 for the operator and request the date and time of incorporation. You are allowed three inquiries per call.

Have ready the exact name of the company such as Texas Instruments Incorporated, CDI Corp., (you must have commas, hyphens, and exact abbreviations, use Moody's or Value Line for this information). Be sure that the company is incorporated in Delaware. If it is incorporated in its state capitol, they may give you a date at which time the company began doing business in Delaware (this is NOT a Delaware incorporation, it's known as a foreign incorporation).

Another area of delineation is the area of real estate transactions. One of the classic business cycles is the cycle of real estate. Having been in the real estate business in California for several years and still having my real estate license, a large portion of my clientele is involved in this industry as agents and brokers, both real estate and mortgage. The timing in a real estate transaction is imperative for a successful transaction to transpire.

I began learning about this cycle from Alice Q. Reichard in the early 1970's and subsequently learned from various sources and after years of observation, began to put together some formulas and projections for these cycles. Over the years I have applied that information and incorporated my own. In the following chapter, I cover the career horoscopes of those in the industry, some transaction charts, as well as some long-term projections for the industry based on its 18.6-year cycle.

[14] Bill Meridian, Planetary Stock Trading, Revised and Updated, (New York: Cycles Research Publications, 1998), Page 7.

This chapter was released, with permission, from Llewellyn Publishing's Financial Astrology for the 1990s, published in 1991, and one of two chapters for which Georgia Stathis was the author.

CHAPTER 11

THE REAL ESTATE PROCESS

It has been said that the base of all wealth is real estate. The condition of wealth involves money, property, abundance and well-being. The ability to purchase, develop, and sell real estate can be seen in the horoscope. This process uses both masculine and feminine energy, with all of the planets involved in the process.

The masculine planets are the Sun, Mars, Jupiter and Uranus and the feminine planets are the Moon, Venus, Saturn, Neptune, and Pluto. Mercury, the planet that rules agents, communication, contracts, and sales, has no particular gender affinity.

The Moon, ruled by Cancer, is the designated ruler of property and the natural fourth house, which usually depicts early home life and family. Moving vertically to the top of this axis, we find Saturn, ruled by Capricorn as the natural ruler of the tenth house. Saturn is the designated ruler of real estate, including the buildings and any improvements on it, and any adjoining assets therein, including minerals, water and petroleum. Saturn is the outward structural manifestation of the Lunar (Moon) principle of containment. Both the Moon and Saturn are feminine. The Moon is concerned with conception; it reigns over fertile territory that is movable and mobile (i.e. watery), whereas Saturn is finite, structured and concrete.

THE LUNAR NODES

The Moon's Nodes transit through one complete cycle approximately every 18.6 years. The real estate industry calls this the Brenner cycle, but astrologers refer to it as the Nodal Cycle. It is important to remember that the Nodes are the points formed where the Moon's orbit intersects the path of the Earth's orbit around the Sun (the ecliptic). The Moon displays public response. When the North Node transits through Cancer prices and interest rates peak. As the demand for property escalates there becomes a subsequent inventory shortage. While Cancer rules property, the North Node shows the trend in the marketplace. As the Node moves backwards into Capricorn, over nine years later, interest rates, prices and activity decline. Inventory of available housing is relatively high but there are fewer buyers.

The most recent examples of the real estate cycle of the Nodal transit through Cancer were in the late fall of 1981 and the spring of 2000. In 1981 the interest rates went as high as 20 + %! Because of the slowdown, real estate agents unable to make their margins abandoned the industry and thus there was a correction in activity. This coincided with of the election of a Republican Presidential administration and the start of Reaganomics. In the spring of 2000 that same cycle of the Node reoccurred. Correspondingly, interest rates have risen in an effort to slow the economy, but did not peak as to the same levels as in the 1980's. Housing prices rose markedly during the same period and in several San Francisco Bay Area counties increased 176% over the course of a few months! A severe housing shortage ensued despite a booming employment economy. Similarly, we are at the end of one presidential cycle and the beginning of another. This could forebode a republican president. In January 2001 we will have a new president as well as having just completed the latest Saturn/Jupiter conjunction on May 28, 2000, which always kicks off new economic cycles and thus, the downward trend in prices may begin again.

As the North Node moves closer to Capricorn it is a good cycle to buy property and hold it, allowing it to grow in value. When the Node is in Cancer it is a good time to liquidate since people tend to pay higher prices for property regardless of how high the interest rates. Houses are popular during cycles of the North Node in Cancer.

Of course planets that either square their transiting positions or conjunct the North or South Node positions influence Nodal Cycles. For example, when Jupiter is in Cancer (property), Capricorn (real estate), Scorpio or Taurus (the natural eighth and second house signs), activity is high and people are willing to pay higher prices. The same is true when Jupiter conjuncts, trines or sextiles the North Node. The activity is heightened since there is public confidence.

The converse is true if Saturn is aspecting the North Node. Activity declines with only a small sector of the populous participating in distress sales (i.e. foreclosures). In times when the North Node is in Capricorn or there is a strong Saturn influence, there is a possibility that properties will be available from the banks at a good price because they have gone into foreclosure. This is a buy cycle if you can hold the property as a long-term investment.

Transactions

Real estate transactions require the use of both masculine and feminine energies. After a period of incubation the buyer of property must examine several economic factors to determine the feasibility of a real estate purchase particularly when it is residential property. Is there enough income to support the purchase? Is there work available in the area? Are the schools the right ones for the children?

Upon deciding this and other personal factors, a real estate professional is engaged. The qualified agent must possess both assertive and receptive qualities. They must know the property inventory (a sixth house matter), the market, prices, and existing interest rates. Both sides of the brain the logical, rational left-brain, which is referred to as the masculine side of the brain, and the right-brained intuitive, feminine function are utilized in the decision-making process. (Both men and women have equal access to either the left or right brain.)

The agent must know to query about income, outstanding debts, and how many bedrooms, baths, etc., the buyer requires. This is called the probe, a Plutonian process.

The search begins when masculine Mars is engaged. Much time is spent moving about from one property to the next in an automobile. Automobiles are ruled by Mars and are an integral part of real estate sales. (Ed. Note: I feel Mercury and the third house have some jurisdiction over cars since they represent means of transportation.)

The agent must know when and how to close the deal so that when they find a property best suited to the buyer and the buyer's qualifications they proceed to ask the question, "Do you want to buy this property?" Ultimately, the final decision about a piece of property is formulated through a gut-level response. After the decision is made, the numbers and closing costs are calculated and then the intuitive mode kicks in. This final emotional calculator is critical in closing a sale. Remember, the Moon rules property and it represents the feminine, receptive side that helps in the final determination. The neutral Mercury principle finalizes the transaction as escrows are opened and/or lawyers are consulted. (On the East Coast, attorneys generally process the transaction, whereas on the West Coast, the processing of a transaction takes place through a title company and its escrow department.)

The Planets and Real Estate

The **Sun** usually represents speculative matters and conditions that represent some type of gamble due to its relationship to the 5th House. If the Sun is prominent and well placed by natal position or well aspected by transit, then the time might be appropriate to take a "gamble" on a piece of property.

The **Moon** reflects how the public sees you. If, for example, the Moon is in the 10th House at birth, the public might see you as one who deals in property, particularly if the Moon also rules the natal 4th House. Even the progressed secondary Moon has a great bearing on moves and home changes in some capacity. The other progressions are also significant, but you primarily use the progressed secondary Moon because it moves so rapidly and it aspects the natal chart frequently. Particularly watch when the secondary Moon moves from one sign to the next. This often indicates a change in residence of the home situation. A progression moving over one of the angles can also trigger a move.

Aspects to the Moon may move you, change the way your home might look or create an emotional explosion or change in the home. The Moon may involve one particular property — occupied or leased — while Saturn can involve several properties as well as the sale, purchase or development of property.

Mercury, the fast moving planet and the one closest to the Sun, rules communications, sales and written legal agreements — contracts. A successful transaction must have a well-placed Mercury. Individuals who do well in sales transactions usually have Mercury well-aspected.

If there are negative aspects to Mercury, the contract may be difficult to negotiate. For example, if transiting Mercury is opposing or squaring natal Jupiter or even transiting Jupiter, then you may pay too much for the property. Your judgment might be off. If Mercury is square transiting or natal Saturn, you may worry yourself needlessly concerning this particular real estate matter, no matter how long you own it! The other manifestation of Mercury square Saturn might be that something was forgotten in the contract at the time of its writing.

A good time to sign a contract is when either the Moon (property) or Saturn (real estate) is well aspected by Mercury through a trine or sextile. Always look at both the natal and the transiting planets and how they interact with each other.

If the Moon or Mercury is void of course at the time of the sale, the sale might not complete. When the move is scheduled, watch for challenging aspects to Mercury, particularly from Neptune or Jupiter, as there may be a tremendous disorientation.

Much has been said about *Mercury retrograde periods,* and they do have an effect on real estate transactions. If a new contract comes in during such a time, there may be a problem with finalizing the sale or purchase. Sometimes a particular word or paragraph is inadvertently left out when the contract is written. At other times, the intention of the purchaser to purchase may be based on some type of financial assistance from family or friends. When Mercury moves into direct motion, the missing paragraph is discovered or the funding is no longer available.

Mercury retrogrades approximately three times a year for about three weeks at a time. This is an excellent time to wrap up details in a contract or an escrow and uncover any problems about the property. One-way Mercury retrograde "works" in a real estate transaction is perhaps the property was viewed prior to the retrograde, but the buyer or seller was not necessarily sure this was what he or she wanted. In presenting the offer, precautions still need to be exercised, but sometimes if care is taken this will work out during Mercury retrograde periods.

Even if Mercury is well aspected at the time of the retrograde, there could still be a delay in the transaction. Watch the degree and minute at which Mercury begins its retrograde motion. Watch when it returns to the direct position. Particularly watch when it returns to the original "shadow" position — the same degree and minute at which it went retrograde. This is when any differences or problems are usually resolved.

Venus, the natural ruler of the 2nd and 7th Houses, governs money, cash flow, legal papers, and contracts. If Venus is well placed, it often indicates a natural ability to make things happen, particularly if it is well aspected at the time of a transaction in either the natal or event chart. If it is moving in retrograde motion, it may indicate either a delay in receiving funds or an inability to get the funds necessary for a purchase. Luckily, Venus only retrogrades about once every two years for about six weeks. When it does, however, you must be cautious, because the purchase you decide on may not be entirely appropriate to your needs, or the buyer or seller might change his or her mind. Venus retrograde may also indicate that you settle for less than you really want.

Mars is the planet that triggers the gun. The entire sky can be set up for action, but action only occurs when Mars comes along and sets it off. Where Mars is placed in the event chart is where stress will be experienced or where action takes place. For example, if it is placed in the 1st House of the chart, the seller might be agitated. Placed in the 4th House, the final outcome, the deal might not close or there may be trouble with the structure or the plumbing. Placed in the 2nd House of cash flow and resources, there could be difficulty in raising the capital to purchase the property.

This is not to say that wherever Mars is placed, you will find trouble. The other side of Mars' energy is that of courage and confidence. Mars placements in the chart may indicate areas in which you keep your nose to the grindstone.

Mars in the 2nd House, while it can indicate difficulty in getting funds, may also indicate your all-out effort to pursue and obtain those funds for a successful completion of purchase.

In a horary chart, if a question is asked about signing a contract and the Moon's last aspect was to Mars, some feel it is not a good time to close. If transiting Saturn is squaring Mars, people might easily be upset or angered.

Jupiter well-aspected to the 4th House ruler or placed in the 4th House of the horoscope can indicate luck in real estate matters. If this is found in a chart for a transaction, it might indicate a successful consummation of the deal. If transiting Jupiter is positively aspecting natal Saturn or the ruler of the 4th House, it often indicates a positive move in a real estate transaction.

Jupiter in flowing aspect to the Sun or Moon often indicates a positive outcome for a transaction. With the Moon (property) and Mercury (contracts) well-aspected, it is an indication of a good contract — a good buy. Mercury rules sales, so if Jupiter is in negative aspect to Mercury, you should check to see that you are not paying too much for the property.

Saturn was mentioned earlier as the ruler of real estate. It invariably takes an aspect to Saturn to purchase or let go of real estate or to enter a career in the building or real estate industry. Positive aspects by transit or natally between Saturn and Jupiter indicate positive real estate potential. Transiting Jupiter conjuncting, trining or sextiling Saturn indicates great times for property purchase.

Prior to telescopes and the discovery of the outer planets, Saturn was also assigned the rulership of Aquarius. In modern times the rulership of Aquarius has been given to Uranus. **Uranus** also has its place in the delineation of real estate matters. It rules the "big dealers": subdivisions, developments, commercial property, REITS (real estate investment trusts) and leasing specialists, particularly if strong Pluto energy is also indicated.

Uranus prominent in the horoscope indicates an individual who has the ability to put together in an innovative way, groups of people who collaborate on large real estate projects and work with syndications. Transiting Jupiter conjuncting, trining, or sextiling Uranus could indicate a very lucky, almost windfall-like possibility for any large project, development or leasing.

Neptune has had a lot of bad press concerning financial transactions. It may show confused judgment, misinformation and looking at deals through rose-colored glasses, particularly if it is poorly aspected by transit at the time of the transaction. A property may be over inflated price-wise, or you as the purchaser may misjudge what you can afford to pay. You could purchase at a times when things are beyond your current means.

The positive side of Neptune is the ability to visualize the potential in a property and to realize your vision. In a lecture about the pre-natal eclipse, Buz Meyers talks about Neptune/Pisces energy. He states that the nature of this energy is to act as a bridge and to reprocess negative into positive.

A strong Neptune placement, well-aspected natally or by transit, can give those involved in the transaction insight into how to improve the property, but favorable aspects to Saturn or Pluto must also be operating. Transiting Jupiter positively aspecting Neptune can help you realize your vision and aid in your inspiration.

A prominent **Pluto** might indicate a talent in renovating large shopping centers or building complexes that need refurbishing before they exhibit profitability.

Strong aspects to Uranus or Pluto can indicate the development or transformation of pieces of property as well as redevelopment. Strong, positive aspects to Pluto by itself may also enhance the ability to acquire loans and funding. The converse is also true. If there are negative aspects to Pluto, you may miss out on the opportunity to acquire funds or even have to declare bankruptcy if other factors in the horoscope confirm this.

THE HOUSES

In defining the houses both the natal horoscope and the event chart can be used. The time to use to set up a chart for the real estate transaction, the event, can be found on the final contract. When a transaction is consummated, the date and time are recorded next to the signatures of the purchasers and the sellers. At that moment, the **event chart** can be erected.

The **1st House** represents the seller — how he or she views the transaction.

The **2nd House** is the immediate cash at hand — the cash flow. It also represents other resources that are available in a transaction in other property for trade; tangible assets like valued stones, furniture and refrigerators can be compensation for a transaction.

The **3rd House** represents the signing of the contract, the communication in the transaction. Negatively it shows the loss of property (the 12th House from the natal 4th).

The **4th House** represents the property itself, as well as how one deals with it. It also indicates vacant property and property damage particularly in the plumbing. In corporation charts it represents warehouses and factories held by a company. As in horary Astrology, the 4th House can also indicate the outcome of an event.

Many planets in your 4th House often suggest that real estate might be a suitable choice for your profession or that you could profit from real estate holdings. This is particularly true if natal Pluto is placed here and is well aspected.

Traditionally, the **5th House** signifies speculation or taking a gamble on property. It is also an indicator of income from real estate (the 2nd from the 4th House). Sometimes recreational property is suggested by this house or income from recreational property. For example, a man was part owner of a duck club, and the income generated from the club plus the pleasure the individual received from going to his "investment", was a perfect combination of how this house works. When transiting Jupiter passed through his natal 5th House, the government offered to pay his group for NOT planting rice, which many clubs grow to attract the ducks. At this point they turned around and sold the surplus rice for profit!

The **6th House** of the chart reveals the agent, the tenants in a leasing situation, income property and the logistics of the real estate contract.

The **7th House** is simply the buyer of the property. It can also designate legal contracts.

The **8th House** represents the estate, a will, a settlement, or a business or marriage partnership's assets (the 2nd from the 7th). It depicts the joint holdings of a couple or a business partnership. In an individual's chart, it also indicates whether there is positive or negative financial support from the partner as well as inheritance possibilities. It can define the qualities of the mortgage, the interest rates, and the insurance required. Probate is represented by the 8th, as well as the escrow itself, which includes the title search.

Taxes are also an important part of real estate transactions, and anything related to taxes comes from the 8th House. Jupiter in this house or Sagittarius on this cusp can indicate luck in investment matters with a partner, inheritance, or investments that prosper. So can Venus in or ruling this house.

The **9th House** shows the money that comes from an estate or settlement as well as the care taking and any legal situations surrounding property.

The **10th House** indicates landowners, landlords, land developers, land dealers, and land in general.

The **11th House** designates money that comes from the individual's business or career, the treasury, and it can also indicate, if negatively aspected, the loss of property. Sometimes loss is also assigned to the 12th House.

The **12th House** denotes property in foreign countries (in the Hindu system, the 12th is the house of gestation and foreigners), or it can indicate the end of a situation.

Rulerships, Transits and Delineation

One of the most important delineation devices that can be used when interpreting a horoscope is to observe the planets, the house in which they are placed and the houses they rule. This is particularly true concerning real estate matters. Transits to these points set things in motion. The following are some case studies that demonstrate this concept. (All charts shown use the Koch House System). The first chart illustrates how to interpret a real estate event. This person (Illustration 55) is a woman born on November 19, 1943.

For several years she had been a manufacturers' representative for various furniture lines. Energetic and industrious she decided two and a half years before the following event that she wanted to purchase old properties and then refurbish them. This is an excellent choice with her natal Pluto in the fourth house sextiling both Venus and Uranus thereby indicating an uncanny ability to work hard and fix property (Venus in the sixth house) and turning it around to

Illustration 55

Female: Rebuilt Homes, Nov. 19, 1943, 4:15pm PWT + 7:00, Los Angeles, CA, 34°N03'08" 118°W14'34"

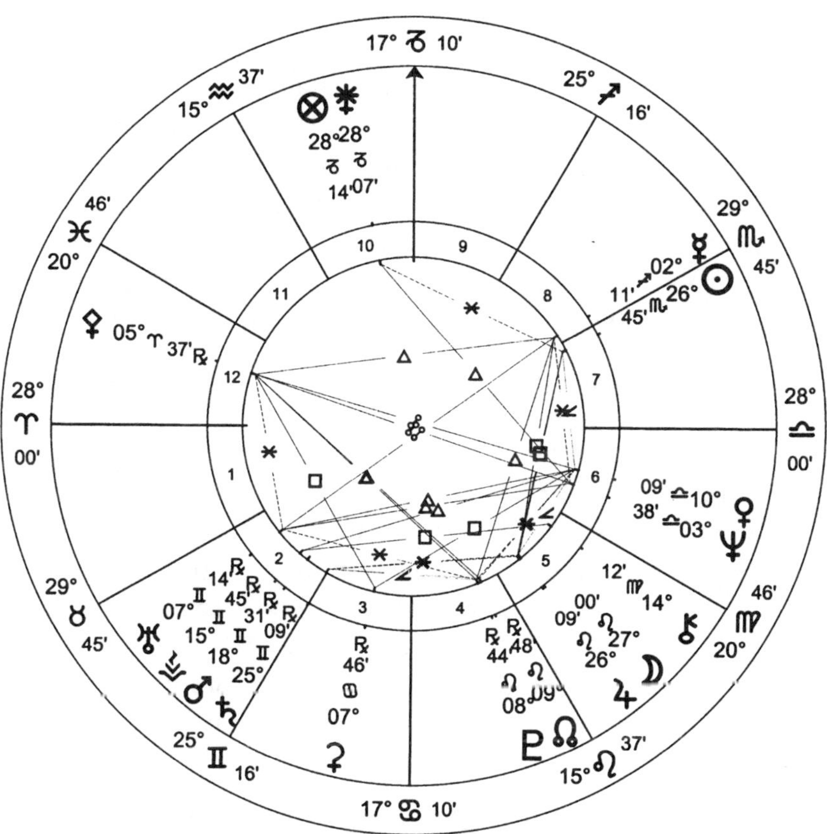

make it financially profitable (Uranus in the second house). The high degree of fire elements in her chart gives her the needed physical stamina required to complete the work.

In 1987, she purchased a huge, older home with tremendous character and true potential. Note her Leo Moon, which loves elegance. For one year she and a friend tore out walls and floors, built new decks and refinished, repainted and restored the home. The home turned out to be an exquisite piece of art, produced through a labor of love. Note the Moon (property and ruler of her fourth house) conjunct Jupiter (ruler of luck in the fifth house of artistic ability). Even though she had purchased her materials wholesale, did the work herself and budgeted carefully, she found herself needing funds at the end of this incredible project and was prompted to sell the property. However, she was resistant to part with the house.

She received an offer on the property when transiting Venus (her second and seventh house rulers) turned retrograde. A few weeks later Mercury was also to transit retrograde. Transiting Venus and Mercury were in Gemini. When Venus began retrograde motion she had second thoughts about selling the property in spite of having accepted an offer (Venus rules the seventh house and represents the buyer).

During our consultation I advised her to prepare for the buyer to ask for some type of change in the contract when Mercury (contracts) turned retrograde. This would void the original contract allowing her to back out of her legal obligation and to retain the property. The buyer did indeed counter with a demand for an additional reduction of $6500 on the selling price, thus enabling her to cancel the contract. She wrote me a letter a few weeks later, "...sometimes you have to come close to losing something before you can decide to commit to it!" an appropriate Scorpio/Pluto response.

Another way to look at this transaction was to see whether the fourth house (her property) was stronger at the time of the contract than that of the buyer (represented by the seventh house). When the fourth house is stronger at the time of a transaction the seller often retains the property.

Another woman whose birth date is April 28, 1950 (Illustration 56) was involved in the following transaction. Note the emphasis of planets in the fourth house with Saturn, the Moon (the chart ruler) and Mars in Virgo and Neptune in Libra. While transiting Uranus opposed both her Uranus and Saturn in early 1988, she suddenly inherited a house from a friend who had died (Uranus often rules windfalls). When

Illustration 56

Female: Former Pilot, Apr. 28, 1950, 9:16am EST + 5:00, Royal Oak, MI, 42°N29'22" 083°W08'41"

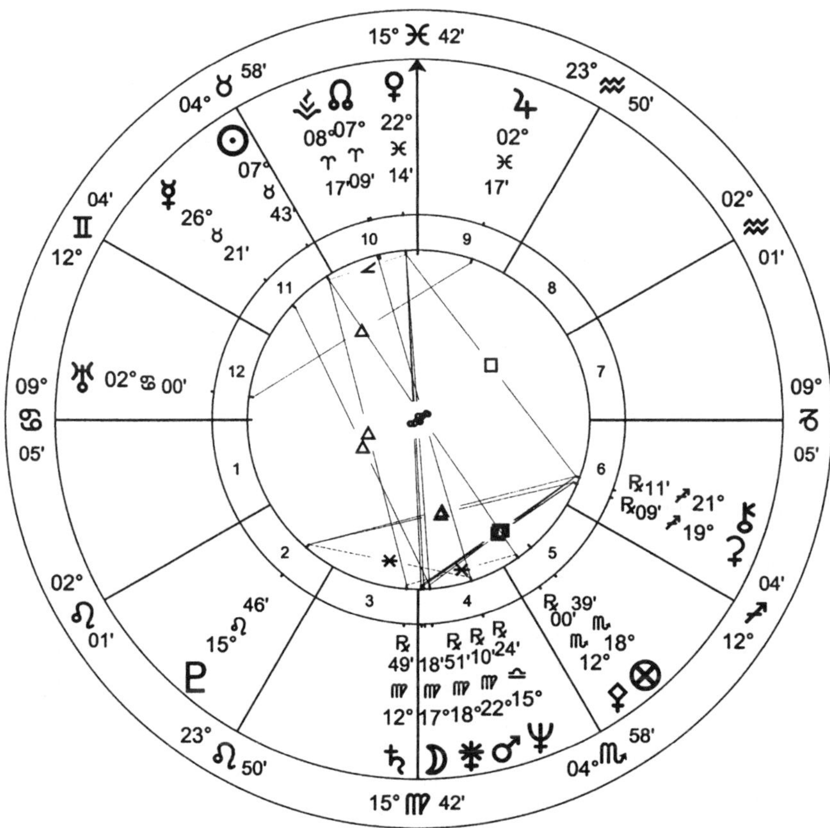

Jupiter transited over her Mercury in Taurus (ruler of her fourth house of real estate) the title was transferred to her and she had the option of either moving into the house or allowing the current renter to stay through the end of that year. Because the client was a pilot with a complicated schedule, she elected to delay the move until January of 1989 when transiting Jupiter would turn stationary direct at about 26° Taurus on her Mercury and the ruler of her fourth house of property. This was a better choice for her in light of an exact Lunar Eclipse on her Moon at 17° Virgo on September 10, 1988.

When an eclipse hits a planet at an exact degree in the natal horoscope, there is a change occurring in both the house(s) ruled by the planet and the house where the planet is posited. As noted earlier, the Moon signifies the property or the home. The change transpires either within a few days of the eclipse or 90 to 100 days following when squaring (about 90 degrees) the original point of the eclipse. An event may also happen as late as six months after the initial eclipse at the opposition point.

In her case, the alignments suggested she would experience the event three to four months later or at the beginning of 1989. Her secondary progressions for July 1, 1988 showed the Moon (the ruler of her chart as well as the assigned ruler of the home and property) at 24° Aquarius. The progressed secondary Moon moves at approximately 1° per month so when her Moon entered Pisces approximately six months later, she moved.

In the case of the progression, if the progressed Moon is changing to the next sign, there is generally a change in the way the home looks (including structural transformations) or a physical move may be imminent. At the time this woman sought advice the transiting Node in Pisces was traveling through her tenth house and soon would enter her ninth while the transiting South Node in Virgo was moving through her fourth house. Sometimes when the transiting South Node is situated in the fourth house you relinquish property and change your habits in regard to the property. She had just started having transiting Uranus opposing her Uranus at 2° Cancer in the twelfth house. When transiting Uranus begins opposing Uranus between the ages of 38 and 41, the individual awakens to the soul's purpose often presenting bigger opportunities if the person is willing to open themselves to the new experiences.

Since Uranus rules her eighth house of investments, the transiting opposition was already signaling thoughts of transforming property, and then leasing or selling it for her future retirement security. This is an excellent example of a positive use of a Uranus transit. Since Uranus seems to be the "antenna to God", messages are always coming in during this time to break out (Uranus lies outside of Saturn's visible orbit) of the box in terms of experience. When experiencing Uranus transits, there is a need to visualize them in a positive light. Many things fall into place in life when visions are followed.

Real Estate Vocational Indicators

The following are charts of individuals involved in real estate in different positions. Included are a manager who started out as an agent, an investor who is still an agent, a real estate marketing expert, and two people who work with subdivisions — one sells and the other owns and sells.

The first example is a woman born on October 27, 1937 (Illustration 57). Her Ascendant is Sagittarius, ruled by Jupiter, an excellent rising sign for people in the sales professions. She has Saturn (ruler of real estate) in her fourth house. This placement seems to be fairly common in the real estate profession. Most of her fourth house is Aries, ruled by Mars, which falls in her second house of cash flow, earned income and money. It conjuncts Jupiter, which is her chart ruler. She immediately became a high-powered agent and then a manager. Venus, the ruler of money and funds, falls in her tenth house of career; it is also the ruler of her sixth house of work. This is another indicator of professional involvement in tangible assets.

Notice the high concentration of earth and water elements in this chart. The earth planets form a grand trine, and Saturn opposes Venus, another indicator of a structured profession. This opposition indicates someone who can manage quite unemotionally and effectively. She can also per-

Illustration 57

Female: Real Estate Manager, Oct. 27, 1937, 10:17am CST +6:00, Amarillo, TX, 35°N13'19" 101°W49'51"

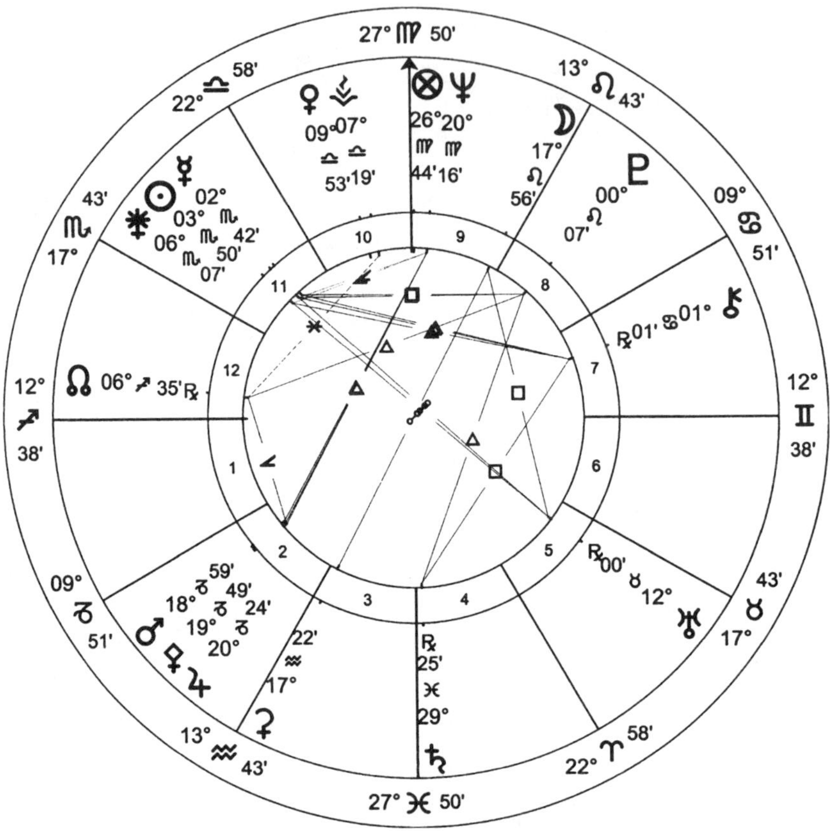

suade people to cooperate with her because Venus falls in the tenth house; she is viewed as responsible and effective, and is also well liked.

The following chart (Illustration 58) is of a man who is a real estate broker and investor. The case study about his career is covered in the chapter on the Saturn/Jupiter Career Cycle. He was born on June 19, 1941. In the early 1940's Saturn and Uranus were conjunct in Taurus, which is ruled by Venus, and is placed in his chart along with Jupiter in Gemini. There is a strong earth concentration in this chart, particularly in the fourth house of property.

His Ascendant is Capricorn, ruled by Saturn, which also falls in his fourth house. Land, property and real estate are a very tangible part of his life. Since Uranus is in his fourth, forming a grand earth trine with the Ascendant and Neptune in the eighth house of investments, this indicates excellent intuition about money and property matters. Natal Jupiter in the fifth house of speculation rules both Sagittarius and Pisces. Pisces is intercepted in his second house of cash flow. His Moon is also in Taurus and rules property, but in his chart it also rules his seventh house of how he deals with other people. It is placed in his third house of communication and sales.

Illustration 58

Male: Agent/Broker, Jun. 19, 1941

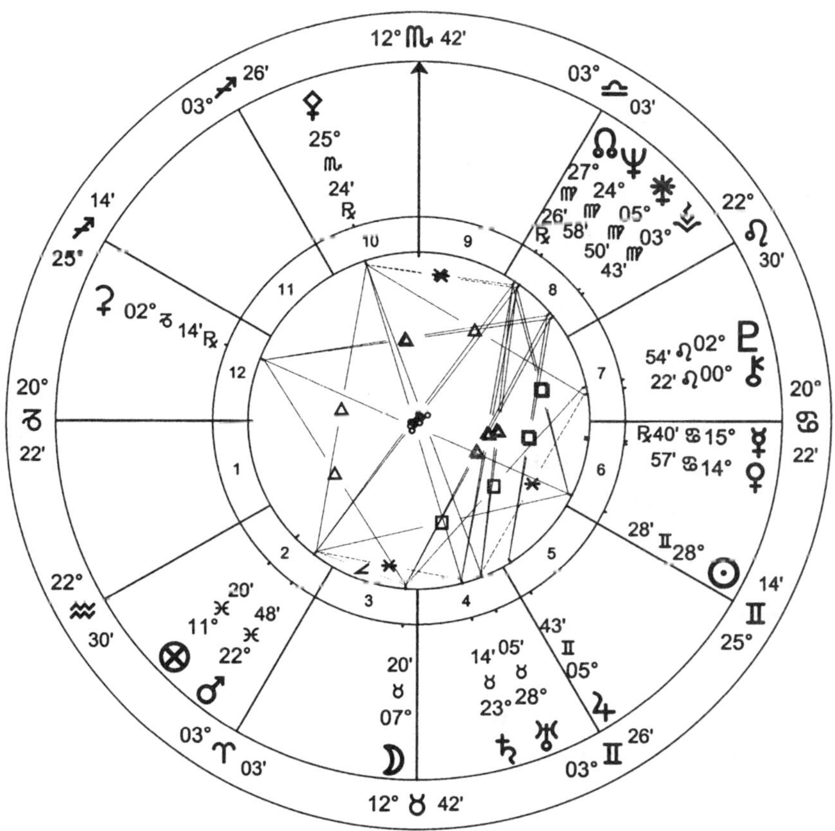

The Sun in Gemini, the sign of communication, Mercury, the planet of sales, and Venus, ruler of money, are all placed in the sixth house of service and work. He operates in a service profession, which involves a tremendous amount of detail work (sixth house), but he is also an agent. The sixth signifies the agent and also income property. He and his family own income property, which they lease. Note the Uranus placement (leasing) in the sixth house of both real estate and family. As mentioned earlier, Uranus also rules the big deals and the developers. At the time that Jupiter transited through his fourth house, his family decided to invest in a very large piece of property that needed subdividing. As the transit continued, they completed the subdividing with relative ease and sold it for a profit very shortly thereafter to a developer (Uranus).

A woman born on December 31, 1937, which can be seen again in Illustration 59, was a marketing specialist. Note the high concentration of planets in her ninth house of sales and marketing. Her fourth house cusp is Cancer (property), and her tenth house cusp is Capricorn. She is a real estate marketing expert for a large developer. Uranus is in the first house in Taurus. Venus, which rules her second house, is conjunct Mercury in the ninth house of marketing. She is able to communicate effectively and promote sales. Venus, Mercury, and the Sun in Capricorn, all trine Uranus in Taurus, are excellent aspects for big projects. On a more personal note, she has Pluto in her fourth house in Cancer. She has bought and sold a lot of property, each time at a profit. She refurbishes the properties herself (Aries Ascendant) through painting, building decks and reconstructing rooms. The refurbishing guarantees her a tremendous amount of profit over a fairly short span of time. Pluto trines Saturn, an auspicious aspect for making money with real estate, particularly since Pluto rules Scorpio her eighth house of investments.

The next chart (Illustration 60) is of a woman born on July 31, 1952, who sells subdivisions. Note her Aries Ascendant with the ruler Mars in the seventh house of buyers trining her

Illustration 59

Female: Marketing Director. Builder, Dec. 31, 1937, 12:03pm PST + 8:00, Portland, OR, 45°N20'27" 122°W37'

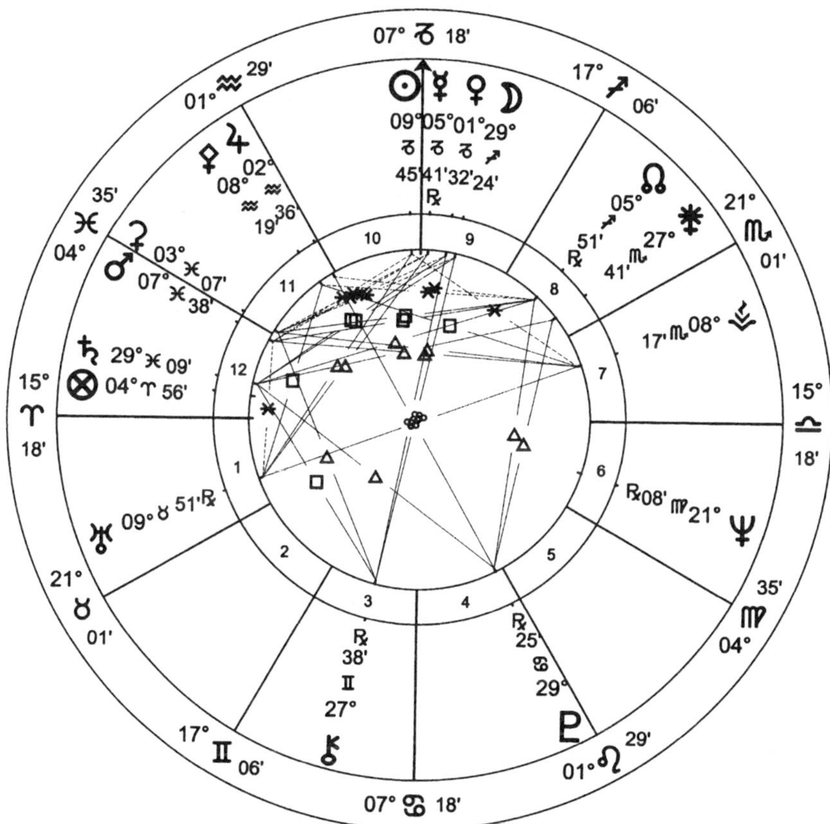

Uranus, which rules subdivisions. Uranus is angular in her fourth house in Cancer, the sign of property. Her Sun is in Leo in her fourth. Leo is on the cusp of her fifth house of speculation. The property signs Cancer and Capricorn are on the fourth and tenth house cusps, respectively. The rulers, the Moon and Saturn, are sextile. The Moon is in the eighth house of other peoples' monies, and Saturn is in the sixth house of the agent conjunct Neptune. She helps people to achieve their vision.

A potent Jupiter is one indicator of strong sales abilities. It is in her first house and has challenging squares to Venus, Pluto and widely to Mercury, all in Leo in the speculative fifth house.

Illustration 60

Female: Subdivision Sales, Jul. 31, 1952, 11:17pm PDT + 7:00, Whittier, CA, 33°N58'45" 118°W01'55"

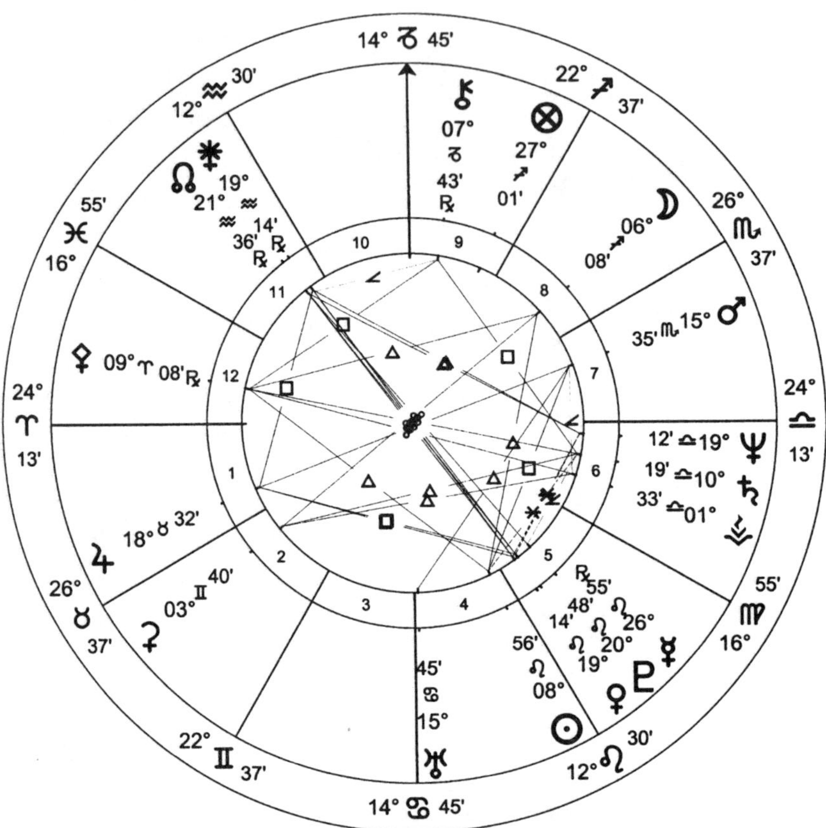

One of the ventures she considered was investing in recreational property, buying properties that need work and turning them into healing and health facilities. Note the above-mentioned concentration of Leo planets in the fifth house of speculation, fun and recreation. Note also the wide Saturn conjunction to Neptune in the sixth house. She has a strong interest in healing, and when transiting Saturn and Neptune conjuncted in 1989 and 1990, her sixth house became activated for the first time since birth as an adult so that she could integrate her investment knowledge with her healing interests. A Saturn conjunction to Neptune can indicate an ability to crystallize (Saturn) one's vision (Neptune)

once you believe in yourself. During the course of this conjunction from 1989 to 1990, she was able to sell some land and purchase property in another state, most of which she was planning on leasing to organic produce growers. The remainder of the land she planned to use for a healing institute. This was the plan she had at the time of this writing.

The last chart is of a woman born September 18, 1934 (Illustration 61). She used to sell and own subdivisions, was very good at this, and became quite wealthy with assets she acquired as the result of this profession. She has a Libra Ascendant, and Cancer/Capricorn tenth/fourth house cusps.

Illustration 61

Female: Subdivision Owner, Sep. 18, 1934, 7:45am CST + 6:00, San Antonio, TX, 29°N25'26" 098°W29'36"

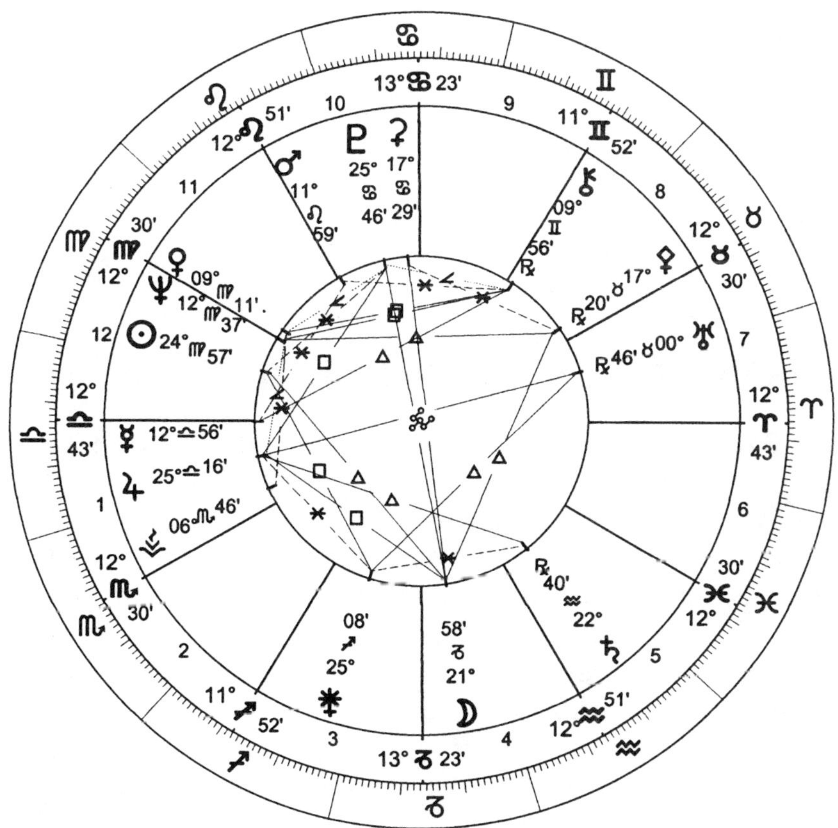

The ruler of her tenth, the Moon in Capricorn, is in her fourth house of real estate. The trine between Moon and the Sun suggests fortunate speculation. The ruler of her chart is Venus, and it trines Uranus, indicator of subdivisions, again angular. Saturn, the ruler of real estate and her fourth house, is in Aquarius in the fifth house of speculation. Saturn forms a trine to Jupiter in Libra in the first house—an excellent combination for success in real estate. Jupiter again is placed in the first house of the seller. So is Mercury, indicative of communication and sales ability.

She, too, has an angular Pluto in Cancer in the tenth house of career. She is a powerful woman in the eyes of the public (tenth house). Note the angular Mars, ruler of her seventh house of buyers, sextiling her Mercury, ruler of communications and contracts. This is an excellent configuration for the successful consummation of transactions. These are just a few examples of charts of people in various levels of the real estate industry and are presented here as an example of how to discover vocational potential in this particular industry.

Long-Term Projections for the Real Estate Industry

The outer planets (Uranus, Neptune and Pluto) have to do with future and outer trends in various industries. They are beyond physical sight and for this reason we look at them as indicators of the future. For example over the last two decades there have been a series of synodic cycles involving the planet Saturn, the ruler of real estate. By synodic, we mean relatively rare alignments of the outlying planets, which only occur once every so many years. In 1981, Saturn and Jupiter conjuncted in Libra as they did in 2000 in Taurus; in 1982, Saturn conjuncted Pluto also in

Libra; in 1988, Saturn conjuncted Uranus three separate times in Sagittarius and Capricorn; and in 1989, Saturn conjuncted Neptune in Capricorn.

When Saturn was conjunct Jupiter in the early 1980s, interest rates and property values expanded out of sight in terms of affordability, as did property values again in 2000. When the interest rates jumped outrageously in the early 1980s, many in the profession fled the field. Jupiter represents the professional sales field and the conjunction of these two planets might imply some sort of exodus or a new vision or philosophy (Jupiter) in the field. The same was true in the following years as banks tightened their belts and loans for property ended up being as difficult to obtain as water in the desert.

Whenever Saturn conjuncts Uranus, major changes occur in the real estate industry. This occurred during the early 1940s when they were conjunct in Taurus. Contractors changed from building one home at a time to building tract housing in order to accommodate the influx of the post-war population.

In the 2000 conjunction of Saturn and Jupiter in Taurus, we witnessed large growth patterns towards the development of assisted living facilities for the aged. In Contra Costa County, in Northern California, the assisted living facilities are becoming increasingly sophisticated in terms of what they offer residents as the competition for high-end facilities continues. Since Saturn rules the elderly, Jupiter rules opportunity, and Taurus rules land and property, assisted living facilities will prove to be major moneymakers during the course of the next twenty years as aging baby boomers vie for housing.

It was also during this time that a new co-housing movement began laying down roots. This is a concept whereby people buy regular homes or condominiums, but the complex is designed around a central garden and/or central cooking facility in which owners may or may not participate. Think of it as the new extended family scenario.

During the early 1940's, an innovative idea that promised to improve vehicular travel was conceived and executed. It was the Interstate highway system. It was developed to accommodate the growing population. Now with these upcoming conjunctions, we see people traveling a different way, via telecommuting on their computers as the information highway and its technology has moved us to new levels of travel and communications.

Since the last conjunction of Saturn and Uranus in late Sagittarius/early Capricorn, real estate professionals have been required to become computer literate. The Multiple Listing Services are accessible nationwide on computers.

Meanwhile, the paperwork involved in real estate transactions has become so complicated that it easily compares to the paperwork required of a qualified attorney. In California, future real estate agents are now required to have several hours of college credit in order to take the real estate licensing exam. Because of the added dimension of computer requirements in this industry, it is very likely that at some point the licensing will consist of not just agents versus brokers, but, perhaps Level 1, Level 2, or Level 3 agents who also have computer technology as part of their training. There are also courses offered on-line for people to take their real estate license. This has happened quite suddenly with 1988's conjunction of Saturn and Uranus in Sagittarius, which rules education. In the industry itself, there is a greater need for an "official education." For years there has been talk of making a real estate license a four-year degree and grandfathering in those agents who already have licenses. Since Uranus, the planet of motivation, is involved in this conjunction, the education required is somewhat different from a conventional education. The idea of an advanced Bachelor or Master's degree in real estate is not as inconceivable as it has sounded in the past.

Since Uranus rules commissions, one of the things we have seen is a change in the commission structure of the industry. Most companies carry errors and omission insurance for their agents so that, if there is any conflict, the company as well as the agent is protected. For this, the broker usually takes half of the commission on one side or the other of the transaction. The commissions are negotiable, but generally speaking the agent receives roughly one-quarter division of the total commission. The possibility of giving the real estate agent a larger piece of the pie along with more of the responsibility is a possibility in real estate companies in the coming years. Some agents are even charging a per hour fee for the information they now give free in order to make a sale. Remember, Uranus rules public information, consulting and commissions! The accessibility to a higher volume of commissions has also become possible due to the full access agents have to properties being bought and sold not only through other real estate companies, but also through such government programs as H.U.D., whose properties can be found at such websites as www.goldenfeather.com.

Uranus rules awakening, invention, and revolutionary new ways of doing things, and with Saturn, which also rules construction and building materials, we see new materials everyday that improve the quality of construction, particularly those in earthquake-prone zones, such as California. I have already mentioned the connection between Uranus with computers and electronics. Not only are the local boards of realtors hooked up to their agents' computers, but also agents now have options of purchasing memberships in other adjacent local boards of real estate, which gives them a greater demographic market from which to buy and sell property. An agent has more freedom now, since they can work from their office, their home, and their car or from another state!

Uranus' other recent innovations include the now common and indispensable cellular phone and Palm Pilot. Even the signs that are posted in front of a residence to announce that it is available for sale are changing because agents now place their email addresses and their websites where they used to post phone numbers. There are even "drive by" signs that are on a radio frequency allowing an agent driving by in a car with the necessary equipment to hook up to that sign and get the details about that particular piece of property! Not very popular yet, but they are available.

Portable computers are used so that a salesperson on the road has accessibility to information such as current closing costs, and the status of loans, escrows, and interest information. The real estate agent entering the industry is being challenged in quite a different way than in the past. If an agent is computer-phobic, he or she has to get over this quickly. An agent is now required to input all the new sales data directly into the computer in the office, which in turn connects to the main computer bank, making the information instantly available to the entire real estate community through the Multiple Listing Service or, for some very large real estate companies, in their mainline computers that hold all listings for all offices in a region.

In Northern California Boards there has been what was called a "daily hot sheet", which listed properties available in the last 24-hour period. They still have it, but it is now on computer. The new technology requires real estate agents to learn different skills involving the ability to work with equipment and input information. Certain real estate companies are requiring their agents to pay monthly fees for computerized marketing programs that make flyers, send birthday cards, or do form letters using their agents' listings directly off the listing program.

Since the industry standard is computerized, licenses from one state are honored by some of the other states in a kind of reciprocal agreement. The statute was called the Non-resident Reciprocity Statute. Some of the states that were involved in the past were: Washington (Scorpio), Florida (Pisces), Alabama (Sagittarius), and Alaska (Capricorn). This statute allows an agent from a cooperating state to operate in other states.

It is very possible that in the future we might have as a

standard a Global Marketplace for real estate as we do for manufactured goods. With the increasing travel that people are required to do as part of their jobs, it is possible that instead of timeshare for vacation purposes, we may witness a new term "property share" for those who have to live bi-coastally or in two different countries.

The dissolving of borders has been the result of the outer planets forming multiple conjunctions with one another. Quickly moving us from one fixed mindset to new vistas opening the doors wide for not only the real estate industry, but also many industries.

In this first book on Business Astrology (this is only the tip of the iceberg), I have attempted to cover the basics that we use in Business Astrology. Business Astrology includes vocational analysis as well as corporate and real estate planning. Financial Astrology covers the movements and cycles of the stock market. In the following chapter, I present two important case studies. I have attempted to include as part of these analyses several of the insights and techniques presented in this book.

My purpose in presenting this material is to act as a bridge over which I invite you to cross, to paraphrase one of my favorite Greek authors, Nikos Kazantzakis. Upon crossing this bridge, it is my hope that you will discover new techniques and methods in this exciting study of Business Astrology. Enjoy.

(Information found in this chapter, was first published in Llewellyn's Financial Astrology for the 1990s in 1991 and was released by written permission from Llewellyn's. Portions of this chapter have been updated from that time. I want to thank Alice Q. Reichard and Grace Morris for teaching me so much in the very early years of my career. Their wise ways spurred me on to use that initial information as the seed in the work I have done over the last 25 years).

Chapter 12

Two Case Studies

Following are two case studies. They are very basic and presented with the hope that many of the techniques presented in this book can be applied to these horoscopes. Between what you have learned and can apply and what you can see for yourself as the result of what you have learned, you should be able to see how to approach an analysis when someone comes to you as an astrologer for vocational analysis or timing ideas. Both these parties have been clients and were kind enough to allow me to interview them for use as case studies in this chapter.

Case Study #1: A Woman

(see Illustration 62)

One of the greatest struggles we all have to overcome is to wrestle with a fear. Fear is either learned or remembered. That fear is the thing that divides us and holds us frozen in a self-imposed box of terror. When we finally are conscious, we realize that the walls of those boxes are only paper and that they are thin. It is then and only then that we can step out of our self-inflicted hell. This is the challenge of Saturn as well as its gift.

Presented here is a female born in 1945 that learned to conquer a deep-seated fear. The time used is taken directly off of her birth certificate, but the data is not revealed here in

Illustration 62

Female: Case Study One, 1945

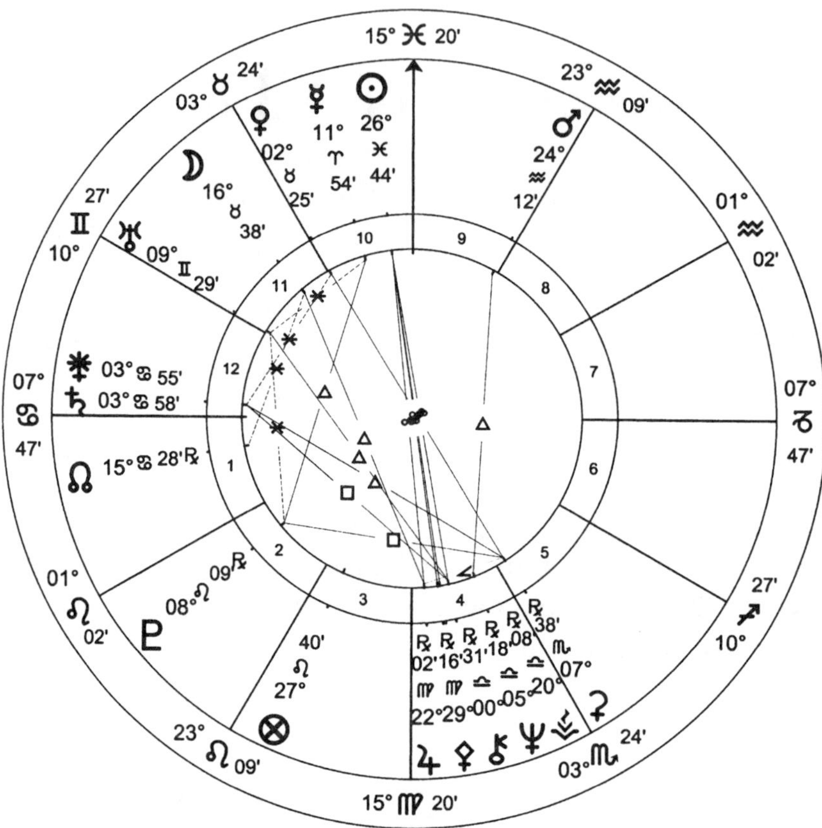

order to respect the subject's privacy. In fact, all specific chart data for the case studies was not included in this book, in order to respect the privacy of the individuals. By looking at her horoscope, you will note that she is balanced in terms of her elements and her modes or qualities. I am using the asteroids and Nodes as part of this measurement. For example, she has her Mercury, Saturn, Neptune, Chiron, Vesta, Juno, and North and South Node in cardinal signs totaling eight points. She has her Moon, Venus, Mars, Pluto, Ceres, and Part of Fortune in fixed elements totaling six points. And, she has her Sun, Jupiter, Uranus, and Pallas all in mutable modes totaling four points.

There are three fire placements, which include her Mercury, Pluto and Part Fortune. There are five earth placements, which include her Moon, Venus, Jupiter, Pallas, and South Node. There are five air placements, which include Mars, Uranus, Neptune, Chiron, and Vesta. And, finally, there are five water placements, which include the Sun, Saturn, Juno, Ceres, and North Node. By using all of these points we see a mixed signature. Other astrologers just use the planets. This is a personal decision to be made by you as to what to use. I have found that both the asteroids and the Nodes, after someone is 45 years of age, provide a deeper resonance with the individual's horoscope. In keeping with the above theme, she is natally quite capable of doing a great deal in her life. However, her strongly placed Saturn conjuncts the Ascendant, semisquares the Moon, and is square to her Neptune. There has been disillusionment, dismemberment, as well as the ability to imagine and create related to this Saturn. The latter traits having emerged in more recent years.

Her Saturn sits precariously on the twelfth house side of her Ascendant, which is 7° Cancer. Her Saturn at 3° Cancer is the first planet that crosses her birth path right before she was born. This marker has had a tremendous impact on her life. In her first seven years of life, her Sun placed at 26° Pisces 44' slowly progressed to an exact square to her Saturn by the time she entered primary school.

Her memory (twelfth house) was Saturn. She was an only child for sixteen years before her brother was born. Her mother was a homemaker and her father was an insurance adjuster. Her mother eventually went to work as a school secretary right before her brother was born. She states that her father handled the income responsibly, but that her mother (the Moon in Taurus) handled the distribution of the resources. Her recollection was that her mother was always complaining to her daughter that they didn't have any money. She also recalls that they moved some 23 times in the 18 years she lived at home because her father kept being promoted.

Since her mother always complained that they had no money, her perception (Saturn-perceived limitation semisquare the Moon) was that her parents were poor and as she states, "there was never anything there". In childhood, the years associated with the Moon, she developed a fear of ample financial security.

The first seven years of someone's life the person is in the Moon Phase of his or her life. Note the natal position of the Moon at 16° Taurus 38' semisquare to Saturn. Her Moon is in the Crescent Phase to her Sun. Therefore, we are immediately confronted with someone who has, in the course of her lifetime, had many pre-conceived psychological battles and obstacles to overcome. The difficulty that accompanies maturation in life is that we cannot really learn until we have some experiences.

In her early twenties she fell deeply in love. She knew when she married her first husband that he had a hereditary congenital heart problem. Quite suddenly, on August 29, 1969, as transiting Uranus went direct at 0° Libra 08' on her Chiron in the fourth house and, as transiting Saturn stationed at 8° Taurus 50' squaring her natal Pluto in the second house at 8° Leo 09', her first husband died of heart failure. Note that Saturn is the ruler of her seventh house, which rules partnerships. Since the Moon is associated with childhood and its memories, this sudden tragedy triggered childhood memories of not having enough security.

At the time of her husband's death, she had two children less than four years of age. As transiting Jupiter started here at early degrees of Libra, it began the First Quarter Square to her Saturn. This was the beginning of her realizing that she had two mouths to feed and no marketable skills. Terror set in. Security needs were plaguing her. She remarried in December 1970, as transiting Saturn went over her Moon. The motivation for doing this was unclear at the time of this interview. As the interviewer, I suspect that with Saturn (fear) transiting the Moon (security), part of the decision might have been based on security issues. She married a widower (Saturn) who was in the real estate business (Saturn and Moon). She adopted his one child and they had a child together on December 29, 1971. They had another child who died soon after birth in May 1973. In 1974, she was diagnosed with cervical cancer and underwent a hysterectomy, followed shortly after by gall bladder surgery.

At this time transiting Pluto was conjuncting her Chiron/ Neptune midpoint in the fourth house of the chart and squaring her Saturn in the twelfth house. Transits of Pluto move you from darkness into light and prompt sudden discovery. Transits of Pluto to Saturn can help us, through some sort of creative pursuit, heal and dismiss our fears.

In spite of these losses there were new beginnings in terms of career choices for her between 1974 and 1975. She opened a decorating business, which was an appropriate choice with the sign of Pisces on her Midheaven along with the Sun, Mercury and Venus placed in her tenth house. Her 15° Pisces 20' tenth house cusp is in the Cancer decanate of Pisces, which is ruled by the Moon and rules property. This transpired while transiting Jupiter entered the last quarter square to her Saturn. Her husband, the real estate broker, joint ventured a project with her to save money. He had her take the box seats from a stadium investment, in which he was involved, and transform them into a far more appealing venue. As the people invested in the box seats, it was her job to redesign them. These box seats were featured in the film, "Middle Age Crazy". Throughout she was unaware of the financing and income streams, just as she had been in her first marriage.

Still she cultivated individual clients for her new design business. During late 1975, she separated from her husband and continued to conduct her design business while also rearing her four children.

As transiting Jupiter passed over her Saturn in September 1977, she moved across the country. She bought a house and intended to marry after the move. However, after moving she opted not to remarry and instead built a life for herself with her children in the new home. During this new career cycle she began to find herself. There was a major turning point for her in 1980 during the first quarter square of transiting Jupiter to her Saturn. She moved, yet again, to a new home that she remodeled and started a new landscaping business with her children in March 1981. This coincided with the Synodic conjunction of Saturn and Jupiter in Libra in her fourth house, which triggered an approximate twenty years worth of work on properties.

Her landscaping business evolved into commercial work with some lucky breaks from friends and associates. Uranus in the eleventh house of friends and in its own house was being trined by the Jupiter/Saturn conjunction in the sign of Libra. Uranus rules her eighth house of income, which came from referrals from friends and acquaintances. The ruler of the Ascendant the Moon is also co-ruler of the Cancer decanate of Pisces, which is on the MC. The last large job was a condominium complex with a drainage problem. Several planets had been challenging her with squares to her Saturn the planet of fear and survival issues. Transiting Pluto, in late degrees of Libra, had been traveling through her fourth house and had just squared her North and South Nodes all of the while when she was reconstructing, reshaping, and working on the plumbing and drainage problems. Pluto rules plumbing and drainage.

She kept a close rein on her children by working seven days a week with them. This continued through 1982 until she began having trouble with her oldest child, now about 16, and she realized she had to let something go (a Pluto issue). She closed down the landscaping part of her business and returned to doing only interior design.

Late in 1982, she met and married her high school sweetheart to whom she remains married. She refocused on raising her family and remodeling home after home. In her late thirties, as transit Uranus traveled through her fifth house of speculation and opposed her natal Uranus, she became adept with financing methods and building techniques. Slowly, she began to dispel her fears surrounding money and she awoke to investing. Note, too, natal Vesta, associated with investing, in the fourth house of family and home.

Around 1985, she started to get involved with her husband's finances and realized that although he was financially successful, he wasn't the least interested in managing his money. This was an old ghost that had come back to haunt her (Pluto in the second house). Wherever Pluto is placed in the chart is where we hold a dark shadow of vulnerability and as we mature and face this shadow, become powerful and face our fears head-on and confront the cobra. At forty years of age, with transiting Pluto square Pluto, it was time to grapple with her long held fear.

She began to redirect her husband's Keogh funds in 1985 because he had been borrowing against them. This particular event forced her into dealing with all of her finances. She started new investment accounts and learned by, "...asking any man at any cocktail party that was involved in finance. I learned a lot. They gave me a lot of information. I would pick anybody's brain about finance or money." She was, for all intents and purposes, going to school and this transpired while transiting Pluto was first opposing her natal Venus. This cycle encouraged her to review her worth and what was of value to her. Her husband finally expressed to her that he really was unhappy with managing the money and that he wanted to retire at some point. He asked her to help him figure out how to make that happen.

In addition to investing their monies she opened a lady's boutique on November 9, 1988 as transiting Neptune hit her seventh house cusp and as transiting Pluto began the opposition to her Moon. She didn't give a reason for doing this in our interview. However, transiting Chiron had been traveling through her twelfth house and had just conjuncted her Saturn and it may have been an attempt to see if she could apply her newly learned skills to something that was hers independent of another's finances.

Regardless, it turned out that it was too much. Her attempts to open the boutique, manage the family finances, oversee strip malls and apartments they owned was becoming overwhelming. Still the transit of Chiron over her Saturn, the originating point of fear, and then Ascendant, which promises a new identity, kept her from letting up. It was one year later as transiting Pluto was completing the opposition to her Moon that she sold the boutique and returned to remodeling and investing in their homes for profit and pleasure and to simplify her life.

As transiting Uranus began to oppose her Saturn in 1990 and pushed the envelope even further, she got involved with large remodel projects. Uranus is the sign of the "big-dealers", it breaks us out of our fixed structures (Saturn) and this was the case here. The two remodels she dealt with during this time were their private homes on vast acreages. She hated the houses calling them "huge money pits". She didn't use a general contractor and micro-managed each sub-contractor.

Uranus is the ruler of her eighth house of investments and income. It was also moving into Capricorn and beginning to trine her Venus in Taurus, as well as her Moon in Taurus. Uranus would, eventually, trine her fourth house Virgo which contains her Jupiter, and is the ruler of her tenth and sixth houses. Thus, she did wind up profiting from these projects.

In the last couple of years as Uranus has entered Aquarius and her eighth house, which it also rules, her children have "awoken" her to beginning to do her own trading via computers. She says she is a neophyte and that she is just beginning to learn. On the day I interviewed her, her children had just installed her laptop computer with trading software. Transiting Neptune, the ruler of Pisces and her Sun as well as her tenth house, had just stationed at 6° Aquarius having trined her Neptune in the fourth. She was excited, but cautious.

The recent Saturn/Jupiter conjunction of 2000 occurred in her eleventh house of friends, the community and goals having completed its 20-year cycle in her fourth house, which represented her involvement in the construction and design aspects of property. The conjunction now occurring in her eleventh house is trining her Jupiter in Virgo, which rules her sixth house of systems, equipment and methods as well as her tenth house of career. She is good at systems and details and may study technical analysis, which is an appropriate choice for sixth house transits. Note, too, that Pluto, the ruler of investments, has just entered her sixth house suggesting a transformation in the use of techniques and methods. Transiting Jupiter is trining her Neptune, the ruler of her tenth and conjuncting her Uranus, which rules computers and information and provides new insights that are refreshing and out of the ordinary.

Eventually, the upcoming transits of Jupiter, Saturn, Uranus, and Neptune, all in air signs will trigger continued transformations in her thinking and focus. Ultimately, as her thinking grows and evolves, she is slipping out of her shackles of fear, and with her versatility is beginning a new phase of confidence and joy. This is the result of tackling and moving through her darkest fears.

Case Study #2: a Man

(see Illustration 63)

In this case study the subject, born in 1952, named himself "The Rebel with a Clue", which seemed appropriate in light of the many markers in his horoscope. The remainder of the data is concealed in order to respect the life of the subject. He is in the real estate sales and service business.

In examining the chart we include the asteroids, the Nodes and his part of fortune and see a high degree of Cardinal and Mutable placements. One of his difficulties in executing his

Illustration 63

Male: Case Study Two, 1952

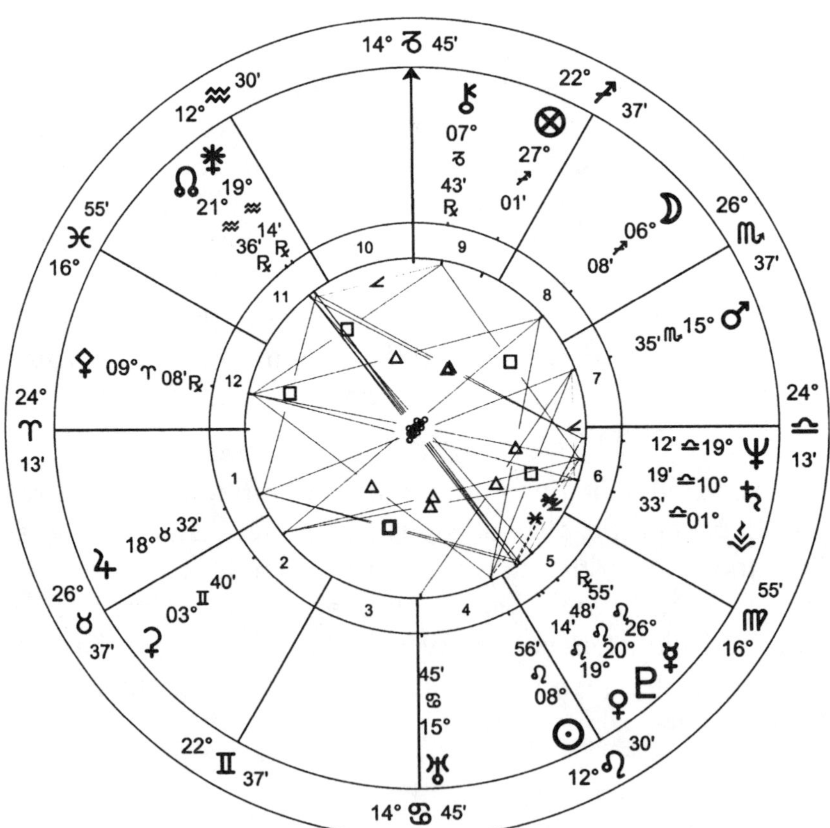

business is his poor attention to detail and record keeping. He has successfully overcome this with his spouse (a Virgo) working steadfastly beside him and attending to the business details.

When I first reviewed his chart, I noted that his tenth house revealed a 00° Aries cusp. In Horary Astrology something at the early degrees of a sign, up to about 2° or 3°, is defined as something that is too early to tell. When I began talking with the subject, he immediately told me that he had worked for himself his entire life, which is in keeping with an Aries Midheaven. The statement that he made regarding being "the rebel with a clue" was intriguing in that those very early degrees of Aries could suggest an individual who jumps into life either by choice or by circumstances without knowing why, or simply in pursuit of adventure.

His tenth house is ruled by Mars, which is in Scorpio and does suggest the eventual move into the property business (ruler of the tenth placed in the fourth house), as well as working at or from home. Note that Mars squares the Sun, which is placed in the seventh house and rules the second house. As we move through this case study, you will note the many affiliations he has had in his career life. His earning power (the second house) is tied with his associations with others (the seventh house).

Jupiter rules his sixth house of service and is placed in his tenth house. He succinctly stated that, "I could sell anything to anyone". He demands freedom in his work and always desires a handsome financial return for his efforts.

His original motivation to go to work was to escape the crowded household of seven people crammed into 800 square feet. His family was poor and he wanted money to spend so he got a job while in the first grade!

He made his first sale when Jupiter conjuncted his Midheaven by progression; he sold his leather boots. After that he sold newspapers door to door for a local publishing house (Jupiter ruled). He used his earnings to buy soda and candy. Simultaneously he embarked on a lifelong struggle with extra weight (Jupiter).

At eight years old, he started working "illegally" at a local car wash. Jupiter and Saturn were transiting his sixth house and both were preparing to make their planetary conjunction in 1961. This event officially triggered his career life in the service businesses. He was supposed to be fourteen years of age to dry cars, but was able to convince the owner that he could do a lot of work for him at a much lower rate. He worked at the car wash until his Saturn opposition approached.

At age 13 he went to work for a local grocery store. The food business is associated with the Moon, which rules his Cancer Ascendant. Saturn, the ruler of his sixth and seventh houses, was traveling through Pisces approaching a conjunction to Ceres (food, grains and agri-business) at 21° Pisces 49' that is a focal point of the yod involving both his Pluto and Neptune. This job came along as Saturn transited the focal point of the yod and as Jupiter moved from Gemini to Cancer over his Ascendant. Interestingly, the job offered perks like potato chips and sodas that helped keep him overweight (Jupiter and the Ascendant) despite the long hours (Saturn) stocking shelves. As Saturn transited the ninth house, he struggled in school, but discovered that he was a great salesman during the course of his stint in the food business. So great that he was working 30 to 35 hours a week while only 15. This continued into his senior year.

I think that it was probably during the initial struggles with his schoolwork that some unidentified learning disabilities were emerging, but those difficulties were not discovered. Note that Mercury, ruler of his third house, is square to Saturn and Neptune. The ability to create economic possibilities through imagination and need (Neptune and Saturn) was the lesson he was learning in his life.

In his senior year he was suddenly fired because of a misunderstanding. He had made a key at the grocery store and forgot to pay for it and the security guard there saw it and had him immediately fired. Transiting Pluto was in the late degrees of Virgo on the midpoint of the sextile between Pluto and Neptune, the reaction point of the yod. It was also opposing his Ceres. Transiting Uranus was just entering Libra, his fourth house cusp, and Chiron had just transited his tenth house cusp. Not only did he lose his job, but also his ability to eat anything he wanted (Moon rules the Ascendant and is placed in his fifth house of pleasure, which could denote pleasure through food). He was very angry as transiting Saturn squared his Pluto and transiting Neptune was just entering Sagittarius squaring his North and South Nodes. Various "deceptions" began to collapse and, thereby, change his life.

This coincided with transiting Jupiter moving through Libra about to cross over his Saturn, signaling a new career cycle. It was hardly surprising that this job was ending. He had just worked during the last quarter phase of transiting Jupiter to his Saturn, which is the part of the career cycle where there is a breaking down and a need to learn new skills.

During this same a friend, with whom he had worked, found him a job as a manager (Saturn) at an automatic car wash (Neptune related). Transiting Uranus (friends and the planet that rules his eighth house of income) was at 1° Libra, beginning to trine his Sun at 2° Aquarius in the seventh house. Transiting Jupiter was crossing his Saturn, the planet that rules managers. Transiting Saturn was squaring his Sun, an indicator of more responsibility.

Some of his new duties included scheduling people (Saturn), managing the money (Saturn), and counting the end of day returns (again, Saturn). Meanwhile he found a second job at a pizza restaurant cooking and flipping pizzas. Between the two jobs there was not much time dedicated to schoolwork.

He had started drinking alcohol while working at the grocery market and his dependence on alcohol continued to escalate. Transiting Neptune (alcohol) was in the late degrees of Scorpio and squaring his Pluto in the second house and transiting Jupiter (over indulgence) was aspecting his Saturn and Neptune, which is severely aspected. His father was an alcoholic so he carried the genetic marker that he would struggle with for many years.

The summer of 1970 he graduated from high school. It was the summer after the Kent State shootings at Bowling Green, Ohio, when most of the colleges in the United States had just been on strike the previous spring. As he was graduating, Vietnam was escalating. The rule was that if you were in school, you would not be drafted. He quickly applied to various schools in Ohio in order to avoid being drafted. He managed to register in a school in Ohio.

Although a poor student, he studied some fairly interesting subjects, including aviation (Aquarius). As transiting Uranus began conjuncting his Saturn, he began extreme uses of drugs, exacerbating his alcohol addiction. College began to get in the way of working for money in order to sustain his habits. He needed to keep making money.

At this point, transiting Neptune was exactly squaring his North and South Nodes. In one of the earlier chapters it was discussed how a planet either placed natally or by transit, particularly in square to the North and South Nodes can denote profession. Neptune is the planet that rules such activities as art and music and spiritual pursuits, but it is also rules drugs, alcohol and delusions. In his first year at college, while working at yet another pizza parlor, he had an epiphany.

He discovered that many of the students in their first year at school were there to avoid the draft. Some of these students were tough street kids from certain parts of the Midwest. In order to stay in school to avoid the draft they sustained themselves financially by selling drugs. It turned out that hemp was being grown to make rope for the war in Vietnam, in the county in which he lived. The locals that lived there knew how to go down to the fields at night and gather huge amounts of hemp to sell on the streets at $100 per pound or $10 per ounce, a tidy income. For one semester, he dealt drugs.

He was not doing well in school and was broke, which meant if he failed he would go to Vietnam. So, with trepidation, he went back to selling drugs in 1971 just as transiting Neptune was stationing, again, in the early degrees of Sagittarius, again squaring his North and South Nodes. This was something he would continue to do until the war ended.

Between 1973 and 1976, he was in transition. Pluto had just moved into Libra and had begun transiting his fourth house cusp. Usually any major planets crossing into the IC of the chart represent a transformation on a deep level. It is a time when we go inside to find that which works for us and release all else. Pluto is the ruler of his fifth house of creativity. It was now in the sign of Libra, the sign that is ruled by Venus and which rules such diverse things as the arts, weaving, fashion, jewelry, adornments, all Venusian types of occupations. While in Colorado on a visit, he met two women with whom he became good friends. They taught him lapidary as well as jewelry making. Not only was Pluto transiting the fourth house cusp, but also transiting Jupiter was now in early degrees of Aquarius and on his Sun sign, which rules his second house cusp.

Jupiter rules Sagittarius and Pisces, and Sagittarius rules turquoise. He found that he loved jewelry making because he made a lot of money and was able to easily sell exotic stones, particularly the turquoise, which was a giant craze at that time. Note that Jupiter rules part of his fifth house where the ruler of his chart, the Moon, is placed. He also has natal Mars square natal Sun and Mars can represent working with various metals and some gemstones. Lapidary was becoming his main income source, but because of the continued alcohol and drug use, he admits there were many "blurs" during this period. Saturn was now traveling through his twelfth house and his confrontations with the "Devil" (Saturn ruled) began plaguing him.

As Saturn crossed his Ascendant and entered Leo, he returned to school to obtain a heating (Mars) and air conditioning (Saturn) certification in an attempt to have one more bag of tricks to add to his income artillery and support his habits. This is interesting symbolism when looking at the chart, because transiting Saturn at this point was in the early degrees of Leo squaring his Mars in the early degrees of Scorpio, while it opposed his Sun sign in the early degrees of Aquarius. While studying for his certification, he was doing carpentry (ruled by Aquarius) for four to five hours a night.

From 1977 to 1978, as transiting Jupiter was in a last quarter square to Saturn and opposing his Venus, which rules Libra, in his third house that rules siblings, his older brother presented him with a career opportunity. He and his brother found work as Mud Loggers for oil companies (Neptune) and they were sent to Venezuela. Mud Logging requires working in an analytical trailer next to the oil wells, monitoring gas emissions and borings. By sampling the dirt, you get the readings.

During this last quarter phase, many people go to school to learn something new because they are breaking down the structure of their old lives. It was during this phase that he was sent to Mud Engineering School in the Southwest for three months. As soon as he finished his training, he quit the first company for whom he worked and began working for more money at another firm in January 1980.

By checking the ephemeris you will see significant transits occurring around this period. He was approaching his Saturn return, the coming of age cycle for adults and Saturn was squaring his Uranus in the twelfth house. Uranus is the ruler of his eighth house, which describes how we share resources with a partner.

Reality was setting in harshly on all fronts as transiting Pluto was conjuncting his Neptune in his fourth house and ruler of his ninth house of philosophy and belief systems. Transiting Neptune was conjuncting Venus (his values and his desires) and approaching a conjunction to his Moon (his emotional security issues), the ruler of his chart. Transiting Chiron was in middle degrees of Taurus about to square his Pluto in the second house. Something big was happening.

He decided to start his own company as transiting Jupiter transited his Saturn beginning a new career cycle. Since Saturn is the ruler of his seventh house of partnerships, he took a partner who had the know-how that complemented his knowledge. As mentioned earlier, transiting Neptune was conjuncting his Venus, which is the planet that rules partnerships. Transiting Neptune was also squaring his first/seventh house axis of relationship and partnership agreements. Neptune rules the oil business as well as grand visions. It also rules deception, drugs and alcohol. In the first year they made tremendous amounts of money, enough to buy a home and to support his family. But the partnership quickly dissolved after the partner absconded with $750,000 in funds! In true Neptunian fashion he lost everything: his home, his assets and his money in foreclosures just as transiting Pluto was entering Scorpio in 1984 and conjuncting his Mars, which rules his tenth house (his standing in the world). Pluto squared his Sun in the seventh of partnerships, which also rules his second house of values, cash flow, and earning power. Neptune was entering Capricorn and squaring his tenth/fourth house cusps. It began to all wash away.

He had married during this time and now had two stepchildren to support, as well as a new baby to, but he was still drinking hard. His wife became frightened as he was continually falling off of the wagon. She became detached (Neptune transiting the seventh), but continued to stay with him in hopes that he would change. As Jupiter crossed over his Sun sign in Aquarius and as Saturn was squaring his Pluto in the second and beginning to square his North and South Nodes, he went to Real Estate (Moon, Saturn rulerships) school and became a licensed agent. As Neptune continued to teeter and square his tenth/fourth house cusps, he turned to his parish priest (Neptune) for guidance. Here he found someone who "mentored my spiritual reawakening". With Saturn squaring his Pluto and his Pallas Athena (wisdom) and about to square his Nodes, he finally arrived at a harsh reality check. He stated, "I was a chronic alcoholic, I had no money, I had a growing family, and the real estate industry was not a thriving industry where he lived. I was in trouble."

In late October 1985, there was a Total Solar Eclipse at 20° Scorpio entering his fifth house and squaring his Pluto at 20° Leo in the second house. His wife confronted him, took the children and left him for a while. Six months later on April 15, 1986 he became sober and has remained sober ever since. His family is in tact and happy to this day.

In 1990 he and his wife began investing in their own properties and land. In September 1994 transiting Saturn entered early Pisces, hitting his North Node in Pisces in the eighth house and his wife joined him in their business as a partner.

In 1996, as transiting Uranus re-entered Aquarius and conjuncted his Sun sign, he purchased a second vacation home for his family to which they periodically retreat from their work. It is next to a wonderful lake where he boats and fishes frequently. (See the Neptune in the fourth house, which suggests living by bodies of water). In November 1998, he became a licensed real estate broker as Saturn had just entered and retrograded in the early degrees of Taurus squaring his Sun and opposing his Mars.

In October 1999, as Uranus conjuncted his Sun, he developed a website (Uranus) to increase his visibility and his earning power. Currently he focuses on the sales of high-end homes. Still he has another career transition in mind (Uranus). He plans to next develop multi-media (Uranus or Aquarius) programs on satellite to motivate people and help them change their lives based on his own experiences. He wants to incorporate the various mediums such as speech, software, video and music and is working with family members (Moon in the fifth) on developing these projects. His timing is impeccable as transiting Chiron in early Sagittarius along with Pluto is traveling through his fifth house of creativity.

I believe that when they conjunct his natal Moon, the ruler of his chart, and then, when he hits his Chiron return in his sixth house of service and facilitation, this dream will materialize. Without knowing it, he is on track. Chiron is the maverick or the rebel of the zodiac. His Chiron conjuncts his Mercury, which rules most of his eleventh house of groups and his third house of communications. It squares his Saturn (work). Ultimately, he, the wounded healer (Chiron), will heal others who enter Chiron's path after their 50th year. He is becoming what he called himself, "the rebel with the clue", or, the maverick, whom by virtue of his experience, can mentor, or, teach others. This is the ultimate task for Chiron.

Afterward

There are so many more techniques that we can use after we learn the basic principles upon which to base our delineations. This book is a platform for basic methods. Over the years as we grow as astrologers, we add different techniques to our bag of delineation tricks, but in the end, we always revert to a few formulas that work for us. The "formulas" presented in this first book, are just that, "formulas". They are my basics. There are other techniques too, and I look forward to presenting more in the future. For now, try practicing these.

To make your life as a business astrologer easier, it is important that you screen your clients to see what specifically they need to have done. This way you can pare down their needs and save you time and them money thereby charging appropriately. This work involves a great deal of time and it is highly unlikely that you can accomplish in a ninety minute consultation all that they need. You will usually find yourself spending at least five hours preparing and presenting, depending on what they require you to do. As a result, you need to charge them accordingly. This is not the standard "reading" or "individual consult" fee that you charge for your regular clients. Generally speaking, you need to up your per hour fee for corporate clients and charge them for your preparation time as well as your presentation time, whether you meet with them or write them a report. Allowing for payments with a Visa or Mastercard is an excellent idea, particularly for Sole Proprietorships.

There is a very helpful questionnaire I use in the appendices of this book that follows the bibliography and resource page. By presenting your client with a questionnaire, they take you seriously and realize the amount of time that is needed to do the job. A tool like this can help separate serious clients from people who are just shopping. If you don't like this questionnaire, or any of the other worksheets like the planning grids, then you can use them as a model for something that is more suited to your practice. At recent Astrological conferences, I presented a booklet entitled Marketing Your Practice, which is available for $12 by writing or calling us.

Hope you have enjoyed this book and I hope to present more information down the road. Our email is: venus2@ix.netcom.com or write us at: 200 Gregory Lane, Bldg. C-2, #5, Pleasant Hill, CA 94523-3389. Phone: (925) 689-7827.

BIBLIOGRAPHY

Ashley, Wendy. Email: astromythology@juno.com.

Bills, Rex E. The Rulership Book. Richmond, Virginia. Macoy Publishing & Masonic Supply Co., Inc. 1976.

Binder, Jamie. Planets in Work. San Diego, California. ACS Publications, Inc. 1988.

Doane, Doris Chase. Vocational Selection and Counseling, Volumes 1 and 2. Tempe, Arizona. American Federation of Astrologers. 1981

Esclavon-Hardy, Pat. "Energies, Trends, and Cycles." Clearwater, Florida. Email: patetc@aol.com. Phone: (727) 573-0755.

George, Demetra with Bloch, Douglas. Asteroid Goddesses. San Diego, California. ACS Publications, Inc. 1986.

Gillen, Jack. The Key to Speculation on the New York Stock Exchange. San Antonio, Texas. The Bear Publishers, Inc. 1979.

Greene, Liz. Saturn: A New Look At An Old Devil. New York. Samuel Weiser, Inc. 1976.

Hamilton, Edith. Mythology. Boston, Massachusetts. Little, Brown and Company. 1942.

Hirsch, James S. Hurricane-The Miraculous Journey of Rubin Carter. Boston-New York. Houghton-Mifflin Company. 1999.

Howell, Alice O. Jungian Symbolism in Astrology. Wheaton, Illinois. The Theosophical Publishing House. 1987.

Jansky, Robert Carl. Interpreting the Eclipses. San Diego, California. Astro Computing Services. 1979.

Kanchier, Carol. "Dare to Change." San Francisco, California. San Francisco Chronicle. October 10, 1999.

Koval, Barbara. Time & Money. St. Paul, Minnesota. Llewellyn Publications. 1993.

Lehman, J. Lee, Ph.D. Essential Dignities. West Chester, Pennsylvania. Whitford Press. 1989.

Luntz, Charles E. Vocational Guidance by Astrology. St. Paul, Minnesota. Llewellyn Publications. 1942. Second Printing. 1992.

Mason, Joyce. "Chiron." Rocklin, California. Email: chironicle@aol.com.

McEvers, Joan, Editor. Financial Astrology for the 1990's. St. Paul, Minnesota. Llewellyn Publications. 1989.

Meridian, Bill. Planetary Stock Trading. New York. Cycles Research and Publications. Second Printing. 1998. Email: cyclesresearch@aol.com.

Merriman, Raymond A. Evolutionary Astrology. West Bloomfield, Michigan. MMA/Seek-It Publications. First Edition. 1977.

Merriman, Raymond A. Geocosmic Correlations to Investment Cycles, Volume 2. West Bloomfield, Michigan. MMA/ Seek-It Publications. 1999.

Michelsen, Neil. Tables of Planetary Phenomenon. San Diego, California. ACS Publications, Inc. 1990.

Morris, Grace K. How To Choose Stocks That Will Outperform the Market, 2001. Chicago, Illinois. Astro-Economics Publications. 2000. http://www.astroeconomics.com.

Mull, Carol S. Standard and Poor's 500. Tempe, Arizona. American Federation of Astrologers. 1984.

Ornstein, Robert E. The Psychology of Consciousness. New York. Penguin Books. 1975.

Reichard, Alice Q. PMAFA. Studio City, California.

Reinhart, Melanie. Chiron and The Healing Journey. Middlesex, England. Arkana Publishing. 1989.

Rodden, Lois. Profiles of Women. Tempe, Arizona. American Federation of Astrologers. 1979.

"Rorschach Test." Funk and Wagnall's Standard Dictionary. New York. New American Library. 1980.

Rudhyar, Dane. The Lunation Cycle. Berkeley, California. Shambhala Publications, Inc. 1975.

Silver, Morris, Editor. Ancient Economy In Mythology: East and West. Savage, Maryland. Rowman & Littlefield Publishers, Inc. 1991.

Stathis, Georgia. "Delineating the Corporation." Financial Astrology for the 1990's. McEvers, Joan, Editor. St. Paul, Minnesota. Llewellyn Publications. 1989.

Stathis, Georgia. The Other Side of the Paradigm: Man's Personal Equation. Malibu, California. Pepperdine University Press. Faculty of the School of Business and Management. 1978.

Stathis, Georgia. "The Real Estate Process." Financial Astrology for the 1990's. McEvers, Joan, Editor. St. Paul, Minnesota. Llewellyn Publications. 1989.

Tyl, Noel, Editor. How to Use Vocational Astrology for Success in the Workplace. St. Paul, Minnesota. Llewellyn Publications. 1992.

Added Resources

Professional Organizations

AA: Astrological Association of Great Britain
www.astrologer.com/aanet

AFA: American Federation Of Astrologers, Inc.
www.astrologers.com

AFAN: Association for Astrological Networking
www.afan.com

ISAR: International Society for Astrological Research
www.isarastrology.com

ISBA: International Society for Business Astrologers
www.businessastrologers.com

NCGR: National Council for Geocosmic Research, Inc.
www.geocosmic.org

OPA: Organization for Professional Astrologers.
Contact BOBMULLIGA@aol.com

Software

A.I.R. Software
115 Caya Avenue
West Hartford, CT 06110
(800) 659-1247
www.alphee.com

Astrocybernetics
John Woodsmall
Pathfinder Software
www.astrocye.com

AstroDatabank Company
25 Raymond Street
Manchester, MA 01944-1614
(978) 526-8864
www.astrodatabank.com

Astrolabe
Box 1750
Brewster, MA 02631
(800) 843-6682
www.alabe.com

Cosmic Patterns
6212 N.W. 43rd Street Suite B
Gainesville, FL 32653
(352) 373-1504
www.patterns.com

Matrix Software
315 Marion Avenue
Big Rapids, MI 49307
(800) PLANETS
www.astrologysoftware.com

Tape Recording and Catalogue Services

Conference Recording Services, contact: Michael Brant or Richard Page at 1308 Gilman Street, Berkeley, CA 94706, Tel. (510) 527-3600 or www.conferencerecording.com.

Starcycles Publishing, contact: Georgia Stathis at 200 Gregory Lane, Bldg. C-2, Room 5, Pleasant Hill, CA 94523-3389, Tel. (925) 689-STAR or www.starcycles.com.

Sun Recording Service, contact: Steve Pincus at PO Box 4184, Mountain View, CA 94040 Tel. (650) 968-4513 or stardial@best.com. Represents Georgia Stathis' tapes and many more.

University

Kepler College in Seattle, Washington. Accredited Bachelor and Masters programs providing Degrees in Astrological Science. Contact them at www.kepler.edu.

Further Studies

ONLINE College of Astrology at www.astrocollege.com. Contact: Ena Stanley.

Instructional Audio Tapes

Available from StarCycles

The Myths and the Signs of the Zodiac,
Special Twelve-Tape Set

ISBN: 1-881229-30-0, Twelve-tapes, also sold as individual tapes

"Elegantly Produced with Imagination & Stories for all of the signs of the zodiac."

Volume One —The Planets

ISBN: 1-881229-31-9, Twelve Tapes

Volume Two — Basic Interpretation

ISBN: 1-881229-32-7, Twelve Tapes

- Interpretation
- The Rulership Workshop
- Progressions and Solar Arcs
- Analyzing the Chart Using Stories
- Eclipses and Timing (Short Version)
- What Will I Be When I Grow Up?
- Shadow Points

Volume Three — Advanced Techniques

ISBN: 1-881229-33-5, Twelve Tapes

- Seeing the "Other" in the Horoscope
- Issue Charts
- Weird and Wild Techniques in Understanding Relationships
- Relationships (3 Tapes)
- Saturn/Jupiter Career Cycle (1 Tape)
- Eclipses & Timing (2 Tapes)

Volume Four — Business Astrology Techniques

ISBN: 1-881229-34-3, Six Tapes

- Business and Career Directions
- Financial Counsel in the Horoscope
- Saturn in Taurus & You

Volume Five — Teachings

ISBN: 1-881229-35-1, Six Tapes

- Spiritual Values, Material Gifts
- Global and Spiritual Collaboration
- Age Cycles and You
- Mid-Life Crisis
- The Search for Freedom and the Holy Grail
- Cracking Up or Cracking Open

Volume Six — Eclipses and Prediction

ISBN: 1-881229-36-x, Three Tapes

Volume Seven — Aspects

ISBN: 1-881229-37-8, Three Tapes

Volume Eight — The Houses

ISBN: 1-881229-38-6, Three Tapes

- Interpretation of Houses (includes Corporate, Mundane, and Real Estate Delineations)

Volume Nine — Synodic Cycles

ISBN: 1-881229-39-4, Three Tapes

- The intervals between the Conjunctions of any two Planets. How do these and others trigger your chart?

Volume Ten—Saturn/Jupiter Career Cycle

ISBN: 1-881229-40-8, Three Tapes

Volume Eleven—Business Astrology Weekend

ISBN: 1-881229-41-5, Six Tapes

- Two-day workshop that covers a wide variety of topics including general financial timing, corporate analysis
- Some on real estate and interest rate cycles, financial management in the horoscope

Volume Twelve—The Chiron Tapes

3 Tapes

Volume Fourteen—Saturn in Taurus: Options and Possibilities

3 Tapes

Volume Fifteen-Cycles of Abundance

4 Tapes

- Presented at ISIS Institute
- Includes Saturn in Taurus information in Volume Fourteen, and more

ORDER THROUGH:

Sun Recording Service
Steve Pincus
PO Box 4184
Mountain View, CA 94040
Tel. (650) 968-4513
Fax:(650) 968-9433;
EMAIL: Stardial@best.com
Visa, MC, AMEX, Discover accepted.

Twelve Tapes: $89.95
Six Tapes: $59.95
Three Tapes: $25.00

Please add Shipping/Handling plus 8 % tax for CA residents

Wholesale Prices available.

APPENDIX I

VOCATIONAL WORKSHEET

Vocation	Some of the Planetary Ruler(s)	Sign(s)	Corresponding House(s)
Accessories, Adornment	Venus	Libra or Taurus	2
Accountant	Mercury	Virgo	3
Activist	Uranus	Aquarius	11
Actor	Sun or Moon or Neptune	Leo or Cancer or Pisces	5, 4, 12
Adventurer	Mars	Aries	1
Advertising	Jupiter or Neptune	Sagittarius or Pisces	9, 12
Advertising Executive	Mercury or Sun	Gemini or Leo	3, 5
Advertising Sales	Mercury or Venus	Gemini or Virgo or Taurus	2, 3, 6
Aerobics	Mars	Aries	1
Agents, Real Estate or Escrow	Mercury	Virgo	6
Agriculture	Moon or Venus	Cancer or Taurus	4, 2
Analyst	Mercury	Virgo	6
Animal Husbandry	Venus	Taurus	2
Antiques	Moon or Venus	Cancer or Taurus	4, 2
Arbitration Specialist	Venus	Libra	7
Aromatherapy	Neptune or Venus	Pisces or Taurus or Libra	12, 2, 7
Artist, Art	Neptune or Jupiter	Pisces or Sagittarius	12, 9
Asset Manager	Pluto	Scorpio	8
Astrologer	Uranus or Mercury	Aquarius or Virgo	11, 6
Athlete	Sun or Mars	Leo or Aries	1, 5
Autistic Work	Neptune	Pisces	12
Autonomy	Mars	Aries	1
Aviation	Uranus or Jupiter	Aquarius or Sagittarius	11, 9
Baker	Mars or Ceres or Moon	Mars or Virgo or Cancer	1, 4, 6
Banker	Venus or Pluto	Taurus or Scorpio	2, 8
Big Dealer	Uranus	Aquarius	11
Biofeedback	Neptune	Pisces	12
Body Worker	Saturn or Mars	Capricorn or Aries	9 or 1

Vocation	Some of the Planetary Ruler(s)	Sign(s)	Corresponding House(s)
Bone Work, Orthopedics	Saturn	Capricorn	10
Bookkeeper	Mercury	Gemini or Virgo	3, 6
Breath Work	Mercury	Gemini	3
Broker	Uranus	Aquarius	11
Budget Analyst	Venus or Mercury	Taurus or Gemini or Virgo	2, 3, 6
Builder	Saturn	Capricorn or Aquarius	4, 10
Burglar	Mars or Pluto	Aries or Scorpio	1
Butcher and Meat Cutter	Mars or Pluto	Aries or Scorpio	1
Caretaking	Moon	Cancer	4
Carpenter	Uranus	Aquarius	11
Cash Flow Specialist	Venus	Taurus	2
Caterer	Mercury or Ceres or Moon or Venus	Gemini or Virgo or Cancer or Libra	4, 6, 7
Chairman of the Board	Sun	Leo	5, 10
Chef	Moon	Cancer	4
Chemistry, Alchemy	Mercury or Uranus	Virgo or Uranus	3, 11
Chiropractors	Saturn or Chiron	Capricorn or Virgo	10, 6
Chocolatier	Venus	Libra or Taurus	2
Civil Engineer	Moon	Cancer	4
Clergy	Neptune or Jupiter	Pisces or Sagittarius	12
Clothing Designer	Venus	Libra or Taurus	2
Coaching	Jupiter or Mercury	Sagittarius or Gemini or Virgo	3, 9
Coffee Industry	Saturn	Capricorn	10
Collector	Moon	Cancer	4
Comedian	Sun or Saturn	Leo or Capricorn	5, 10
Commerce	Mercury	Gemini	3
Commissioned Work	Uranus	Aquarius	2, 11
Communication	Mercury	Gemini	3
Community Relations	Uranus	Aquarius	11
Composer	Neptune or Uranus	Pisces or Aquarius	12, 11
Computer Work	Mercury or Uranus	Virgo or Aquarius	3, 11
Concrete and Masonry	Saturn	Capricorn	10
Conservator	Pluto	Scorpio	8
Consultant	Jupiter	Sagittarius	9
Container	Moon	Cancer	4
Contract Writing	Mercury or Venus	Gemini or Virgo or Libra	3, 6, 7

Vocation	Some of the Planetary Ruler(s)	Sign(s)	Corresponding House(s)
Copper Manufacturing	Venus	Taurus	2
Cosmetics	Venus or Neptune	Taurus or Libra or Pisces	2
Counselor	Moon or Venus	Cancer or Libra	4, 7
Cowboy	Mercury or Jupiter	Gemini or Sagittarius	3, 9
Dancer	Neptune	Pisces	12
Death Business	Pluto	Scorpio	8
Debt Specialist, Mergers	Neptune or Pluto	Pisces or Scorpio	8
Decorators	Moon	Cancer	4
Dentist	Saturn	Capricorn	10
Design	Venus or Neptune	Taurus or Pisces	2, 12
Desktop Publishing	Jupiter	Sagittarius	9
Developer	Uranus	Aquarius	11
Diamond or Gem Cutter	Mars	Aries	1
Diplomacy	Venus	Libra	7
Director	Sun	Leo	5
Dispatcher	Mercury	Gemini or Virgo	3, 6
Dream Therapist	Neptune	Pisces	12
Drug Rehabilitation	Neptune or Pluto	Pisces or Scorpio	12, 8
Efficiency Expert	Mercury or Saturn	Virgo or Capricorn	6, 10
Elder Care	Saturn	Capricorn	10
Electronics	Mercury or Uranus	Gemini or Aquarius	3, 11
Employee	Moon	Virgo (esoteric ruler)	6
Engineer	Mercury	Gemini or Virgo	6
Entertainer	Sun	Leo	5
Entrepreneur	Saturn or Uranus	Aquarius	10, 11
Environmentalist	Mercury	Virgo	6
Epicurean	Venus	Taurus	2
Equipment Sales	Mercury or Mars	Gemini or Virgo or Aries	6, 1
Escrow Officer	Mercury	Virgo	6
Essayist	Mercury	Gemini	3
Estate Liquidator	Pluto or Mercury	Scorpio or Gemini	8
Estate Manager	Pluto or Saturn	Scorpio or Capricorn	8
Esthetic Pursuits	Venus	Taurus or Libra	2, 7
Executive Position	Sun	Leo	5
Facilitator	Mercury or Venus	Virgo or Libra	6
Family Business	Moon	Cancer	4

Vocation	Some of the Planetary Ruler(s)	Sign(s)	Corresponding House(s)
Farming	Ceres or Moon	Virgo or Cancer	6, 4
Father	Sun or Saturn	Leo or Capricorn	5, 10
Film Making	Mercury or Neptune	Gemini or Virgo or Pisces	3, 12
Financial Services	Pluto	Scorpio	8
Fishing	Neptune	Pisces	12
Fitness	Mars	Aries	1
Flowers	Venus	Taurus or Libra	2
Food Business	Moon or Mercury or Ceres	Cancer or Virgo	4, 6
Food Supply Businesses	Mercury or Ceres	Gemini or Virgo or Cancer	4, 6
Foreign Exchange	Venus	Taurus or Libra	2, 7
Foreign Service and Agencies	Jupiter or Neptune	Sagittarius	9, 12
Foster Caregiver	Chiron	Virgo through Sagittarius	6, 7
Franchises	Uranus	Aquarius	11
Furnishing	Venus	Taurus or Libra	2
Futurist	Uranus	Aquarius	11
Gambler	Sun or Jupiter	Leo or Sagittarius	5, 9
Genealogist	Moon or Saturn	Cancer or Capricorn	4, 10
Genetic Engineering	Chiron or Pluto	Virgo or Scorpio	6, 8
Gentrification	Pluto	Scorpio	8
Global Specialist	Jupiter or Uranus	Aquarius or Sagittarius	11, 9
Gold and Precious Metals	Sun	Leo	5
Golfer	Sun	Leo	5
Government Work	Jupiter or Saturn	Sagittarius or Capricorn	9, 10
Grains, Farming	Mercury or Ceres	Virgo	6
Group Work	Uranus	Aquarius	11
Hands, Working with	Mercury	Gemini or Virgo	3, 6
Healer	Neptune or Mercury	Pisces or Virgo	12, 6
Herbs	Venus	Taurus	2, 6
Hero or Heroine	Mars or Sun	Aries or Leo	1, 5
Holistic Health Practitioner	Mercury or Chiron	Virgo	6
Home Designer	Moon or Venus	Cancer or Taurus or Libra	4, 2
Horses	Jupiter	Pisces or Sagittarius	9, 12

Vocation	Some of the Planetary Ruler(s)	Sign(s)	Corresponding House(s)
Hospice Work	Pluto or Chiron	Scorpio or Virgo	8, 6
Hospital Worker	Mercury or Neptune	Virgo or Pisces	6, 12
Hosting	Venus	Taurus or Libra	2, 7
Human Rights	Uranus	Aquarius	11
Hunter	Mars	Aries	1
Hybrid Thinking	Chiron	Virgo through Sagittarius	6, 8
Hypnotherapists	Neptune or Pluto	Pisces or Scorpio	12, 8
Ice and Frozen Food	Saturn	Capricorn	10
Importer and Exporter	Jupiter	Sagittarius or Pisces	9, 12
Independent Contractor	Uranus	Aquarius	11
Industrial Engineer	Saturn	Capricorn	10
Institutional Work	Neptune	Pisces	12
Insurance Industry	Pluto	Scorpio	8
Interior Designer	Venus	Taurus or Libra	2, 7
International Business and Relations	Jupiter	Sagittarius	9
Internet Design	Mercury or Uranus	Gemini or Virgo or Aquarius	3, 6, 11
Inventor	Uranus or Neptune	Aquarius or Pisces	11, 12
Inventory Control	Mercury	Virgo	6
Investigator	Pluto	Scorpio	8
Investment Banker	Sun or Pluto	Leo or Scorpio	5, 8
Investor	Mars or Pluto	Aries or Scorpio	1, 8
Jewelry Design	Venus	Taurus or Libra	2, 7
Journalism	Mercury or Jupiter	Gemini or Virgo or Sagittarius	3, 9
Judge	Venus or Jupiter or Saturn	Libra or Sagittarius or Capricorn	7, 9, 10
Jungian Symbolism	Neptune or Pluto	Pisces or Scorpio	12, 8
Late Bloomer	Saturn	Capricorn	10
Leader	Sun or Mars	Leo or Aries	5, 1
Leather Goods	Venus	Taurus	2
Legal and Paralegal Services	Venus or Pallas	Libra	6, 7
Legal or Justice System	Venus or Jupiter	Libra or Sagittarius	7, 9
Liaison	Mercury or Venus	Virgo or Libra	6, 7
Licensing	Mercury	Gemini	3
Lighting Contractor	Saturn or Uranus	Aquarius	10, 11
Lottery	Sun	Leo	5

Vocation	Some of the Planetary Ruler(s)	Sign(s)	Corresponding House(s)
Lyrics	Mercury	Gemini	3
Machinist	Mars	Aries	1
Manager	Saturn	Capricorn	10
Manufacturing	Mars	Aries or Scorpio	1, 8
Marketing	Jupiter	Sagittarius	1
Martial Arts	Mars	Aries	9
Mass Production	Pluto	Scorpio	8
Mathematics	Mercury or Uranus	Gemini or Virgo or Aquarius	3, 11
Mechanical Engineer	Mars or Mercury	Aries or Gemini or Virgo	1, 3, 6
Media	Mercury or Uranus	Gemini or Virgo or Aquarius	3, 11
Mediation	Venus or Pallas	Taurus or Libra	2, 7
Medical Supplier	Mercury	Virgo	6
Meeting and Convention Planner	Sun	Leo	5
Mental Health Professional	Mercury or Moon or Neptune	Virgo or Cancer or Pisces	6, 4, 12
Military Strategist	Mars or Pallas	Aries or Libra	1, 7
Mining	Pluto	Scorpio	8
Ministers	Jupiter	Sagittarius	9
Mortgage Broker	Mercury or Pluto	Gemini or Virgo or Pluto	3, 6, 8
Mortician	Pluto	Scorpio	8
Mother	Moon or Ceres	Cancer or Virgo	4, 6
Motivational Speaker	Jupiter or Uranus	Sagittarius or Aquarius	9, 11
Multi-Level Marketing	Uranus	Aquarius	11
Multi-Media	Mercury or Uranus	Gemini or Virgo or Aquarius	3, 11
Musician	Uranus or Neptune	Aquarius or Pisces	11, 12
Native American	Jupiter	Sagittarius	9
Negotiator	Venus	Taurus or Libra	2, 7
Networker	Uranus	Aquarius	11
Newsletter Writing	Mercury	Gemini or Virgo	3, 6
Nuclear Energy	Pluto	Scorpio	8
Nurturing	Moon or Ceres	Cancer or Virgo	4, 6
Nutritionist	Mercury	Virgo	6
Office Furniture Supplier	Mercury	Gemini or Virgo	3, 6
Oil and Petroleum	Neptune or Pluto	Pisces or Scorpio	12, 8

Vocation	Some of the Planetary Ruler(s)	Sign(s)	Corresponding House(s)
Olive Trees, Olive Oil Industry	Sun or Pallas	Leo or Libra	5, 7
Orange and Citrus Growers	Sun	Leo	5
Organizational Management	Saturn	Capricorn	10
Organizer	Uranus	Aquarius	11
Painting Contractor	Uranus or Neptune	Aquarius or Pisces	11, 12
Paralegal Service	Venus or Pallas	Libra	7
Petroleum	Neptune	Pisces	12
Pharmaceutical Industry	Neptune	Pisces	12
Philosopher	Jupiter	Sagittarius	9
Photographer	Neptune	Pisces	12
Physical Education	Mars	Aries	1
Piercing Artist	Mars	Aries	1
Plastics	Neptune	Pisces	12
Pleasure Business	Venus or Sun	Taurus or Libra or Leo	2, 7, 5
Poetry	Mercury or Neptune	Gemini or Virgo or Pisces	3, 12
Police	Mars	Aries	1
Politics	Jupiter or Saturn	Sagittarius or Capricorn	9, 10
Precious Metal	Sun	Leo	5
President	Sun	Leo	5
Press Relations	Mercury	Gemini or Virgo	3, 6
Priest	Neptune	Pisces	12
Prison Work	Neptune	Pisces	12
Probation Officer	Neptune	Pisces	12
Problem Solver	Mercury	Gemini or Virgo	3, 6
Product Development	Moon or Venus	Cancer or Taurus or Libra	4, 2, 7
Professional Sales	Jupiter	Sagittarius	9
Professional Speaker	Jupiter or Uranus	Sagittarius or Aquarius	9, 11
Professor	Jupiter	Sagittarius	9
Promotional Work	Jupiter	Sagittarius	9
Property	Moon	Cancer	4
Property Development	Saturn or Uranus	Capricorn or Aquarius	10, 11
Prosecutor	Venus or Saturn	Libra or Capricorn	7, 10

Vocation	Some of the Planetary Ruler(s)	Sign(s)	Corresponding House(s)
Psychic	Neptune	Pisces	12
Psychotherapist	Pluto	Scorpio	8
Public Figure	Saturn	Capricorn	10
Public Housing	Moon	Cancer	4
Public Information	Saturn or Uranus	Aquarius	11
Publisher	Jupiter	Sagittarius	9
Radio	Mercury or Uranus	Gemini or Aquarius	3, 11
Ranching	Venus or Moon	Taurus or Cancer	2, 4
Realtor	Moon	Cancer	4
Rebirthers	Pluto	Scorpio	8
Reconstruction	Pluto or Mars	Scorpio or Aries	8, 1
Recycling	Mercury or Saturn or Pluto	Virgo or Capricorn or Scorpio	6, 8, 10
Redevelopment	Pluto	Scorpio	8
Rehabilitation	Neptune or Pluto	Pisces or Scorpio	12, 8
Religion	Jupiter	Sagittarius or Pisces	9, 12
Renovation	Pluto	Scorpio	8
Rental Property	Moon or Mercury	Cancer or Virgo	4, 6
Research and Development	Neptune	Pisces	12
Researcher	Mercury or Pluto	Gemini or Virgo or Scorpio	3, 6, 8
Restaurant Supply Business	Mercury or Ceres	Gemini or Virgo or Cancer	6
Rock and Roll	Neptune or Sun	Pisces of Leo	12, 5
Royalty Work	Uranus or Venus	Aquarius or Taurus	11, 2
Sales	Mercury or Jupiter	Gemini or Virgo or Sagittarius	3, 6, 9
Salvage Specialist	Moon or Pluto or Saturn	Cancer or Scorpio or Capricorn	4, 8, 10
Science	Uranus	Aquarius	11
Screenwriting	Mercury	Gemini	3
Sea, Products of the Sea	Neptune	Pisces	12
Self-Employment	Mars	Aries	1
Service Business	Mercury	Gemini or Virgo	3, 6
Serviceman	Mercury	Virgo	6
Sex Therapist	Pluto or Venus	Scorpio or Taurus or Libra	8, 2
Shamanic Work	Pluto	Scorpio	8
Shelters or Safe Houses	Neptune	Pisces	12
Shipping and Fishing	Neptune	Pisces	12

Vocation	Some of the Planetary Ruler(s)	Sign(s)	Corresponding House(s)
Short Story Writer	Mercury	Gemini or Virgo	3, 6
Singer	Venus or Neptune	Taurus or Libra or Pisces	2, 12
Skin Specialist	Venus or Saturn	Taurus or Libra or Capricorn	2, 10
Social Activism	Uranus	Aquarius	11
Social Welfare Worker	Neptune	Pisces	12
Soldier and Soldier of Fortune	Mars	Aries or Scorpio	1, 8
Soul Work	Neptune	Pisces	12
Speaker	Mercury or Jupiter	Gemini or Virgo or Sagittarius	3, 9
Speculator, Lottery	Sun	Leo	5
Sports	Sun or Mars	Leo or Aries	5, 1
Stock Broker	Venus or Pluto	Taurus or Scorpio	2, 8
Strategic Planner	Mars	Aries	1
Sugar	Venus	Taurus or Libra	2, 7
Surgeon	Mars or Pluto	Aries or Scorpio	1, 8
Syndication	Uranus	Aquarius	11
Systems Manager	Mercury or Saturn	Gemini or Virgo or Capricorn	3, 6, 10
Tattoo Artist	Mars	Aries	1
Teacher	Mercury or Jupiter	Gemini or Virgo or Sagittarius	3, 9
Telecommunications	Mercury or Uranus	Gemini or Virgo or Aquarius	3, 11
Textile Designer	Venus or Neptune	Taurus or Libra or Pisces	2, 7, 12
Therapist	Pluto	Scorpio	8
Toolmaker	Mars	Aries	1
Tourist Work	Mercury or Sun	Gemini or Leo	3, 5
Trader	Mercury	Gemini or Virgo	3, 6
Traffic	Mercury	Gemini or Virgo	3, 6
Trailblazer	Mars	Aries	1
Transportation	Mercury or Jupiter	Gemini or Virgo or Sagittarius	3, 6, 9
Traveler, Travel Industry	Mercury or Jupiter	Gemini or Virgo or Sagittarius	3, 6, 9
Trend Setter	Jupiter or Uranus	Sagittarius or Aquarius	9, 11
Two Careers	Mercury	Gemini or Virgo	3, 6
Union Liaison or Worker	Mercury or Venus	Virgo or Libra	6, 7

Vocation	Some of the Planetary Ruler(s)	Sign(s)	Corresponding House(s)
Upholstery	Venus	Taurus or Libra	2, 7
Venture Capital Funding	Neptune or Pluto	Pisces or Scorpio	12, 8
Veterinarian	Mercury or Neptune	Virgo or Pisces	6, 12
Videography	Uranus	Aquarius	11
Visionary	Jupiter or Neptune	Sagittarius or Pisces	9, 12
Vocational Trainer	Mercury	Gemini or Virgo	3, 6
Voicework	Venus	Taurus or Libra	2, 7
Weapons and Munitions	Mars	Aries	1
Weaving and Textiles	Venus or Pallas	Taurus or Libra	2, 7
Web Master	Mercury	Gemini or Virgo	3, 6
Weight Lifter	Mars	Aries	1
Welder	Mars	Aries	1
Welfare Worker	Neptune	Pisces	12
Wholesaler	Uranus	Aquarius	11
Wilderness Guide	Jupiter	Sagittarius	9
Wine Merchant	Mercury or Neptune	Gemini or Virgo or Pisces	3, 6, 12
Wish Fulfillment	Uranus	Aquarius	11
Women's Issues	Moon	Cancer	4
Writing	Mercury or Neptune	Gemini or Virgo or Pisces	3, 6, 12
Youth Worker	Sun	Leo	5

Appendix IIa

Corporate House Worksheet, Alphabetical Order

House Meanings	House	Placement of House Ruler
Ability to be Profitable	2	
Activities Abroad	9	
Adjustments	7	
Administrative Department	10	
Advertising	3	
Advertising Department	9	
Advertising Failure	5	
Advertising Success	5	
Agricultural and Agricultural Products	6	
All Legal Affairs	9	
Allied Organizations	11	
Amusements	5	
Assistance received from other Employees	6	
Attitude towards Competitors	1	
Attitude/Actions of Board of Directors in opposition to President	5	
Attitude/Actions of Shareholders in opposition to President	5	
Audits	9	
Banquets	5	
Base of Operations, Field of Activity	4	
Boards of Directors	8	
Bulletins, Newsletters, Magazines & Technical Manuals	3	
Business Fixtures and Furnishings	6	
Code of Ethics and By-Laws	9	
Colleagues, Friends, Acquaintances	11	
Commercial Radio	3	
Committees	5	

House Meanings	House	Placement of House Ruler
Community Connections	11	
Company Business Objectives	1	
Company Morale	1	
Company Philosophy	9	
Competitors and Their Activities	7	
Competitor's Financial Condition	8	
Completion of Merger Contracts	9	
Constitutional Policies	11	
Contacts with the Public	3	
Contracts with other Companies	9	
Conventions	5	
Corporations associated with Hotels or Inns-Hostelries	6	
Credit	8	
Demand for Stocks and Bonds	3	
Direct Competition	4	
Disposition towards Investments	2	
Dissolutions and Negotiations	12	
Dividends	8	
Donations to Nonprofits	8	
Dramatic or Theatrical Ventures	5	
Earnings	2	
Education	3	
Educational Enterprises	5	
Effective Presentation of Products	7	
Effects of Litigation	12	
Employee Attitudes	6	
Employee Cooperation	6	
Employee Incomes and Payroll	7	
Employee Performance	6	
Employee Strikes and Labor Troubles	6	
Employees/Workers Voluntary or Paid	6	
Enemies and Secret Organizations Against the Organization	12	
Equipment	6	

House Meanings	House	Placement of House Ruler
Executive Personnel (does not include President or CEO)	5	
Figureheads	10	
Financial & Trade Relations with adjacent Countries/States	3	
Financial and Trade Publications	3	
Financial Conditions involving Partnerships	8	
Financial Relations with Competitor	8	
Financial Responsibilities in general	8	
Foreign Relations	9	
Fraternal and Club Groups	11	
Future Designs	12	
General Business Conditions presented to the Public	10	
General Membership	1	
Governing Body	5	
Government Relations	10	
Handling of Legacies	8	
Hazards involving Property	4	
Health Conditions of Personnel	6	
Health Policies and Insurance	6	
Income from Invested Capital	5	
Incubation of Ideas	12	
Indebtedness of Organization	11	
In-House Information Dissemination	3	
In-house Policies and Platforms	3	
Insurances	8	
Intangible Assets	11	
Inter-Company Communication	9	
Internal Agreements	3	
Inter-Office Communication	3	
Inventories	6	
Lawsuits and Legal Affairs	7	
Library	3	
Lighting and Heating Bills	6	
Liquid Assets	2	

House Meanings	House	Placement of House Ruler
Liquidation of Frozen Assets	8	
Literary Works	3	
Loans and Income from sources not under immediate control of the Organization	8	
Location and Condition of Factory	4	
Long-Distance Communications	9	
Long-Range Goals of Organization	11	
Losses and Gains through closing of Corporation	8	
Mail-Order Campaign Results	9	
Management Teams	5	
Meeting Planning	5	
Merger Finances or Lawsuits	8	
Mergers	7	
Mindset of President or CEO	12	
Money-Making Activities	2	
Mortgages	11	
National Reputation	10	
Neighboring organizations	3	
Net Earnings	8	
News Distribution Methods	3	
Nonprofit Status of Company	8	
Officials	9	
Open opposition to growth	7	
Original home of company	4	
Personnel of Corporation	1	
Place of Deposit of Capital, Safes, Vaults, Banks	5	
Place of Incorporation	1	
Political and Commercial Affiliates	7	
Political Connections	11	
Power	10	
Power of competitors	4	
President or Chairman of the Board	10	
Private Conferences	8	
Professional Consultants	9	

House Meanings	House	Placement of House Ruler
Public Accounting	7	
Public Image	10	
Public Relations	9	
Public Relations through Group Involvement	11	
Publications	9	
Publicity	9	
Rails, Telephones, Telegraphs	3	
Raw Land	4	
Real Estate Investments/Holdings	4	
Relations with Educational Institutions	9	
Relations with other Organizations	7	
Relationship to Public	1	
Research and Development	12	
Resources available through Head of Company	11	
Results of Speculative Ventures	5	
Revenue from Investments	8	
Revenues	2	
Roots of Company	4	
Sabotage	12	
Sales Appeal	7	
Secret Assistance	12	
Secret Intelligence Department	12	
Seminars	5	
Shareholder View	1	
Shareholders	1	
Shipping	9	
Short-Distance Travels	3	
Social Affairs	5	
Speculation	5	
Strikes and Labor Troubles	12	
Supportive or Hostile Relations with others	7	
Supreme or Governing Authority	10	
Tangible Assets of corporation	4	
Teaching	5	
The Treasury	11	

House Meanings	House	Placement of House Ruler
Trade Agreements	7	
Trade Formulas	12	
Trade Secrets	8	
Trade Secrets	12	
Trade Volume (Amount of stock being purchased)	7	
Trade Volume Figures/Numbers	3	
Traffic, Transportation	3	
Treasurer-Company Treasurer	8	
Type of Work	6	
Voluntary Expenditures	2	
Warehouse or Office Buildings	4	
Work Schedules and Routines	6	
Workshops	5	

Appendix IIb

Corporate House Worksheet, Numerical House Order

House	House Meanings	Placement of House Ruler
1	Attitude towards Competitors	
1	Company Business Objectives	
1	Company Morale	
1	General Membership	
1	Personnel of Corporation	
1	Place of Incorporation	
1	Relationship to Public	
1	Shareholder View	
1	Shareholders	
2	Ability to be Profitable	
2	Disposition towards Investments	
2	Earnings	
2	Liquid Assets	
2	Money-Making Activities	
2	Revenues	
2	Voluntary Expenditures	
3	Advertising	
3	Bulletins, Newsletters, Magazines & Technical Manuals	
3	Commercial Radio	
3	Contacts with the Public	
3	Demand for Stocks and Bonds	
3	Education	
3	Financial & Trade Relations with adjacent Countries/States	
3	Financial and Trade Publications	
3	In-House Information Dissemination	
3	In-house Policies and Platforms	
3	Internal Agreements	

House	House Meanings	Placement of House Ruler
3	Inter-Office Communication	
3	Library	
3	Literary Works	
3	Neighboring organizations	
3	News Distribution Methods	
3	Rails, Telephones, Telegraphs	
3	Short-Distance Travels	
3	Trade Volume Figures/Numbers	
3	Traffic, Transportation	
4	Base of Operations, Field of Activity	
4	Direct Competition	
4	Hazards involving Property	
4	Location and Condition of Factory	
4	Original home of company	
4	Power of competitors	
4	Raw Land	
4	Real Estate Investments/Holdings	
4	Roots of Company	
4	Tangible Assets of corporation	
4	Warehouse or Office Buildings	
5	Advertising Failure	
5	Advertising Success	
5	Amusements	
5	Attitude/Actions of Board of Directors in opposition to President	
5	Attitude/Actions of Shareholders in opposition to President	
5	Banquets	
5	Committees	
5	Conventions	
5	Dramatic or Theatrical Ventures	
5	Educational Enterprises	
5	Executive Personnel (does not include President or CEO)	
5	Governing Body	
5	Income from Invested Capital	

House	House Meanings	Placement of House Ruler
5	Management Teams	
5	Meeting Planning	
5	Place of Deposit of Capital, Safes, Vaults, Banks	
5	Results of Speculative Ventures	
5	Seminars	
5	Social Affairs	
5	Speculation	
5	Teaching	
5	Workshops	
6	Agricultural and Agricultural Products	
6	Assistance received from other Employees	
6	Business Fixtures and Furnishings	
6	Corporations associated with Hotels or Inns-Hostelries	
6	Employee Attitudes	
6	Employee Cooperation	
6	Employee Performance	
6	Employee Strikes and Labor Troubles	
6	Employees/Workers Voluntary or Paid	
6	Equipment	
6	Health Conditions of Personnel	
6	Health Policies and Insurance	
6	Inventories	
6	Lighting and Heating Bills	
6	Type of Work	
6	Work Schedules and Routines	
7	Adjustments	
7	Competitors and Their Activities	
7	Effective Presentation of Products	
7	Employee Incomes and Payroll	
7	Lawsuits and Legal Affairs	
7	Mergers	
7	Open opposition to growth	
7	Political and Commercial Affiliates	
7	Public Accounting	

House	House Meanings	Placement of House Ruler
7	Relations with other Organizations	
7	Sales Appeal	
7	Supportive or Hostile Relations with others	
7	Trade Agreements	
7	Trade Volume (Amount of stock being purchased)	
8	Boards of Directors	
8	Competitor's Financial Condition	
8	Credit	
8	Dividends	
8	Donations to Nonprofits	
8	Financial Conditions involving Partnerships	
8	Financial Relations with Competitor	
8	Financial Responsibilities in general	
8	Handling of Legacies	
8	Insurances	
8	Liquidation of Frozen Assets	
8	Loans and Income from sources not under immediate control of the Organization	
8	Losses and Gains through closing of Corporation	
8	Merger Finances or Lawsuits	
8	Net Earnings	
8	Nonprofit Status of Company	
8	Private Conferences	
8	Revenue from Investments	
8	Trade Secrets	
8	Treasurer-Company Treasurer	
9	Activities Abroad	
9	Advertising Department	
9	All Legal Affairs	
9	Audits	
9	Code of Ethics and By-Laws	
9	Company Philosophy	
9	Completion of Merger Contracts	
9	Contracts with other Companies	

House	House Meanings	Placement of House Ruler
9	Foreign Relations	
9	Inter-Company Communication	
9	Long-Distance Communications	
9	Mail-Order Campaign Results	
9	Officials	
9	Professional Consultants	
9	Public Relations	
9	Publications	
9	Publicity	
9	Relations with Educational Institutions	
9	Shipping	
10	Administrative Department	
10	Figureheads	
10	General Business Conditions presented to the Public	
10	Government Relations	
10	National Reputation	
10	Power	
10	President or Chairman of the Board	
10	Public Image	
10	Supreme or Governing Authority	
11	Allied Organizations	
11	Colleagues, Friends, Acquaintances	
11	Community Connections	
11	Constitutional Policies	
11	Fraternal and Club Groups	
11	Indebtedness of Organization	
11	Intangible Assets	
11	Long-Range Goals of Organization	
11	Mortgages	
11	Political Connections	
11	Public Relations through Group Involvement	
11	Resources available through Head of Company	
11	The Treasury	
12	Dissolutions and Negotiations	
12	Effects of Litigation	

House	House Meanings	Placement of House Ruler
12	Enemies and Secret Organizations Against the Organization	
12	Future Designs	
12	Incubation of Ideas	
12	Mindset of President or CEO	
12	Research and Development	
12	Sabotage	
12	Secret Assistance	
12	Secret Intelligence Department	
12	Strikes and Labor Troubles	
12	Trade Formulas	
12	Trade Secrets	

Appendix IIIa

Real Estate House Worksheet, Alphabetical Order

House Meanings	House	Noted Comments
Accumulation or Loss	11	
Agent	6	
Assets of Seller, Tangible	2	
Behind the scenes for Seller	12	
Buyer	7	
Buyer, Physical Description	7	
Buyer's Cash Flow	8	
Buyer's Cash on Hand	8	
Buyer's End of Escrow	12	
Buyer's Escrow Agent	12	
Buyer's Real Estate Agent	12	
Communication in Signing	3	
Contract Signing	3	
Details of Real Estate Contract	6	
Escrow	8	
Estate, Money that comes from	9	
Estates	8	
Factories of Corporation	4	
Foreign Country Associations	12	
Health Issues of Buyer	12	
Income from Individual's Career	11	
Income from Real Estate	5	
Income from Recreational Property	5	
Income from Speculative Investments	5	
Income Property	6	
Insurance required	8	
Interest Rate	8	
Joint Holdings of Seller	8	
Land Dealers	10	

House Meanings	House	Noted Comments
Land Developers	10	
Land in general	10	
Landlords	10	
Landowners	10	
Legal Contracts	7	
Legal Situations around Property	9	
Loss of Property (12th from 4th)	3	
Mortgage Qualities	8	
Motivation for Sale of Property	12	
Outcome of the Transaction	4	
Partnership Assets, Business	8	
Partnership Assets, Marital	8	
Physical Description of Seller	1	
Plumbing	4	
Probate Conditions	8	
Property Damage	4	
Property itself	4	
Psychological frame of Seller	12	
Recreational Property	5	
Resources available in transaction from Seller	2	
Resources available in transaction from Buyer	8	
Seller's Cash Flow	2	
Seller's Cash on Hand	2	
Settlements	8	
Speculation	5	
Tenants in Leasing Situation	6	
Title Search	8	
Transaction, How Buyer Sees It	7	
Transaction, How Seller Sees It	1	
Treasury	11	
Vacant Property	4	
Warehouses of Corporation	4	
Wills	8	

Appendix IIIb

Real Estate House Worksheet, Numerical Order

House	House Meanings	Conditions in House
1	Physical Description of Seller	
1	Transaction, How Seller Sees It	
2	Assets of Seller, Tangible	
2	Resources available in transaction from Seller	
2	Seller's Cash Flow	
2	Seller's Cash on Hand	
3	Communication in Signing	
3	Contract Signing	
3	Loss of Property (12th from 4th)	
4	Factories of Corporation	
4	Outcome of the Transaction	
4	Plumbing	
4	Property Damage	
4	Property itself	
4	Vacant Property	
4	Warehouses of Corporation	
5	Income from Real Estate	
5	Income from Recreational Property	
5	Income from Speculative Investments	
5	Recreational Property	
5	Speculation	
6	Agent	
6	Details of Real Estate Contract	
6	Income Property	
6	Tenants in Leasing Situation	
7	Buyer	
7	Buyer, Physical Description	
7	Legal Contracts	
7	Transaction, How Buyer Sees It	

House	House Meanings	Conditions in House
8	Buyer's Cash Flow	
8	Buyer's Cash on Hand	
8	Escrow	
8	Estates	
8	Insurance required	
8	Interest Rate	
8	Joint Holdings of Seller	
8	Mortgage Qualities	
8	Partnership Assets, Business	
8	Partnership Assets, Marital	
8	Probate Conditions	
8	Resources available in transaction from Buyer	
8	Settlements	
8	Title Search	
8	Wills	
9	Estate, Money that comes from	
9	Legal Situations around Property	
10	Land Dealers	
10	Land Developers	
10	Land in general	
10	Landlords	
10	Landowners	
11	Accumulation or Loss	
11	Income from Individual's Career	
11	Treasury	
12	Behind the scenes for Seller	
12	Buyer's End of Escrow	
12	Buyer's Escrow Agent	
12	Buyer's Real Estate Agent	
12	Foreign Country Associations	
12	Health Issues of Buyer	
12	Motivation for Sale of Property	
12	Psychological frame of Seller	

Annual Planning Chart for:

First Quarter of the Year

	Date	*House Where Activity Begins*
New Moon Starting Point		
First Quarter Moon		
Full Moon		
Last Quarter Moon		
	Date	*House Where Activity Begins*
New Moon Starting Point		
First Quarter Moon		
Full Moon		
Last Quarter Moon		
	Date	*House Where Activity Begins*
New Moon Starting Point		
First Quarter Moon		
Full Moon		
Last Quarter Moon		

Appendix IV, Illustration 30b

ANNUAL PLANNING CHART FOR:

Second Quarter of the Year

	Date	*House Where Activity Begins*
New Moon Starting Point		
First Quarter Moon		
Full Moon		
Last Quarter Moon		
	Date	***House Where Activity Begins***
New Moon Starting Point		
First Quarter Moon		
Full Moon		
Last Quarter Moon		
	Date	***House Where Activity Begins***
New Moon Starting Point		
First Quarter Moon		
Full Moon		
Last Quarter Moon		

Appendix IV, Illustration 30c

Annual Planning Chart for:

Third Quarter of the Year

	Date	House Where Activity Begins
New Moon Starting Point		
First Quarter Moon		
Full Moon		
Last Quarter Moon		
	Date	**House Where Activity Begins**
New Moon Starting Point		
First Quarter Moon		
Full Moon		
Last Quarter Moon		
	Date	**House Where Activity Begins**
New Moon Starting Point		
First Quarter Moon		
Full Moon		
Last Quarter Moon		

Appendix IV, Illustration 30d

ANNUAL PLANNING CHART FOR:

Fourth Quarter of the Year

	Date	***House Where Activity Begins***
New Moon Starting Point		
First Quarter Moon		
Full Moon		
Last Quarter Moon		
	Date	***House Where Activity Begins***
New Moon Starting Point		
First Quarter Moon		
Full Moon		
Last Quarter Moon		
	Date	***House Where Activity Begins***
New Moon Starting Point		
First Quarter Moon		
Full Moon		
Last Quarter Moon		

Appendix V

Business Questionnaire from Georgia Stathis

It is important that you submit an RFP (Request for Proposal) to Georgia Stathis at 200 Gregory Lane, Bldg. C-2, Suite #5, Pleasant Hill, CA 94523-3389. Phone: (925) 689-7827 or email: venus2@ix.netcom.com or fax: (925) 686-3196. It need not be more than one page. Please indicate budget and whether or not you foresee this as a one-time analysis or as an ongoing service, which can be handled via retainer.

The Request for Proposal provides us with the specifics of what you wish to accomplish. This questionnaire is designed to clarify those factors for you. Once we receive the proposal and review your needs, we will contact you with some of the ideas we have concerning your request.

The following questionnaire is designed to help you focus on your company needs and the more precise your information the better quality of the analysis you will receive. This requires some work on your part but in the end it saves you time and money, and helps us to work together effectively.

If you wish for us to calculate a good time in which to start a venture or business, use this questionnaire as a guide. Give us the rough time frame in which you care to open the business and then submit the RFP. We will contact you after reviewing your material(s).

1. What is the original incorporation date of your business? ______________________________

2. In what city and state was it legally incorporated?

____

3. List all other incorporation dates and their locations:

____

____

____

4. If you are not incorporated, when did you open the doors of your business or take in your first dollar? ________

____

5. What are the date, time, and place of birth of the head of your company? If you are not the head of the company, then we will need written permission from the head of the company to review this data. __________

____

6. List all other dates, times of birth, and cities and states of births of employee charts, or major figures in your company with which we need to work. We need their written permission for this. ____________________

____

____

____

7. In what city and state is your head office located?

____

8. When did you open the doors of this head office?

____

9. Describe the major service(s) or product(s) of your company? ______________________________

____

____

10. If you are not a service or manufacturing business, what is your business? ______________________________

____

____

11. What date(s) were these products or services introduced? ______________________________

____

____

12. What products or services are you planning to introduce? ______________________________

____

____

13. Do you have the dates in which you plan to begin development? ______________________________

____

____

14. Do you have the dates in which you project releasing these products to the public? ______________________________

____

15. Are there any mergers or collaborations that recently occurred with your company? ______________________________

____

____

16. If so, please list the times and dates in which these occurred? ____________________

____

____

17. In this portion of the questionnaire, please list the major areas of stress or problems in your company which you would like addressed in this initial consult:

____

____

____

____

18. In each of the following categories, circle one or two areas which are the most important issues:

    a. Company identity and morale; stockholders' perceptions.

    b. Revenues; liquid assets; cash flow; spending; profitability.

    c. Contact with the public; inner-office communications; communication equipment; trade volume.

    d. Property or real estate holdings; buildings in which business is housed; tangible assets; hazards or improvements regarding the property.

    e. Subsidiaries or branches of your company; advertising success(s); income from the capital; the place of deposited capital such as bank safes, vaults; conventions; workshops; seminars; social affairs and meeting planning.

    f. Employees; inventories; utility bills; workers' performance while on the job; health policies; health insurance; circumstances around labor or union.

g. Employee spending and payroll; sales volume; best style for sales appeal; mergers; oppositions to growth; legal affairs and lawsuits.

h. Financial responsibilities; insurances; board of directors; company losses and debt; frozen assets; net earnings.

i. Audits, professional consultants, publications, long-distance affiliations (across country or across the sea); advertising /public relations department.

j. President, head of company, or CEO; relations with government; public image.

k. Long-range goals of company; the treasury and its strength or weakness; legislation of the governing body; standing and referrals from community.

l. Research and development; confidentiality; possible hidden saboteurs; inefficiency; effects of litigation; motivation behind company identity.

m. What are your top three concerns; listing the most important as #1:

Index

A

B

C

D

E

F

G

H

I

J

K

L

M

P

Q

R

S

T

U

V

W

Y

Z

Ms. Stathis, a first generation Greek American born with the name Georgianna Stathopoulos, worked in sales, marketing, real estate, and public relations, as well as acting and dance, prior to hanging up her hat to become a full-time astrologer in 1981, when she had her first of two children. She opened her first office in 1982 and after the birth of her second child in 1984, opened her second office seven years later in 1991. Her resulting body of work is a cross section of information, which applies differently to varied groups of clients whom she arms with tools based on a synthesis of art, culture and statistics.

Currently, Ms. Stathis is teaching for Kepler College in Seattle, Washington, and is one of their charter faculty members. Kepler is the first, fully accredited B.A. and M.A. program offered in a university setting since the 17th century. For more information on Kepler, go to their website at www.kepler.edu. She is also a popular lecturer at many local and national organizations as well as frequently interviewed by such publications as Los Angeles Times, Fortune Magazine, Shape Magazine, and the London Economist.

An exiting board member of I.S.A.R., International Society for Astrological Research, she currently heads up the Ethics Review Committee and is also a member of such astrological organizations as OPA (Organization for Professional Astrologers), NCGR, AFAN, and ISBA (International Society for Business Astrologers), all of whose websites may be reached through her website at www.starcycles.com.

A single mother, she credits the success of her work to the unwavering support of her two children, Alexandra and Gus Nunes; her former stepchildren; Tanya and Darcie Nunes; their father, John Nunes; and her parents, Mary and Gus Stathis as well as to her many friends, colleagues, organizations and clients, who keep coming back for more work and asking her to try new approaches and explore new ideas. "Every time I had doubts, or, thoughts of starting a new profession, they were all always there as a cheering section, encouraging me to do more, to stretch the boundaries of my mind, to move past my fear, to have faith and to learn to receive and appreciate that which was offered me by the universe," states Stathis.

Ms. Stathis may be reached by calling (925) 689-7827, or, by email at: venus2@ix.netcom.com. Her website at www.starcycles.com has several articles plus a listing of all events and upcoming lectures as well as all astrological teaching tapes, calendars that she offers.